100 Years of Happiness

100 YEARS
OF HAPPINESS

Insights and Findings from the Experts

Nathan Carlin and Donald Capps

Psychology, Religion, and Spirituality
J. Harold Ellens, Series Editor

 PRAEGER

AN IMPRINT OF ABC-CLIO, LLC
Santa Barbara, California • Denver, Colorado • Oxford, England

Copyright 2012 by Nathan Carlin and Donald Capps

Library of Congress Cataloging-in-Publication Data

Carlin, Nathan.

   100 years of happiness : insights and findings from the experts / Nathan Carlin and Donald Capps.

       p. cm. — (Psychology, religion, and spirituality)

   Includes bibliographical references and index.

   ISBN 978-1-4408-0362-8 (hardcopy : alk. paper) — ISBN 978-1-4408-0363-5 (ebook : alk. paper)   1. Happiness.   I. Capps, Donald.   II. Title. III. Title: One hundred years of happiness.

   BF575.H27C372   2012

   158—dc23   2012006421

ISBN: 978-1-4408-0362-8
EISBN: 978-1-4408-0363-5

16   15   14   13   12   1   2   3   4   5

This book is also available on the World Wide Web as an eBook.
Visit www.abc-clio.com for details.

Praeger
An Imprint of ABC-CLIO, LLC

ABC-CLIO, LLC
130 Cremona Drive, P.O. Box 1911
Santa Barbara, California 93116-1911

This book is printed on acid-free paper ∞

Manufactured in the United States of America

To Thomas Cole and Lewis Rambo

I know there is nothing better for them than to be happy
and to enjoy themselves as long as they live.
—Ecclesiastes 3:12

CONTENTS

PART III
SOME QUESTIONS ABOUT HAPPINESS

SERIES FOREWORD

The interface between psychology, religion, and spirituality has been of great interest to scholars for a century. In the last three decades, a broad popular appetite has developed for books that make practical sense out of the complicated research on these three subjects. Freud had a negative outlook on the relationship between psychology, religion, and spirituality, and thought the interaction between them was destructive. Jung, on the other hand, was quite sure that these three aspects of the human spirit were constructively linked, and one could not be separated from the others. Anton Boisen and Seward Hiltner derived much insight from both Freud and Jung, as well as from Adler and Reik, and fashioned a useful framework for understanding the interface between psychology, religion, spirituality, and human social development.[1] We are in their debt.

This series of General Interest Books, so wisely urged by ABC-CLIO-Praeger Publishers, and particularly by its acquisitions editor, Debbie Carvalko, intends to define the terms and explore the interface of psychology, religion, and spirituality at the operational level of daily human experience. Each volume of the series identifies, analyzes, describes, and evaluates the issues of both popular and professional interest that deal with the psycho-spiritual factors at play (1) in the way religion takes shape and is expressed, (2) in the way spirituality functions within human persons and shapes both religious formation and religious expression, and (3) in the ways that spirituality is shaped and expressed by religion.

The books in this series are written for the general reader, the local library, and the undergraduate university student. They are also of significant interest to informed professional persons, particularly in fields somewhat related or corollary to religion, spirituality, and social psychology. They have great usefulness for clinical settings and ethical values as well. I have spent an entire professional lifetime focused specifically upon research on the interface of psychology, sociology, religion, and spirituality. These matters are of the highest urgency in human affairs today when religious motivation seems to be playing an increasing role, constructively and destructively, in the arena of social ethics, national politics, and world affairs.

The primary interest in this present volume by Nathan Carlin and Donald Capps is spiritual, religious, and ethical. In terms of the field and science of theology and religious studies, this volume investigates the operational dynamics of religion and spirituality in their influence upon the universal human quest for happiness. The founding fathers of the United States observed that the freedom to pursue happiness is an inherent right for all humans. However, they knew and we know that happiness itself is not easily acquired. Nonetheless, its pursuit is a human longing that is very personal and close to home.

The authors have seen through the sham and superficiality of modern culture in its narcissistic notion that *possessing* happiness is the inherent right of all humans and the legitimate *goal* of human life. It seems quite clear that when we make happiness the target of our existence, it fades from view as soon as we shoot the arrow of our life at it. Like self-esteem, happiness must be earned through experiencing a new insight, fashioning a good relationship, or accomplishing a useful service for others. Those persons who live life focused on the acquisition of happiness to feed their own narcissism seem never to achieve real authentic happiness.

It is urgent, therefore, that we discover and understand better what the spiritual and psychosocial forces are that empower people of genuine spirituality and wholesome character to give themselves to all the creative and constructive enterprises that have made human life the humane, ordered, prosperous, and beautiful experience it can be at its best, and which has afforded them a relative degree of satisfaction and happiness. The burden of this wonderful new book, *100 Years of Happiness: Insights and Findings from the Experts*, is a sturdy assist in our discovery of what human happiness really is and how we can find it in the relatively short span of a lifetime.

J. Harold Ellens,
Series Editor

PREFACE

We would like to thank J. Harold Ellens for selecting this volume for the Praeger Perspectives series, Psychology, Religion, and Spirituality. We also would like to thank Debbie Carvalko, Senior Acquisitions Editor, for navigating this book through the production process, as well as the many other editors and staff responsible for bringing this book to the light of day. And we would like to thank Angela Polczynski for her help with looking up references. We are pleased to report that working on this book with this press has contributed to our own happiness. We are grateful, too, for the press's commitment to the field of psychology of religion; without such commitment, the field could not survive.

This book is our second coauthored book together. Our first book, titled *Living in Limbo: Life in the Midst of Uncertainty*, dealt with "limbo" situations in everyday life—experiences that are often uncomfortable and experiences that sometimes contribute to unhappiness. This book is a kind of sequel. In *Living in Limbo*, we explored limbo situations by reflecting on our own personal experiences of limbo, by having informal conversations with friends who have had limbo experiences, and by reading about the stories of others who have had their own limbo experiences. In this book, we explore happiness by turning to the "experts," that is, philosophers and scientists who have explored the subject of happiness. To us, both books seem central to the everyday lived experience of most persons; and both books, in their own way, deal with the question of happiness. After we wrote *Living in Limbo*, our friends would often ask how we wrote the book together. They wanted to know who wrote which chapters. In *Living in Limbo*, we wrote each chapter together, taking separate sections within each chapter. In this book, we took a slightly different approach: we divided the chapters equally between us so that each of us would write an initial draft of a whole chapter (Capps wrote chapters 1–5, 7, and 12, and Carlin wrote chapters 6, 8–11, 13, and 14). But because we wrote our chapters simultaneously, chapters that come later in the book were as influential on earlier chapters as earlier chapters were on later chapters. Moreover, we read and commented on each other's chapters at every step along the way, and these comments invariably resulted in significant revisions. So this book has been as collaborative as our earlier book. We have found that working on these projects together and that expanding and varying our methods of collaboration and writing has afforded us four of the greatest pleasures (and ways to find meaning) that life has to offer: reading, writing, collaboration, and friendship. One final word: We have dedicated this book to Thomas Cole and Lewis Rambo; they have made our lives, both personally and professionally, happier.

INTRODUCTION

This book began when one of the authors (Capps) sent a clipping from the *Reader's Digest* to the other author (Carlin). The clipping was from a 1948 issue of the *Digest* that he found in a scrapbook that he compiled when he was about 10 years old. The clipping was titled "Meet the Folks" and was an excerpt from *Time* magazine. It consisted of four brief paragraphs reporting on a recent Gallup poll. It contained data on physical characteristics of men and women; their views on the ideal-size family; what husbands and wives quarrel about; and their views on various other matters, such as spanking children, family pets, alcoholic beverage consumption, smoking, sleeping habits, saying grace before meals, belief in God, beliefs about life after death, and other topics. At the very end of the article, there was a sentence reporting that only 4 percent are convinced that they are unhappy, 57 percent think they are fairly happy, 38 percent consider themselves very happy, and 1 percent can't tell.

We no longer recall why Capps sent Carlin this clipping. Nor, for that matter, does he recall why he saved the clipping in the first place. What we both recall is that Carlin wrote an e-mail to Capps suggesting that our next writing project together might be one on happiness. We were aware that many books and articles on happiness had been published in recent years, and this in itself was significant. Why, we wondered, is there so much interest in happiness, especially in America? What does this say about us as a society? Does it mean that a lot of people are unhappy and need the help of experts to find out how to be happy? Also, are Americans less happy today than they were 60 years ago? If the same Gallup poll were conducted today, would the percentages of unhappy, fairly happy, very happy, and can't tell be significantly different? Would more than 4 percent of respondents say that they were unhappy, thus reducing the percentages of Americans who believe they are fairly or very happy? Would more respondents say that they can't tell whether they are happy or unhappy?

We were especially intrigued by the low percentage of respondents (1%) who didn't know if they were happy or not. This would suggest that 99 percent of Americans felt they had a good idea of what it means to be happy or unhappy. If so, we wondered if this would be as true today. We also wondered if one of the reasons that so many books have been written on happiness in recent years was due, in part, to the fact that there is a lot of uncertainty as to what happiness really is. Are Americans reading these books in order to find out if they are happy or not?

We were also intrigued by the distinction between "fairly happy" and "very happy." We wondered what would make the difference. Perhaps some Americans were reading these books because they were *fairly* happy but wanted to learn how to become *very* happy. Since in the 1948 poll there were substantially more Americans in the fairly happy than the very happy category (but there were, in fact, a lot of Americans who were very happy), the fairly happy might be thinking that they, too, could be very happy. After all, the state or condition of being very happy was not unattainable or limited to the very few.

We were sufficiently intrigued by these questions that we decided to write a book on the subject of happiness. We are aware that what we have written here may appear, at first glance, to be just one more book on happiness, adding to what some may consider a surfeit of books on the subject. However, we believe that our approach is substantially different from that of other books on the subject. This is because our book is not original. It does not tell the reader what will make him or her happy. Instead, it tells readers what the experts on the subject of happiness tell them about happiness. Thus, you can read our book on happiness and save yourself the trouble of reading all the other books on happiness. This could, in itself, contribute to your happiness (unless you like to read a lot of books on a particular topic or simply enjoy buying lots of books on a subject so that you can impress your friends when they come to your home or study and look at your bookshelf). It is worth pointing out that most of the books on happiness are literature reviews of articles on happiness. These books then read this literature through an interpretive lens, such as the lens of evolutionary psychology, and then go on to make a general argument about the nature of happiness. What our book does is take this approach to the next level. That is, if other books on happiness involve literature reviews of *articles* about happiness, our book about happiness is a literature review of *books* about happiness. Yet, as noted, we do not have a particular point of view to advocate for in this book, because we think that the time has come to catalogue major arguments about happiness simply for their own sake.

On the other hand, we do have a personal motive in writing this book. We both felt that if we had responded to the Gallup poll in 1948, we would have wanted those who formulated the questions to provide an option between "fairly" and "very" happy. It might have said "substantially happy" or "quite happy." If there had been such an option, we are pretty sure that we would have checked it rather than "fairly" or "very" happy. No doubt, the 10-year-old who saved the clipping would have done the same. Of course, we appreciate the fact that the Gallup poll did not present its respondents with a forced choice between happy and unhappy as it seems to have done in the case of the question about whether males prefer brunettes and blonds (what about women with red hair or black hair?). Still, we felt that there must be a state or condition of happiness somewhere between "fairly" and "very" to which most of us aspire (and will gladly settle for). So as we began to read the books on happiness we were interested in finding out whether they made similar distinctions between degrees of happiness.

An even more fundamental question that the poll did not address is: What is or constitutes happiness? The 1 percent who said they didn't know if they were happy or not may have been saying that they didn't really know what happiness is. Maybe they thought that happiness is impossible to define. If so, how can one know if one is happy or not? As we began to work on this book, we became aware of the fact that Saint Augustine was concerned with this very question. We knew that Plato was concerned with it, but we thought, "That figures, because, after all, he was a Greek philosopher." But we assumed that the question of what happiness is and how to attain it would be beneath the dignity of a celebrated Christian saint. Not so. He devotes a whole section to the subject of happiness in his *Confessions* (1991), and the topic comes up at other points in the book as well. But what is particularly noteworthy is the fact that Augustine begins his discussion of happiness by noting that his search for God is a quest for "the happy life," and then goes on to explore the question: How should I seek the happy life? He confesses that he is not at all sure how he ought to go about the quest for happiness (p. 196). However, one thing seems true—namely, that one person may be happy at a particular time, a second may be happy in hopes of becoming happy, and a third may not even have the hope of becoming happy. And yet even the third person wants happiness. He or she just doesn't think happiness is attainable. But why is it, then, that everyone seems to desire happiness, whether they have it or not? To Augustine, the best answer to this question is that we all had happiness once upon a time. In other words, happiness is somewhere in our memories. Maybe it is there because we all experienced happiness individually, or maybe it is there because we all experienced happiness corporately or collectively but lost it when the first human sinned against God and, from then on, we were born into a condition of misery. So, if you were to ask everyone if they want to be happy, they would answer that they do. This would not be the case unless that to which the term "happiness" refers continues to exist in our collective memory (p. 197).

Augustine goes on to note that everyone wants to be happy, but people do not agree on what would make them happy. As for himself, he believes that the truly happy life is one in which he sets his joy on God, and his joy is grounded in God because this is the real thing, and nothing else can rival it. In his judgment, those who think that the happy life is found elsewhere pursue false joy. To be sure, their desire is still drawn by some image of the true joy, but they are occupied with things that they believe will bring them true joy because these things have a greater impression on them than their distant memory of that which is the source of true happiness.[1]

We would guess that few of the respondents to the Gallup poll in 1948 thought there was any connection between the question about happiness and their belief in God. In fact, they would probably have seen more of a connection between the happiness question and the ones about their weight, quarrels with their spouses, difficulty getting up in the morning, spanking their children, and preferences regarding their family pets. But at least Augustine acknowledges that people's tendency to associate happiness with some penultimate image of joy is a reflection of their deeply rooted memory (more likely collectively experienced than personally experienced) of the source and ground of true joy. And perhaps he might grant them a certain leeway in this regard if the things that they desire are somehow reflective of the source and ground of true joy.

In any event, the paragraphs in his *Confessions* that focus on happiness suggest that happiness is something that we all desire and that, in fact, we should desire. They also indicate that happiness is what we were intended to have—and did have—before the fall. If we ask, "What did we lose as a consequence of Adam's sin?" Augustine's answer is that we lost our natural state of happiness. No wonder, then, that everyone wants happiness. In fact, there is no reason to be ashamed of the fact that we want happiness. Rather, our very desire for happiness is an indication that we (collectively) remember what we once had and have since lost. To desire happiness, then, reflects the fact that we have some consciousness, however tenuous, of the fact that God created us.

The idea that true happiness was once ours but has since been lost might also explain why the Gallup poll did not give respondents the chance to say that they were "perfectly happy." In this life, at least, "very happy" would seem to be as good as it gets. Perhaps the 76 percent who believe in an afterlife are anticipating that they will regain such perfect happiness in the next life.

Now, a few words about the books we have chosen to review and a few words about how our own book is organized. As noted earlier, we are aware that a great number of books on happiness have been published in recent years. One can consult the Harvard University Library database (as one of us has done) or traipse over to the local bookstore and rummage through the psychology section (as the other has done) and discover the plethora of books on the subject. We had no grounds to assume—much less claim—that some or many of these authors do not know what they are talking about. On the other hand, we needed to be selective and felt that the key criterion for choosing a particular book was that the author is an expert on the subject of happiness. By "expert," we mean a person who is "very skillful or highly trained and informed in some special field" (Agnes 2001, p. 500).

We believe that the authors of the books reviewed here fit one or both of these descriptions as far as the "field" of happiness is concerned. If we were to imagine a colloquium on happiness occurring somewhere in the United States and thought about who would be invited to come to this colloquium and participate in a round-table discussion on happiness, we have no doubt that if this group of authors were the ones selected, the auditors would find the discussion to be informative and thought provoking.

Except for Sissela Bok, the authors of these books are white males. This may suggest that white males are especially preoccupied with the topic of happiness. After all, it was a group of white males who in 1776 declared that all Americans have the right to "life, liberty, and *the pursuit of happiness.*" The fact that we are also white males may also suggest that we share the same preoccupation as the founding fathers and the authors of the books presented here. In any event, we do not assume a positive correlation between being a white male and being a happy person. In fact, as the reader of this book will be informed, there is some empirical evidence that suggests that neither gender nor race are predictors of personal happiness.

The book is organized into three parts. Part 1, "Some Insights about Happiness," focuses on four books: two of which were published just before and after the turn of the 20th century, while the other two were published in the early part of the 20th century. These books are based on insights derived from traditional reflections on happiness by philosophers and writers; on newly emerging social sciences, including psychology; on personal experience and observation; and on common sense. Chapter 1 focuses on Horace Fletcher's *Happiness as Found in Forethought minus Fear-thought* (1898a). A well-known American lecturer on mental health and diet, Fletcher was in his late 40s when he wrote the book. Chapter 2 introduces Karl Hilty's *Happiness: Essays on the Meaning of Life* (1903). A professor of constitutional law at Bern University in Switzerland, Hilty wrote many books on legal matters. But in the 1890s, when he was in his late 50s and early 60s, he began to write about his inner life through a series of small books issued at intervals throughout the decade. In 1891 his first series of essays on happiness titled *Glück* was published. A second series was published in 1895 and a third in 1898. The

English translation of the first series of essays by Francis G. Peabody was published in the United States in 1903. Chapter 3 focuses on Jean Finot's *The Science of Happiness* (1914). Born in Warsaw, Poland, in 1858, Finot spent his adult life in France as a journalist and a sociologist. He died in 1922. In chapter 4, we present Bertrand Russell's *The Conquest of Happiness* (1968b). It was originally published in England in 1930. It became widely available to the American public in 1968 when it was published in a Bantam paperback. Born in Wales in 1872, Russell was from a liberal family of the British aristocracy. He became a well-known philosopher, mathematician, and social critic. He died at the age of 97, two years after the Bantam paperback appeared.

Part 2, "Some Findings about Happiness," leaps forward to the end of the 20th century and beginning of the 21st and centers on books by psychologists and economists. Although the books by psychologists draw on personal experience, they also, and more centrally, reflect the contemporary emphasis in the happiness literature on empirical findings. Chapter 5 focuses on David G. Myers's *The Pursuit of Happiness* (1992). Born in Seattle in 1942, Myers joined the psychology faculty at Hope College in Michigan in 1967, where he continued to teach and write throughout his professional life. Chapter 6 focuses on Martin E. P. Seligman's *Authentic Happiness* (2002). Seligman is a psychology professor at the University of Pennsylvania and is the creator of an approach to psychology known as Positive Psychology. These two books reflect the emergence of psychological studies of well-being in the last decade of the 20th century. Chapter 7 presents Richard Layard's *Happiness: Lessons from a New Science* (2005). Born in 1934, Layard is a program director at the Centre for Economic Performance at the London School of Economics, and he is a member of the House of Lords. Chapter 8 focuses on Daniel Nettle's *Happiness: The Science behind Your Smile* (2005). Nettle teaches psychology at the University of Newcastle. Chapter 9 presents Daniel Gilbert's *Stumbling on Happiness* (2006), and chapter 10 presents Tal Ben-Shahar's *Happier* (2007). Gilbert was born in 1957, received a doctorate in social psychology at Princeton University in 1985, and is professor of psychology at Harvard. Ben-Shahar received his doctorate in organizational behavior at Harvard in 2004 and is on the faculty of the Interdisciplinary Center in Herzliya, Israel. He has been a popular lecturer in the psychology department at Harvard.

Part 3, "Some Questions about Happiness," focuses on three books that stand outside the mainstream of happiness studies. Two take a critical view of the contemporary literature on happiness, and the third offers a careful and objective review of views and theories about happiness, thus encouraging us to think clearly and sensitively about the subject. Chapter 11 presents Ronald W. Dworkin's *Artificial Happiness: The Dark Side of the New Happy Class* (2006). An anesthesiologist at the Greater Baltimore Medical Center since 1989, Dworkin received a PhD in political philosophy in 1995. He is a senior fellow at the Hudson Institute, while continuing to work part time as an anesthesiologist. Chapter 12 focuses on Eric G. Wilson's *Against Happiness: In Praise of Melancholy* (2008). He has been a professor of English at Wake Forest University since 1996. Chapter 13 centers on Sissela Bok's *Exploring Happiness: From Aristotle to Brain Science* (2010). Bok is a senior visiting fellow at the Harvard Center for Population and Development Studies and a moral philosopher. In a final chapter, we offer a few "afterthoughts." We imagine our presence at the aforementioned symposium at which the authors whose books are considered here made presentations and then reflecting together over coffee that evening and a couple of days later. This chapter is intended to encourage readers not only to reflect on what the experts assembled here have to say about happiness but also to consider the relevance of what they have to say for their own personal lives.

PART I

SOME INSIGHTS ABOUT HAPPINESS

CHAPTER 1

CULTIVATING HAPPINESS

The first book on happiness that we have chosen to review is Horace Fletcher's *Happiness as Found in Forethought minus Fear-thought*, which was published in 1898.[1] As noted in the introduction, Fletcher was a well-known American lecturer on mental health and diet. In the preface to the second edition, he informs the reader that he wrote the book in response to the many questions elicited by his first book, *Menticulture or the A-B-C of True Living* (1895), in which he argued that anger and worry are the two roots of all destructive passions.[2] In the happiness book, he notes that he could just as well have used the word "fear" instead of "worry" and devotes several chapters to the subject of fear. As in his earlier book, he uses the image of the garden or field where weeds have grown. To get rid of the weeds one does not simply trim them back: rather, one pulls them out by their roots so that they will not grow back.

Similarly, in the preface to his happiness book, he notes that the normal condition of nature is healthy growth, either by evolution or progression; and our chief function in assisting nature is first the removal of weeds or other deterrents and then maintaining the quarantine against their return. He suggests that if we direct our attention to pulling out the weeds nature will respond quickly and do the rest. He also contends that the "tap-roots" of all unhappiness are not very formidable in light of our present knowledge, so anyone who is not keenly happy is the victim of errors or illusions whose germs are easy to eradicate once they have been located. Thus, the purpose of the book is to help those who are suffering from unhappiness to find "the tap-roots of their troubles" (p. 5).

THE NEED FOR A SCIENCE OF HAPPINESS

In the introduction, Fletcher notes that while everyone wants to know how to be happy, the better question is how to become *happier*, because none of us are so miserable that we don't have some degree of happiness at times, even if this is just a fleeting moment when we forgot to be unhappy. He believes that in the civilized world in which he and his readers live, there is everything to encourage, but there should be nothing to prevent, happiness. In fact, the progress that has been occurring has been accelerating so fast that the possibility of unrestrained and unfettered happiness has come to us in advance of our being prepared to accept it, mainly because we are carrying the weight of traditions under whose habits we continue to struggle, long after the conditions that gave birth to the traditions have ceased to exist (pp. 7–8).

He realizes that readers may think that his belief that unfettered happiness is possible reveals his naivety about the troubles and problems of the world, so he devotes several pages to an account of what he calls his "singularly adventurous career" in which he has witnessed many of the conditions in which discomfort, fear, and unhappiness breed, including the worst situations to which human life is subjected. He has shared the occupations and sympathies of persons of many different nationalities and of every degree of opportunity and intelligence, and he has done this on ships, farms, mines, factories, war camps, schoolhouses, and universities (p. 8). He has traveled the world and in the course of his lifetime has worked in some 38 different occupations (p. 15).

But it was the appreciative response that his earlier book on menticulture received that prompted him to think that he might be qualified to write a book on happiness. Before that, he had thought that his "chronic restlessness," when measured by the common estimate of usefulness, was merely a function of his aimlessness. But the sympathetic response his first book received suggested the possibility of using his varied experiences and observations to good advantage by calling attention to uses of energy, points of view, habits of thought and of action that made for happiness in some persons in some parts of the world but were entirely unknown to others in other parts of the world who could take advantage of them (pp. 16–17). He was also led to the study of happiness because of his observations of the neglect of the science of menticulture, which he calls "the science of fundamental means," and of the science of happiness, which he calls "the science of ultimate desirable ends." This neglect is found in civilized communities where persons have the physical means to comfort and happiness. The problem is that these civilized communities have focused so much on developing material and physical *means* to happiness that they have excluded serious thought about cultivating the *ends* of happiness—or, in other words, the best uses to which these means may be put (pp. 17–18).

WHY ARE PEOPLE UNHAPPY?

Fletcher's diagnosis of the reason why people are unhappy is rather simple: the fundamental cause, heredity and environment notwithstanding, is weak habits of thinking. This is proven by observed instances in which strong habits of thought have enabled persons to overcome inherited and environmental deficits, illness, and other weaknesses, and have redeemed them from failure and misery and enabled them to enjoy success, honor, and happiness.

The root of these weak habits of thought, he believes, is fear. But despite the teachings of Jesus and other great teachers of the world's wisdom traditions, and despite the lessons taught by all of nature's processes of growth, we continue to believe that the things we fear—such as death, disaster, and non-attainment—are afflictions necessary to human life and are eradicable only at the change we commonly call "death" (p. 21). He believes that the theologies of the past are partly responsible for this because they used "the whip of fear" as well as "the attraction of love" to incline persons to religion. Theology today does teach the religion of love, but, Fletcher suggests, it has not yet sufficiently denounced the earlier teaching of fears, and this is probably due to the desire for consistency or to filial respect, because parents once put the label of truth on the religion of fear. Science is also to blame because it has taught, and continues to teach, what he calls the "crowding out stimulant" to growth in which one organism flourishes at the expense of another. To be sure, fear has been useful in the evolutionary process because each species has needed to devote much of its thinking to the threat of predators, but that it should still remain a part of the mental equipment of human civilized life is, he believes, quite absurd and simply not useful (pp. 21–23).

Fletcher notes that he has made a study of the reports of many psychological researchers, both here and abroad, who have been devoting particular attention to the causes and effects of fears in children and of their aftereffects on adults. These studies reveal that the consideration of the future that constitutes *forethought* is a mixture of hope, faith, and fear. Taken together, they are stimulants to action and to progress, with hope and faith being what he calls the "civilized" or "divine" motives, and fear being the "animal" motive. However, he believes that the fear element of forethought is not a positive stimulant for more civilized persons but is rather a weakening element of forethought precisely because it is no longer necessary (pp. 23–24).

He also points out that when he claimed in his earlier book that anger and worry are the two roots of all negative passions, some readers took him to mean that they should not engage in forethought at all because they understood worry to mean any consideration of the future whatsoever (p. 46). Rather, he was viewing worry in a narrower sense as an *apprehensive* consideration of the future, so he has coined the word "fear-thought" to address this misunderstanding. Thus, fear-thought is the tap-root of which anger and worry are the surface roots (pp. 60–61).

The problem, though, is that most people believe that fear-thought is necessary to forethought, and this is simply not the case. His rationale for claiming that it is unnecessary is somewhat unclear, but it seems to be based on the belief that fear-thought is not only unproductive but also adds complications of its own. For example, as he noted earlier in *Menticulture* (1895), in the vast majority of cases, worry's prophecies never come true, or, if they do, their fulfillment is generally caused by the worry itself (p. 14). In any event, in his book on happiness he asserts that fear-thought can be eliminated from forethought as soon as it becomes evident to a person that it is unnecessary. Thus, he advocates "fearlessness" or "freedom from fear," believing that this is the critical step toward the realization of a society in which famine, selfishness, and misery are eliminated, and "happiness becomes enthroned as the ruler of a joyously industrious and universally prosperous people" (p. 26).

Thus, the contention of the book is that there is a way to individual happiness, even under existing conditions. Moreover, the present acceleration of progress, along with certain already accomplished tests of potential industrial and economic reform, coupled with an optimism that proclaims that all *can be* and therefore *shall* be well, offers not just the promise but the assurance of equal opportunities for securing happiness throughout the world, and by means that are honest, honorable, and unselfish (pp. 27–28).

WHAT IS HAPPINESS AND HOW CAN WE CULTIVATE IT?

In chapter 1, titled "Hypotheses," Fletcher states that "happiness is the evidence and fruit of growth" (p. 30). In chapter 3, titled "Prefatory Definitions," he says that happiness is "the evidence and fruit and reward of growth as involved in altruism" (p. 54). Altruism, which is inspired by love, expresses the divine quality in the human person that grows out of appreciation (p. 50). However, this altruism is not a *reciprocal* altruism where one expects that one's loving act will be reciprocated, but a *spontaneous* altruism that is voluntary, uncalculated, and without reward, except as this is experienced in the act itself. He suggests in this regard that Christ is the Perfect Altruist (p. 51).

Following his definition of happiness, he introduces the idea of *egociation*, a word he coined to contrast with *egotism* (which is the effect or product of fear-thought), and suggests that *egociation* is "an [a]ppreciation of self as a creation of God and an instrument of [a]ltruism" (p. 54). Thus, the appreciation is focused on the self, not, however, for selfish ends but for the purpose of the growth that is grounded in altruism. He adds that self-forethought, self-carefulness, self-culture, and self-respect are in no way related to selfishness, but instead afford strength for useful purposes (p. 57).

How does this growth occur? Analogous to the natural world, human growth will naturally occur if it is not impeded or deterred. So our role is essentially that of assistants to the natural growth process. Human beings, he notes, have done all sorts of things to cultivate the natural growth process—such as selecting, arranging, separating, watering, fertilizing, and so forth—but we have not been able to add a single cell to growth itself. Yet, by removing deterrents to growth, we have enabled nature to do its part, and there is overwhelming evidence that nature takes advantage of the opportunity to do so (p. 32).

Thus, if fear-thought and its various expressions, such as anger and worry, are eradicated, then nothing can prevent happiness from occupying its rightful place in our lives. But to eradicate fear-thought, we need to believe that it is separable from forethought, and we also need an effective method for separating the two. He suggests that repression is ineffective because it accepts the fact that fear-thoughts will continue to manifest themselves, although in a diminished or more circumscribed form. In contrast, eradication rejects fear-thoughts altogether (pp. 35–36). The future, then, is the field in which growth must take place and the time for action is not the distant future but the "immediate-next-future" (p. 36). If your mind is concentrated on the action itself, it will be impossible to entertain fear-thoughts or its derivatives, such as anger, worry, suspicion, jealousy, envy, malice, or indifference. Why? Because the mind cannot be occupied with two distinct thoughts at the same time. So if it is focused on the immediate-next future, it will be occupied with what is being enacted and, therefore, it will not entertain fear-thoughts. And if, once eradicated, the noxious weeds of fear-thought threaten to return, your newly acquired knowledge of its capacity to cause harm will aid in your determination to resist it until this resistance itself becomes a habit of mind. And then, and *only* then, will you be free—free to grow, to eagerly serve, and to be altogether happy (p. 37).

WAGING WAR ON FEAR-THOUGHT

Having emphasized that fear-thoughts are the greatest threat to happiness, Fletcher devotes several chapters to waging war against fear-thought and its derivatives. These chapters focus on the analysis of fear, the harmful effects of fear, how to eliminate fear, and how to cure special forms of fear. There are also chapters on pain and worry.

In the first of the three chapters on fear, he cites the work of Angelo Mosso, a physiologist at the University of Turin in Italy, who has demonstrated the negative effects of fear on the tissues of the body. According to Mosso and his students, fear allows or causes inflammation, fever, and other unhealthy conditions that are favorable to the incubation of the microbes of special diseases, such as those that are sometimes found in the air or in the water we drink. He also cites a study by an unnamed English physician who has shown how fear causes the molecules in the body to separate from one another and thus create the "relaxed condition" in which disease originates (pp. 69–70). Finally, he cites the research conducted by American psychologists, such as G. Stanley Hall of Clark University and editor of the *American Journal of Psychology* and Dr. Colin A. Scott, professor of Psychology and Child Study at the Cook County Normal School in Chicago, whose studies of fear in children have exposed the absurdity as well as the sources of children's fears, and whose questionnaires have also exposed the fact that an overwhelming percentage of adult fears are unreasonable and absurd (pp. 73–74). He concludes the chapter by emphasizing the power of suggestion, noting that experiments have shown that a specific fear can be eliminated by the use of a sufficiently powerful countersuggestion (p. 76). If this works for individual and specific fears, it is reasonable to assume that more universal and general fears—including the most basic fear, namely, the fear of death—can be eradicated once and for all.

The chapter on the harmful effects of fear consists of several anecdotes in which fear was either the direct cause of death, a near-death experience, or was responsible for the development of a compensatory bullying personality (pp. 78–88). In the chapter on how to eliminate fear, Fletcher expands on his earlier contention that all fear can be eliminated through countersuggestion of one sort or another. He cites the fear of death as a compelling example because, in his view, this fear is the first of all of the causes of fear-thought. The first step is to do away with any dread of a lifeless human body. Here, the important thing to remember is that the soul and mind count above everything, and the tissue that they once animated counts for nothing when they have left it, no matter what have been the associations, especially if dread of the dead tissue creates emotions that are detrimental to the welfare of the soul or mind (pp. 92–93). The second step concerns the fear we experience when we think of the separation we will experience from the person or persons we love. The way to counter this fear is to think of the separation as unessential when compared with the privilege of having known a beloved one, and that appreciation and gratitude should always outweigh regret in relation to an inevitable change. All the processes of nature teach us that every change results in a better state or condition, and what nature teaches us is supported by Christian and Buddhist beliefs that when death occurs, a new and better life begins (pp. 93–94).

He concludes that any weapon against fear is a good weapon if it is effective. Logic is the most respectable of all weapons. But because many of our fear-thoughts are absurd, ridicule is often more effective than logic.

If a human being is afraid of a mouse, it can be useful to point out how ridiculous it is for a five-foot or a six-foot person to be afraid of a two-inch mouse, especially when one considers the fact that the mouse is more afraid of the human being than the human being could possibly be afraid of the mouse. And finally, if all other suggestions fail, one can use the method of acquaintance. For example, if a person has a fear of a lifeless human body, an apprenticeship in a hospital dissecting room may be a profitable expedient. Or, in the case of fearsome insects and animals, close observation and study of their habits is better than to suffer harm from a needless prejudice against them (pp. 97–99).

In the chapter on how to cure special forms of fear, Fletcher tells about his own experiment with a mother and her children whom he met at the World's Columbian Exposition. They were all afraid of thunderstorms. His experiment was designed to test the effectiveness of exciting their interest in the intrinsic beauties and usefulness of things that are normally considered disagreeable or dreadful. He provided the mother with statistics showing that the chance of being struck by lightning was only one in a many thousands, and that if one wanted to be struck, one would have to wait, on average, about 10,000 years for one's turn. He also noted the greater beauty of the natural fireworks of the summer season over the displays of fireworks at the exposition and emphasized their relative harmlessness (pp. 100–101). These arguments somewhat modified the mother's fear relative to lightning and thunder, but the real change came through appreciative suggestion and acquaintance. So when a storm approached, he asked the children if they remembered the beautiful fireworks at the exposition? Then he said, "Come here quick!" because "We are going to have something ten times more beautiful, and, oh! Such big booms and bangs. Watch now!" (p. 102). He continued in this manner, repeating the word "beauty" and "beautiful" whenever there was a thunderclap or bolt of lightning. He also wondered aloud what sort of Fourth of July "they" were having up there and added that the storm was clearing the atmosphere so that the sun would shine brighter tomorrow than it ever has, and that it would shine for us, for the plants, and for the butterflies. What he had done was to impress on them the real beauty of the storm and teach them appreciation to take the place of fear. His suggestion reversed their way of looking at storms, and they then found great beauty in them and ceased to fear them (pp. 103–104).[3]

He relates another story about a family composed of a widowed mother and several children, including sons and a daughter, as well as nephews and nieces. The mother's sister, an incurable invalid, had come from her northern home to seek relief in the southern climate where the family lived: "It is impossible to imagine more tender care of an invalid. Each member of the family vied with the others in offering gentle attentions, so that the waning life was filled with happiness that made invalidism almost a pleasure, as being the cause of so much loving consideration" (p. 105). When she died, the remains were sent back to her home in the north so that they could be buried in the family burial lot. As the family waited for the body to be removed, the children of all ages walked in and out of the death chamber, by day and night, as if there had been no death, and there was no expression of dread or fear-thought or mourning. Fletcher observes that it was such a beautiful expression of loving consideration, unmarred by dread or fear-thought, that one could hardly have chosen a better time or place or environment for the occasion of one's passing onto the better life. He adds that if one could witness one's own funeral as an observing spirit, egotism would undoubtedly choose a scene of violent mourning, one that would be long drawn out and painful to as many persons as possible, but, in contrast, loving unselfishness would choose a funeral scene such as the one he witnessed in the home of his friends. He asks his readers to consider which of these options they would choose, and he concludes from this illustration that if we cultivate fear and mourning in connection with death we are unjust to the dead, the living, and to ourselves. Above all, we are cruel to the tender and impressionable emotions of children to whom we are constantly leaving legacies either of cowardice and ignorant egotism or of pure suggestion, love, and appreciation (pp. 105–108).

PAIN AND WORRY

In subsequent chapters, Fletcher discusses several other situations in which fear-thoughts are likely to manifest themselves. For example, he devotes a chapter to pain and makes the case that pain is endurable if it is not accompanied by fear-thoughts. He describes his own experience of being in a dentist's chair for three hours during which the dentist used wooden wedges to hold open his mouth. This experience afforded him ample time to test the hypothesis that concentrating his mind on some unrelated subject or object would make him oblivious to the sense of pain. He also points to the experience of childbirth, noting that there are great differences in the ease or discomfort of the process, and these are largely influenced by the feeling of welcome or the attitude of aversion with which the newcomer is greeted by the mother (pp. 155–158). He also tells about a young man who was employed in a publishing house whose proprietor was a great worrier. The young man's health began to deteriorate to the point where he began to consider suicide as the only way out of his misery. Then one day someone suggested to him that his ill health was due to worry and its attendant frustrations and anger. So he began to keep a ledger in which each time a worry entered his mind he wrote it down. At the end of the month he discovered that only 3 percent of the predictions were even remotely realized.[‡] This story, of course, has a happy ending: the old proprietor of the business who was the cause of the younger man's worry is no longer living, and the young man now owns the business, which has become very successful, largely because the sunny optimism of its new owner attracts customers (pp. 201–202).

THE HAPPILY MISERABLE

Fletcher also has a chapter titled "Unhappy Unless Miserable." Here, he notes that there are a great many persons who are unhappy unless they have a real or fancied cause for complaint. For such persons, martyrdom is their recreation, and they tend to be greedier for this form of recreation than those whose recreation is of a joyous sort. Is there anything that we can do to help such persons to develop a more positive and optimistic view of life? Fletcher believes that there is. He suggests that if we believe our pessimistic friends can be happier than they are, and can become better companions and citizens by a change of attitude toward life, we can use the gentle method of countersuggestion to good effect, and even go so far as to laugh at and otherwise ridicule the misery habit if by doing so we stand a good chance of correcting that which logic has failed to cure (pp. 163–164).

He also notes that the misery habit feeds on sympathy. Children will not continue an angry or surly crying spell if they are sure that it is not producing a sympathetic effect. The same is true of grown persons who practice the misery habit in public and give themselves a rest when they are not being observed. If this is true, we should assume that the object of pessimism or the misery habit is generally to secure selfish attentions by dishonest means. There are some persons who have acquired the misery habit through contact with respected persons who have been the cause of perverse suggestions too strong to be resisted. Such persons deserve our pity; and, in their case, the attempted cure should be one of gentle and loving suggestion. But perverse and chronic practitioners of the misery habit deserve no tolerance whatsoever, because they live and thrive on the unmerited sympathy of others (pp. 164–165).

He also points out that sometimes the victim of the misery habit practices it only within the family, and this makes it especially severe on the family and is much more difficult to treat. He suggests that the family is the locus of the greatest liberty but also the home and breeding ground of the greatest tyranny. It is supposed to be under the holy protection of the divine principle of love, but if that principle does not prevail in a given family, there is no protection whatever from the most inhumane of practices; instead, there is the license to cultivate the most discordant passions (pp. 165–166). Furthermore, when the victim of the misery habit is a family member, you can't simply get rid of the problem by getting rid of this person. And who, after all, would have it otherwise? The whole tendency of civilization is to appreciate the family more and more and to cultivate respect for the family model as the basis of good government. But it is the very indissoluble nature of these bonds that gives the selfishly inclined opportunity to practice the misery habit without fear of being thrown out, left behind, or otherwise gotten rid of (pp. 166–167).

Is there a remedy? Yes, according to Fletcher. It is nothing less than the prescription written out, as it were, by Jesus himself, for if Christianity were to be measured by the optimism of the Master, if the gauge of optimism prescribed by him were to be used to measure professing Christians, if cause and effect were to be placed in true relation to each other, and if the ills we cultivate were to be classed as self-imposed causes and not effects, and if the unnecessary and unprofitable were to be ranked as nonrespectable, then the misery habit would cease to be fashionable; and the family, the principal breeding ground of pessimism, would be purified, as befits its holy office (p. 168). In short, the misery habit is a counterfeit form of happiness. It is gained at the expense of others, and it produces unnecessary discord. In effect, it is a blatant violation of the real meaning of happiness.

What, then, for Fletcher, is the real meaning of happiness; and how, in the final analysis, is it cultivated? Happiness, he believes, grows out of an appreciation of self that is not distorted by various forms of fear-thought and expresses itself in spontaneous love in such a way that this expression understands and serves—with enthusiasm—the higher law of harmony (p. 55).

CHAPTER 2

THE DESIRE FOR HAPPINESS

The second book we have chosen to review is Karl Hilty's *Happiness: Essays on the Meaning of Life* (1903). As noted in the introduction, Hilty was a professor at Bern University in Switzerland. This book has chapters on the following topics: happiness, the art of work, how to fight the battles of life, good habits, the children of light and darkness, the art of having time, and the meaning of life. In addition to the chapter on happiness, there are discussions of happiness in the chapters on the art of work and the art of having time, and a brief reference to happiness in the chapter on the meaning of life.

THE DESIRE TO BE HAPPY

Hilty begins his chapter on happiness with the claim that from the first hour of one's waking consciousness until that consciousness ceases altogether, one's most ardent desire is to be happy; and that the moment of our profoundest regret is when we become convinced that perfect happiness cannot be found in this life. He suggests that this is the problem that gives the various periods of human history their special character, for there are periods when young and progressive nations still hope for happiness; but there are also periods when great masses of people are convinced that all the familiar formulas for securing happiness are illusions. Also, there have been persons of the keenest insight who have pointed out that whenever one speaks of happiness it flees, and that happiness, in its very nature, lies beyond the sphere of practical realization (p. 97).

But he does not agree with them. He believes that happiness can be found. If he thought otherwise, he would not make unhappiness even more discouraging by writing about happiness. He acknowledges that those who talk of happiness often do so with a sigh, as if there were reasons to doubt whether happiness can ever be attained; and he also notes that at the present time, irrational views of happiness are expounded by political leaders and others. But instead of merely dismissing these irrational views of happiness, perhaps we can use them to acquire that level of spiritual and material development that is the necessary foundation for real happiness. In other words, imperfect views of happiness and how to acquire it prompt us to develop more adequate views (pp. 97–98).

INADEQUATE VIEWS ON HAPPINESS

As we assess the extant views on happiness and how to secure it, Hilty proposes that we turn to our own experience for guidance. When we do, we encounter what would seem to be a serious contradiction, namely, that what we learn from our own experience is that there is much in life that does *not* bring happiness, and that there is no way to avoid these experiences. Any theory about gaining happiness that suggests otherwise is terribly misleading (pp. 98–99). He also notes that the paths by which people journey toward happiness lie partly through the world around them and partly through the experience of their souls. So, on the one hand, there is the view that happiness comes from wealth, honor, and enjoyment of life or from health, culture, science, or art; and, on the other hand, there is the view that happiness is found in a good conscience, in virtue, in work, in charitable acts, in religion, and in devotion to great ideas. Referring to the former as "outward ways to happiness," he suggests that in one way or another, they are all disappointing. Why? For one thing, not everyone is able to follow these paths, so, for many persons, they don't lead to happiness. For another, those who possess outward blessings cannot help but feel some twinge of conscience unless, of course, they are thoroughly selfish or profoundly unhappy despite their wealth, honor, good health, and so on (p. 100). In Hilty's view, Jesus was thinking of such persons when he said that it is easier for a camel to go through the eye of a needle than for a rich person to enter the kingdom of God (Mark 10:25) (pp. 99–100).

He turns, therefore, to internal notions of happiness and how these are to be secured. They include performing one's duty, personal work for the public good, patriotism, charity, philanthropy, and conformity to the teachings of one's religion. He believes that a great deal of the pessimism in the present day is due to the discovery that none of these ways leads to happiness. On the other hand, the realist philosophies that are skeptical of these idealistic means of gaining happiness are not based on the conviction that realism will make one happy, but only that these philosophies will save one from the despair of attempting to find any other way to happiness, whether external or internal (p. 105). While he does not want to join in the moralists' condemnation of such realism, he does want to reject the realists' conclusion that happiness is unattainable. In fact, he believes that realists have taken the first necessary step on the way to happiness, which is to rid oneself of the belief that if wealth, honor, good health and such do not result in happiness, neither do these expressions of virtue, religious conformity, and so on. They provide, at best, temporary happiness (p. 105).

Concluding that none of the ways discussed thus far can lead to happiness, Hilty takes up the idea that work is essential to happiness. He notes that work is certainly one great factor of human happiness. Indeed, in one sense, it is the greatest: for without work, all happiness that is not mere intoxication is absolutely denied. No one can be happy without some work to do. And yet it is a serious error to suppose that work is in itself happiness, or to believe that every work leads to happiness. After all, one can hardly imagine a heaven or an earthly paradise devoted to unremitting work, and even those who take a great deal of pride in describing themselves as "working people" are interested in reducing their workday. So if work were essentially the same as happiness, these persons would be seeking to prolong their hours of work as much as possible. Moreover, only a fool can be wholly contented with the work that he or she does. In fact, one might even say that the wisest persons among us see most clearly the incompleteness of their work, so that not a single one of them has been able, at the end of his or her day's work, to say of it, "Behold, it is very good." The simple praise of work, therefore, is, for the most part, only a sort of spur or a kind of whip with which one motivates oneself as well as others to the tasks of life (pp. 109–110).

THE ESSENTIAL CONDITION OF HAPPINESS

Hilty concludes his chapter on happiness with a discussion of what he considers to be the first and most essential condition of true happiness, namely, a firm faith in the moral order of the world. If a person lacks this firm faith in the moral order of the world and instead believes that the world is governed by chance or by the unchanging laws of nature, or if a person imagines a world controlled by the cunning and power of members of the human species, then there is no hope of personal happiness (p. 113). He acknowledges that there is no formal proof of this moral order of the world, but if one begins simply to live as if the world is morally ordered, the path to personal happiness lies plainly in view. The door is open, and no one can shut it; and within one's heart there is a certain stability, rest, and assurance that will endure and even gather strength as one encounters life's outward storms. One's heart becomes neither contrary nor fearful but "fixed" (Psalm 108:1).

So the only peril from which one has to guard oneself is that of regarding too seriously the changing impressions and events of each day.

Also, one's desire must be to live resolutely in an even mood and to look for one's daily share of conscious happiness not in one's emotions but in one's activity (p. 115). It is then that a person, for the first time, learns what work really is. It is no longer a fetish to be served with anxious fear or an idol through which one engages in self-worship. It is simply the natural and healthy way of life, and it frees a person not only from the many spiritual evils that are produced by idleness but also from the many physical evils that have the same source. Happy work is the healthiest of human conditions (pp. 115–116).

Hilty concludes that there are two secrets of happiness that are fundamentally inseparable. The first secret is that one's life is directed by faith in the permanent moral order of the world. The other is that one's work is done in that same faith. Beyond these two, all other ways of seeking happiness are secondary. In fact, they come of their own accord, according to each person's own special needs, but only if one firmly holds to these primary sources of spiritual power (p. 116).

In a few remaining paragraphs, Hilty mentions some subordinate rules for happiness that one can readily deduce from life experience. He calls them "maxims of conduct" and notes that many other such maxims could be added to them. He also notes that these are merely maxims and not the foundation for some sort of system of morals. Rather, they are simply suggestions based on observation. They include the following: (1) be brave and humble at the same time, (2) do not make pleasure an end, (3) one can bear all troubles except sin and worry, (4) everything excellent has a small beginning, and (5) the paths that are best to follow are entered by open doors (pp. 116–117).

In addition, among the best sources of happiness is the enjoyment found in small things and among humble persons, for one avoids many of life's bitter experiences by the habit of an unassuming life, and the best way to have permanent peace with the world is not to expect too much of it, on the one hand, nor, on the other hand, to be afraid of it. Also, one must not take this life too seriously. Many people suffer from making their problems out to be more than they merit, and this is especially likely to occur when they are dependent on other people's opinions and validations. This lack of proportion makes each day's work much more difficult than it deserves to be (pp. 117–118).

Finally, he adds "one last and solemn truth," namely, that under the conditions of human life, unhappiness is also necessary. In fact, in a certain sense, unhappiness is essential to happiness. As the experience of life plainly shows, unhappiness is inevitable, and one must, in one way or another, reconcile oneself to this fact, for efforts to ignore this fact of life simply do not work. Furthermore, unhappiness does us good in at least three ways: as a punishment, it teaches us the natural consequence of our misdeeds; as a cleansing process, it inspires in us a greater seriousness and makes us more receptive to truth; and as a spur to self-examination, it fortifies us by disclosing the degree to which we may rely on our own strength and the extent to which we must rely on God's strength (pp. 119–121). Thus, unhappiness lies on the road of life, and one needs to expect to meet it if one is to become happy. He has observed that many persons, when they see this "lion in their path," turn back and content themselves with something less than happiness. But in such situations one should instead continue forward, reminding oneself that in one's misfortunes, as in one's enjoyments, imagination greatly outruns reality and that pain is seldom as great as imagination pictures it. Even so, to continue forward requires courage, and "of all the human qualities which lead to happiness, certainly the most essential is courage" (p. 122).

WORK AND HAPPINESS

As we have seen, Hilty does not believe that work and happiness can be equated, but he does believe that work is essential to happiness. However, whether work is conducive to happiness or not depends on what kind of work it is, for not all work is conducive to it. He begins his chapter on the art of work with a brief discussion of the contemporary situation. He notes that although everyone likes to praise work, pleasure in work does not always come with the praising. In fact, the disinclination to work is so prevalent that it is almost a disease of modern civilization, and as long as everyone tries as soon as possible to escape from the work that they theoretically praise, there is absolutely no hope for any improvement regarding our social condition (p. 3).

Thus, all members of a society need to be engaged in "faithful work," and such work cannot be brought about by compulsion or force. Instead, what needs to be kindled among persons is the desire for work, and this desire cannot be attained by instruction or example. Rather, it is attained by reflection and experience, for reflection on experience reveals that work and rest are not contradictory but are, in fact, mutually supportive. Thus, rest is not to be found in complete inactivity of mind or body, or in as little activity as possible, but in well-adapted and well-ordered activity of both body and mind. We are created for activity, and the inactive person will suffer as a direct result of inactivity. True rest results from work itself. Intellectual rest occurs through the perception of fruitful progress in one's work and through the solving of one's problems, while physical rest occurs through the natural intermissions that are provided by daily sleep and daily food, and the essential and restful pause of Sunday. This condition of continuous and wholesome activity, interrupted only by these natural pauses, is the happiest condition in each case, and no one should wish any other outward happiness.

Also, it doesn't matter all that much what the nature of this activity is, for any genuine activity that is not mere sport has the potential for becoming interesting as soon as one becomes seriously absorbed in it. So, it is not the kind of activity that ensures happiness but the joy of action and attainment. Thus, it follows that the greatest unhappiness that one can experience is to have a life to live without work to do and to come to the end of life without the fruit of accomplished work (pp. 6–7).

Hilty also points out that the right to work is the most basic of all human rights, and that the unemployed are the most unfortunate of all. However, he notes that there are as many of these unemployed persons in the so-called better classes as in the so-called working classes. Whereas working class persons are driven to work by necessity and therefore suffer unhappiness when there is no work to be had, the unemployed among the better classes are condemned to unhappiness because of their mistaken ways of education, their prejudices, and the long-standing custom in certain classes to forbid genuine work. He believes that most nervous disorders would be healed if physicians in sanitariums and mental hospitals would prescribe work (pp. 7–8).[1]

Having argued that work is essential to personal happiness, Hilty mentions one qualification, namely, that not all work is of equal value in this regard. For example, factory labor is not very satisfying because the workers perform only one part of the work and see little of the fruits of their labor. This is why a farmer is usually more contented than a factory worker. On the other hand, the happiest workers are those who have at least the feeling—sometimes, no doubt, without adequate reason—that they are accomplishing real work for the world: a true, useful, necessary work. Thus, the first thing the modern world needs to develop is the conviction and experience that well-directed work is the necessary and universal condition of physical and intellectual health and, for this reason, is the way to happiness (pp. 9–10).

In the remaining pages of the chapter Hilty engages in what he calls "instruction in the art of work" (p. 11). Like every other art, work has its own ways of dexterity by means of which one may greatly lessen its laboriousness. Furthermore, not only the willingness to work but also the capacity to work is often so difficult to acquire that many persons fail to develop this capacity. But the first step toward overcoming a difficulty is to recognize the difficulty, and, in the case of work, what chiefly hinders work is laziness. No one is completely immune to laziness because it comes so naturally and easily, and, conversely, no one is naturally fond of work. Even the most active-minded persons among us would amuse themselves with other things than work if afforded the opportunity (pp. 11–12).

Thus, love of work needs to proceed from a motive that is stronger than the motive of physical idleness, and Hilty suggests that this motive is to be found in either of two ways: it can be a low motive, such as ambition; or it can be a higher motive, such as a sense of duty, a love for the work itself, or done out of love for someone else, such as one's family. These higher motives have the advantage over the lower motives because they are more permanent and not dependent on the mere success of work. In other words, such work does not lose its force either through the disheartening effect of failure or the satisfying effect of success. Ambitious and self-seeking persons are often very diligent workers but are seldom continuous and evenly progressive workers. Instead, they are almost always content with that which looks like work if it produces favorable conditions for themselves, even if it does not do so for others. So if Hilty were to give younger persons who are entering into life a word of preliminary counsel, he would advise them to do their work from a sense of duty, or for love of what they are doing, or for love of certain specific persons. A second piece of counsel would be that the most effective instrument to overcome one's laziness in work is the force of habit, because no virtue is securely possessed until it has become a habit. So if younger persons train themselves to the habit of work, the resistance of idleness constantly diminishes until work finally becomes a necessity; and when this happens, one has become free from a very large portion of the troubles of life (pp. 12–14).

But how does one develop this habit? Hilty suggests that there are a few "elementary rules" that will help one cultivate this habit of work. The first rule has to do with knowing how to begin. The very resolution to set ourselves to work and to fix our whole mind on the matter at hand is really the hardest part of working. Some people, for example, spend so much time with preparing to work that they only begin when they are compelled to do so, often by external forces. The resulting feeling is that there is insufficient time to do the work, and this, in turn, injures the work itself. Other people wait for some special inspiration that, in reality, is much more likely to come by means of, or in the midst of, the work itself. So the first rule is not to postpone work but instead to dedicate a specific and well-considered amount of time every day to particular tasks relating to work (pp. 15–16).

The second rule is not to waste time. This often happens by spending too much time on the arrangement of the work or on the introduction to the work. One should begin without any preamble to one's work because whatever the preamble might be, it invariably turns out to be a weak or poor anticipation of what is to follow. In Hilty's view, this is especially true of writing books—and we could just as easily mention articles, dissertations, and the like (p. 16).

The third rule is that it is best to begin with that part of the work that is easiest for you, because the most important thing is simply beginning work. It is true that one may progress less directly in one's work when one does it unsystematically, but this loss is more than made up for by the gain in time realized from the momentum acquired in simply beginning work early and continuing it on a regular basis (pp. 16–17).

This rule has two subordinate rules. The first is not to get ahead of oneself. Hilty notes that we are endowed with the dangerous gift of imagination, its dangerousness deriving from the fact that it has a much larger realm than that of one's capacity. Thus, our imagination envisions the whole work lying before us as a task to be achieved all at once, while our capacity can complete its task only by degrees and must constantly renew its strength. So, as a rule, one should do one's work for each day. Tomorrow will come when it comes, and with it will come the strength that the new day requires (p. 17).

The second subordinate rule is that in intellectual work one should deal with one's material thoroughly, but one should not expect to exhaust one's material in the belief that when it is finished there should be nothing further to research. No single person's strength is sufficient for absolute thoroughness, and the person who tries to do too much usually accomplishes too little (p. 18).

The fourth rule is that one should not persist in working when work has lost its freshness and pleasure. One may—and should—begin work without pleasure, for otherwise one may not begin at all, but one should stop as soon as one's work itself brings fatigue. This does not mean that one should stop *all* work, but only the specific work that is fatiguing. In fact, change in work is almost as refreshing as complete rest, and were this not the case, we would hardly accomplish anything (p. 18).

A fifth rule is that in order to be able to do much work one must economize one's force. The practical means to do this is by wasting no time on useless activities. One can hardly overestimate how much pleasure and power for work is lost by this form of wastefulness. The first among such ways of wasting time is by excessively reading newspapers (today we might say by spending an excessive amount of time online, e.g., by e-mailing, by reading Internet sites, or by spending time on Facebook). The second is excessive devotion to societies and meetings. Those who want to do good work and experience pleasure in doing it need to avoid all useless occupation of their minds and bodies and reserve their powers for that which it is their business to do (p. 19).

A sixth rule is that one should develop the habit of reviewing and revising one's work. Speaking specifically of intellectual work, Hilty notes that the work is at first grasped only in its general outlines; and then, as one attacks it a second time, its finer aspects reveal themselves, and the appreciation of it becomes more complete (pp. 19–20).

Hilty concludes his chapter on the art of work by noting that the ideal expression of work is when the mind works continuously, for this is the consequence of having acquired the genuine industry that comes through devotion to one's task. In fact, it often happens that after pauses in one's work that are not excessively prolonged, one's material has unconsciously advanced, and everything has grown spontaneously. Many difficulties seem almost miraculously to have disappeared, and one's first supply of ideas is multiplied, lending itself to further expression, so that the renewal of one's work occurs with ease, as though it were merely the gathering of fruit that had ripened in the interval without effort of one's own. This observation about how work advances without one's being consciously aware of it leads Hilty to return to the claim made earlier in the chapter—namely, that work and rest are not contradictory: for only the person who works knows what enjoyment and refreshment are, and the best, the pleasantest, and the most rewarding way of passing the time is to be occupied with one's work (pp. 20–21).

THE ART OF HAVING TIME

Hilty also refers to happiness in his chapter on the art of having time. The chapter begins with this often-heard lament: "I have no time." He thinks the immediate cause of this perceived lack of time is the prevailing restlessness, the continuous mood of excitement, and the excessive haste of the present age. He suggests several ways in which to defend oneself against these pressures in order to recover the sense that one *does* have time for what matters. Not surprisingly, he suggests that the best way to have time is to have the habit of regular work, not to work by fits and starts, but in definite hours of the day. He agrees that for many persons their work is excessive, but he believes that this is most obviously the case when one cares more for the result of one's work than for the work itself, for under such conditions it is extremely difficult to exercise moderation (pp. 73–77).

Much of the chapter goes on to repeat key points of the chapter on the art of work, including the rules he offered for making work a positive experience and the advice he gave for avoiding distractions, such as reading newspapers and going to meetings. Having reiterated these points, he claims that if one tries to use these ways of saving time, one will make another discovery, which is that one of the most essential elements of happiness lies in not having too much time. The greatest proportion of human happiness consists in continuous and progressive work, and the human spirit is never more cheerful than when it has discovered its proper work. So make this discovery, first of all, if you want to be happy. Most of the problems of human life are caused by having either no work, too little work, or uncongenial work, because the human heart, which is so easily agitated, never beats more peacefully than in the natural activity of vigorous but satisfying work (p. 92).

He concludes the chapter with the observation that there are two possessions that may be attained by persons of every condition and are a constant consolation in misfortune—namely, work and love. But contentedness in

continuous work is possible only when one abandons ambition and also
rejects the philosophy of materialism—the belief that one's life ends with
the death of one's material body—because it claims that this brief life is the
end of opportunity. Under such a view, time is indeed too short, and every
art is too long. Rather, the true spirit of work grows best in the soil of that
philosophy (often called idealism) that sees one's work extending into the
infinite world and one's life on earth as but one part of life itself—for then
one gets strength to do one's highest tasks and the necessary patience when
confronted with the grave difficulties and hindrances that one finds within
oneself and in the times in which one lives. When one has this philosophy,
one is calmly indifferent to much that in the sight of this world alone may
seem important, but which, when seen in the light of eternity, loses significance (pp. 93–94).

THE MEANING OF LIFE

Finally, Hilty makes a brief reference to happiness in his concluding chapter on the meaning of life. To the question "What is the happy life?" his answer
is that it is a life of conscious harmony with the divine order of the world,
a sense, in other words, of God's companionship. To the question "What is
the profoundest unhappiness?" his answer is that it is the sense of remoteness
from God which, in turn, produces an incurable restlessness of heart, and
finally the incapacity to make one's life fruitful or effective. As he points out
in his chapter on happiness, if we begin to live as though we are living in a
moral world, our path to happiness lies plainly before us: the door is open,
and no one can shut it. So, in effect, God is the companion who opens the door
for us because God wants us to be happy; and God's presence alongside us can
give us courage to face "the lion of unhappiness" whose presence might otherwise
cause us to turn back and content ourselves with something less than happiness, something less than our desires, and something less than God desires
for us (p. 14).

CHAPTER 3

THE SCIENCE OF HAPPINESS

The third book we have chosen to review is Jean Finot's *The Science of Happiness* (1914). As noted in the introduction, Finot was born in Poland but lived his adult years in France as a journalist and sociologist. The book consists of a brief introduction followed by eight chapters on the following themes: the possibility of a science of happiness, inner happiness, optimism and pessimism, the unhappiness caused by envy and wealth and the benefits of sorrow, universal happiness, a few catechisms of happiness, the morality of happiness, and what is happiness?

RESHAPING OUR IDEAS ABOUT HAPPINESS

Finot observes in the introduction that we have become so accustomed to hearing our misfortunes discussed that we find it difficult to listen to those who speak to us about happiness. Often we are unduly unhappy because we have been told that we are miserable. Our lives have been painted in such gloomy hues that we believe the brighter portraits of life are inferior to the darker ones, failing to realize that it is much easier to color things black. Yet, we yearn for happiness; and, in principle, there is no reason why we should settle for less. To restore happiness, however, we will need to reshape our ideas about happiness, and this is what his book is all about. He assures his readers that he is not an advocate of the view that everything is for the best in this best of all possible worlds, but he does believe that if we consider ourselves happier than we really are, perhaps some additional happiness will follow, and, in any case, misfortune will not have gained anything (pp. 1–3).

Next, he defends his use of the word "science" in the book's title. He assures his readers that the science he intends to employ is free from dogmatism and contains no imperatives. It simply strives to disengage precepts from facts in much the same way that bees draw honey from flowers. Also, among so many useless sciences, it will at least possess the merit of dealing with the essential concerns of the entire human race. He also assures readers that his own personal ambitions relating to the book are of no significance. His only merit, if any, is that he is calling attention to the need for a science of human happiness. If his efforts are rejected as useless, this is unimportant. In fact, it is the nature of any science that it progresses beyond the achievements of its early practitioners. In his view, the science of happiness promises much and will perform still more. It will be a delightful, altruistic, attractive, and free science committed to human equality. On behalf of the life of everyone, it will strive to release the soul of goodness from evil things and the smile of happiness from the wry faces of life. In its presence, everything will harmonize in pursuit of the same object: to simplify, to increase, and to diffuse happiness upon the earth (pp. 4–7).

A SCIENCE OF HAPPINESS: IS SUCH A THING A POSSIBILITY?

In chapter 1, which deals with the possibility of a science of happiness, Finot elaborates on his observation in the introduction that our belief that we are miserable creatures results from a simple misunderstanding. In accepting this view, we become the victims of "a dangerous mirage" that is all the more dangerous because it constantly increases the number of those who are sacrificed. Yet, there are numerous scientists who assert that the woe that burdens the human race will become heavier and ultimately fatal. The moralists are no better, as they usually scorn happiness. It is as though happiness drags along behind ethical systems like an importunate shadow. He also notes that religion teaches that life on earth is only a dung heap and that it displaces our dreams of happiness onto a future invisible paradise. Among the philosophers, Stoics alone have had the courage to exalt happiness, but their happiness is sorrowful and is always mourning lost illusions (pp. 12–13).

So, if these authorities in science, ethics, religion, and philosophy mention happiness at all, they either devalue or dismiss it. And yet, despite this dismissal by these influential social institutions and cultural forces, the idea of happiness returns, as it were, uninvited and invisible, entering through doors thought to be sealed: It is a voice that insists on being heard. This being the case, we should try to direct its power, to study its operation, and to facilitate its beneficent evolution. In other words, we should try to develop a science of happiness. The chapters that follow are designed to do precisely that (pp. 14–15).

HAPPINESS IS WITHIN US

Finot begins chapter 2 with an account of how the suffering from a loss or misfortune tends to diminish over time. After the immediate experience of various losses or misfortunes, we are unable to think and often we do not even want to survive such losses or misfortunes. But within days, when we are released from the brutal influence of the moment, our minds begin to investigate the situation, and as we look within ourselves, we are astonished to see how greatly our feelings have changed.[1] Our sense of irreparable misfortune and of eternal suffering has disappeared. After another interval of time, another surprise occurs—namely, our sorrows and our acute emotions of despair have suffered a further diminution. Their intensity having disappeared, their faded forms are no longer recognizable. Something vague has replaced our grief, and a day comes when we smile indulgently at past misfortunes. We no longer find in them anything except a subject of study of the changing conditions of our soul.[2] This transformation often occurs suddenly under the influence of a person who is dear to us (pp. 26–27).

The fact that the various degrees, intensity, and extent of these transformations in our minds depend on the sensibility of the individual proves that the source of our sufferings is internal. The external world plays a secondary role. Like a singer standing before the notes of a score, the sweet or mournful tones of our voices follow the external signs, but the unhappiness, like the sounds, is within us. This means that in the majority of cases, happiness and misery are only the fruits of our own sensibility and that misery forms only a portion of our mind. So, in effect, we are the authors of our happiness and our grief. External circumstances are difficult to conquer, but the formation of our ego—its mode of existence and its mode of thought—is within our power. And since we find it difficult or even impossible to change external factors, we need to alter the internal ones (pp. 28–29).

Finot suggests that the way to do this (i.e., the way to author our own happiness) is to govern and to direct our desires. If we cannot have servants, palaces, and unlimited funds, it is easier to drive this longing from our hearts. When we reflect thoughtfully and seriously on the things we formerly so ardently desired, we realize, with a smile, that these things are, in fact, empty. Finot compares this mental process to belief in the devil. As long as people believed in the devil, he appeared to them, but the abandonment of this belief was sufficient to make him cease to disturb even their dreams. The happiness that we gain from curbing our appetite for inaccessible things becomes an acquisition equaling all the blessings of this world (p. 29).

Finot also advises us to consider how we acquired these desires. The fact that they are the product of our education is inescapable. Through education we form opinions of things, and these opinions become the source of our beliefs about happiness. And yet, most persons spend more time on the arrangement of their hair than they do in forming or correcting the opinions on which their happiness depends. If we get upset with people who give us bad advice concerning the purchase of furniture, if we are suspicious of a poorly baked loaf of bread, and if we are on guard when eating in a doubtful place, shouldn't we also be suspicious of the purveyors of false opinions about happiness? (p. 32). Finot thinks so. For example, we know that the pursuit of wealth crushes the firmest characters and reduces to fragments the most stable principles of societies and of individuals; yet, once the attractions and charms of wealth enter our minds, we adorn it with invincible and alluring powers. But we need only to examine it from a certain point of view, and its intoxicating beauties will vanish forever (p. 35).

And what is this point of view? Finot relates the parable a teacher told him when he was a boy. It was about a country that no one enters except himself. Once there, he finds a resplendent kingdom, full of mysterious charms, and the moments he spends in this fascinating kingdom are the sweetest of his whole existence. He laments the fact that he is able to go there so rarely but envisions a time when everyone will have the opportunity to spend a large portion of their lives in this happy country. Years later, Finot understood that the parable was about happiness, for the more we reflect, the more we perceive that happiness dwells within us and that through a regrettable lack of comprehension, we wear ourselves out looking for it elsewhere (pp. 35–36).

Finot concludes the chapter with a discussion of the role played by the will in fostering inner happiness. Noting that the power of suggestion is an especially effective ally of the will, he observes that modern science has instituted almost a worship of suggestion. However, when suggestion is utilized as a beneficent force and subordinated to the reasoning and rational will, it can radically transform and improve our lives. In fact, psychotherapy, the new medical method, teaches us that certain diseases vanish, as if by magic, in consequence of suggestions repeated over and over again. However, he cautions that to operate in an efficient manner, suggestion requires a method, a discipline of the mind, the first step of which is to develop a pedagogy that offers young minds suggestions concerning the value of wealth, of ambition, of fame, or of happiness itself (pp. 43–47).

OPTIMISM AND PESSIMISM

Chapter 3, which is on optimism and pessimism, is an excursus on the claim that although religion, philosophy, and literature are frequently at odds, they affectionately clasp hands when the object is to crush the joy and happiness of their faithful friends. We will not discuss this chapter in any detail here because it is mainly designed to support his earlier claim that advocates for happiness face an uphill battle in an age when the brighter portraits of life are believed to be inferior to the darker ones (p. 48). But we do want to note that in the concluding pages of the chapter he makes an interesting connection between happiness and age by contending that pessimism is essentially juvenile. He suggests that we usually fall into its nets before the mind has a chance to mature. Before climbing the mountain, we see only the rocks that block the way; and before appreciating the serene aspects of life, we see only the dark little corners—but age and experience, he notes, almost always tear away the "black bandage" that pessimism places over our eyes (p. 102).

He cites the example of the German poet and dramatist Johann von Goethe, who once wrote that "to be pessimistic in feeling we must be young." At the age of 39, Goethe wrote that he was "not made for this world," but, at the age of 81, he declared, "I am happy," and that his only unhappiness was that he could not live his life over again. Finot concludes that many writers have died pessimists from not having reached the age of optimism. He adds, however, that the mere question of years often plays no part in it: that it is the wise experience of life that counts the most. So his advice to those who are young is that they live as though the mountain up ahead is not as formidable as it may appear to be (p. 102).

ENVY, THE BENEFITS OF SORROW, AND WEALTH

In chapter 4, Finot focuses on the unhappiness caused by envy, the benefits of sorrow, and wealth. In his discussion of envy and its power to make us unhappy, he considers the desire we have to make other people envious of us. He suggests that this is a desire that emerges in childhood, that it increases as we grow older, and that it continues throughout life. It even manifests itself after death in the form of mausoleums and tombs intended to create envy among those who survive us. The author who tells us about his wonderful books; the woman who boasts of her success with men; the politician who dazzles us with his influence; and the financier, the physician, and the lawyer who proclaim the amount of their income are all acting under the domination of the same motive—the desire to be envied—that urges a snobbish person to sit in the front boxes at the theater or to drive around in an expensive automobile (pp. 110–111).

In Finot's view, history has proven that envy has been the most detestable factor in the march of human affairs, for it has generated all the great social and political revolutions and it has created more suffering than poverty. If the dominant groups had been able to resist the deceptive charms of envy, human society would have taken a very different course. The problem is that those who take pleasure in creating envy seem oblivious of its poisonous character. Nor do they seem to be aware of the fact that it humiliates and creates bitterness in others, and that it also stifles the development of feelings of justice, benevolence, and sympathy, as well as the will of those who are its target. The pleasure one derives from making others envious, he suggests, is not true happiness. When Finot asked a famous psychologist why he boasted of his success as an author when his other achievements—that is, his achievements as a psychologist—would have been more than sufficient to make him feel good about himself, the man replied: "The potion of envy which we make friends and enemies drink affords us delicious sensations." But over time, his colleagues became exasperated with his bragging, and they took steps to diminish his success and ridicule his fame. Now he curses the fatal envy that prompted him to pour poisons for others and that now compels him to swallow it himself (pp. 111–113).

Finot rejects the argument that envy is innate, because he observes that the behavior of young children attests to the fact that we are not born with it. This being the case, we need to modify our pedagogy so that instead of sowing envy, we learn to extirpate it from our minds and souls, for to be rid of envy is almost the equivalent of being certain of happiness. He cites the Roman author Ausonius whose father said to him, "I have always thought that happiness consisted not in having everything that we desire, but in not desiring what fate has not bestowed." Animated by this thought, Ausonius desired only the things within his reach, and all his life he asked of God only the favor of having nothing to covet. He died happy because he had lived a life free from envy (pp. 119–120).

Finot next takes up the subject of the benefits of sorrow. In his view, our pleasures, joys, sorrows, and sufferings are all part of life, and together they lend it value. If anyone believes that a life in which sorrow is absent is as close as we can come to a life of happiness, this person should consider those mentally ill persons who are insensible to sorrow. A fixed smile on their lips bears witness to the aberrant condition of their minds. They are sheltered from suffering, but are they happy? Or better yet, who of us would wish to accept their happiness as our own? (pp. 122–124).

Sorrow, he believes, ennobles the soul, forcing it to reflection; and, during the constant march to the future, it serves as a stopping point. It purifies the soul and plays the role of the soul's mirror, reflecting its faults, sins, deficiencies, and negligence. It also serves a pedagogical purpose, showing us the mistakes in the path we are pursuing and revealing to us new and better paths. When it does not destroy, sorrow strengthens us (pp. 126–127). In support of this claim, he cites recent research studies on the nerves that are specifically affected by sorrow, and notes that a reciprocal and often decisive action of the mind tends to neutralize physiological pain. By using various instruments, researchers have succeeded in demonstrating that joy, sadness, and pain are dependent on our energy. We feel pain when the energy of one of our faculties finds it impossible to move freely, but we experience pleasure and joy when the opposite is the case. Similarly, modern physiologists tell us that joy is the consciousness of the circulation that is acting easily in our nervous systems. Therefore, we need to keep the energy of our minds in reserve so that sufferings and sorrows assume beneficial forms. Then these sorrows will circulate freely through our minds, like the sensations of physical pain that flow without suffering through the nervous centers, for moral or physical pangs can do nothing but retreat before the intense energy of our souls and bodies. Pain, then, is united with our happiness, and the question is not how to destroy it but how to draw strength from it. On the other hand, there must not be too much of it. In endurable doses, pain is our teacher of energy, for, if pleasure enervates and if long continued joy exhausts us, sorrow strengthens us. It is like the shower–bath administered to neurasthenics who shriek while receiving it, and yet they emerge from it feeling rejuvenated and regenerated (pp. 131–135).

Finally, Finot discusses what he calls "the prejudice of wealth." He notes that ancient thought and modern ideas agree that riches do not secure happiness. Yet the attainment of wealth nevertheless exerts a powerful effect on our imaginations, and we all too often sacrifice our human individuality—our autonomy—in exchange for it. Wealth commands a certain respect that it does not deserve; society, for example, always treats a wealthy thief with more respect than a poor honest person. This being the case, a reaction has become necessary, and the current struggle against the worship of wealth offers hope. He cites in this connection the efforts of President Theodore Roosevelt in his attack on dishonest millionaires. However, the problem is that even though we endorse the view that wealth does not procure happiness, and we use it to console friends who are in economic distress, we lack the strength of soul to apply it to ourselves. As a result, we destroy our health by fretting because we do not have at our disposal all that the rich possess, and we add envy to our regrets, which is like quenching thirst by eating salt (pp. 135–145).

The question, then, is how do we rid ourselves of a desire that we know will not secure our personal happiness? One way to do this is to challenge the feelings of envy that we experience when we hear about the wealthy, their activities, and so forth. But how does one do this? Finot suggests that making the acquaintance of those we envy can be very helpful. He relates his conversation with the richest man in Paris. It took place in the man's drawing room, which contained furnishings and paintings equaling the value of a small provincial city. He asked his host point blank: "Are you happy?" The man replied:

Very happy in the opinion of others. But what constitutes happiness? If it is a series of pleasures and gratifications, I very rarely experience any of these. Everything yields or appears to yield before the power of our wealth. Disappointments cause us annoyance as they do others, but we are not delighted by success. The increase of our riches—for is it not said that we are constantly increasing them?—leaves us indifferent, for we well know their part in our happiness. (p. 139)

In response, Finot asked him about the acquisition of the treasures of art for which he was the envy of other art connoisseurs. His host replied, "They undoubtedly afford intense delight—to the man who sells them to me!" And then he added, "There is one rare joy that very wealthy people experience almost never. It is labor crowned with success, a goal attained after the efforts of long years. We lack, in short, that which gives life its zest: its troubles, its difficulties" (pp. 139–140). But Finot persisted, "Is not your case exceptional?" His host answered, "Look around me. See the members of my family, who are so generally envied. Examine their colorless existence, their hopeless melancholy, the lowering of their energy, and you will behold the wrong side of time-honored wealth." Finot comments: "On that day I had the effrontery to pity the richest man in Paris" (pp. 139–140).

On the other hand, Finot cautions against an overreaction that teaches contempt for wealth. The abolition of its excessive worship will suffice. Thinking in pedagogical terms, he imagines a school in which teachers would endeavor to imbue young minds not with contempt for wealth but a sensible comprehension of its merits. They should be shown that wealth and happiness are rarely found on the same path, and that goodness, the soul's inestimable treasure, will obtain for its possessor a happiness that wealth is in no position to bestow. They should also be taught that true wealth lies solely in spiritual independence, for through such independence we can satisfy our every desire because these desires will come only when called by the voice of the soul. Parents should also support the instruction of the teachers by constantly reiterating the same ideas. If they did so, our youth, thus transformed, would be better able to resist the malign influences of life (pp. 156–157).

HAPPINESS THROUGH GOODNESS

In chapter 5, "Happiness for All," Finot discusses happiness through goodness, the affections as sources of happiness, the active life and happiness, the accessibility of happiness to everyone, and religion and religiousness. We will confine our discussion to the themes of goodness, the affections, and religion and religiousness.

Finot begins his reflections on happiness through goodness with an account of how "the conscious principle" that presided over the creation of humankind may have engaged in the following course of reasoning:

The feeble creature which, in developing, will become man will be exposed to every peril. He will suffer from contact with his fellow-creatures. Envy and wickedness will cause him numerous pangs. In the struggle for life, the weak will be crushed by the strong. A prey to constant discouragements, man will lose faith in the future. He will need a companion to brighten his life with the softest rays. He needs a warm hearthstone to vivify his depressed mind. (p. 158)

So we received the gift of a beneficent power and this gift, the tireless partner of our joys and sorrows, has never since that time abandoned us.

What is this gift? It is the gift of *goodness*, a gift that is accessible to all. Its germ exists in all human beings, and, like the sun, it contains an inexhaustible energy and shines for the entire world. Moreover, it makes no distinction between the lofty and the lowly, between religions, sexes, ages, the poor or the rich, the person of talent, or the person of genius. Furthermore, it brightens our lives. The sight of goodness renders faces serene; lavishes strength upon the weak; hope on the despairing; and, like providence, it creates much from nothing. And it is the primary key to happiness because the answer to the question as to how to be happy often resolves itself into the question: "How are we to exercise goodness?" (pp. 159–161).

Finot's account of the creation of the feeble creature who becomes humankind suggests that goodness is innate, but he actually believes that goodness is largely acquired. At least, he suggests that it needs directing toward worthy subjects and to be turned away from things that would make it lose its dignity. He imagines a course on goodness in high schools, and suggests that such a course, among the sciences taught, would be the most useful to the students' happiness and to that of the community. He thinks of the many subjects that could be brought into the teacher's lectures on goodness. The art of serving our neighbor would play the dominant part, but there are a vast number of ways that one can render service to others. In any case, foremost among these subjects would be that of love, for we love better those to whom we have rendered service, and we render service to those whom we love. Goodness and love accompany each other, and together they form one of the necessary conditions of happiness (pp. 162–165).

Unfortunately, people have preached the duty of loving, but they have forgotten to teach us its moral advantages, and especially its effects on happiness. To love means to live a multiple life. We come out of ourselves, but we return far richer than at the moment of departure. We reenter our souls accompanied by delightful companions. Our kindly affections return to our hearts, and when they do so, our ego is multiplied, holds to existence with more ties, and existence is more closely united to us. Thus, affection renders the poorest human beings the equal of sovereigns. It assures us boundless power. We can love, even against the will of the object of our affection. The pleasure of loving, as well as its benefits, lies within us. No one can deprive us of these benefits for they are hidden in the depths of our individuality, and they furnish the most efficacious remedies for the troubles of life because they breathe on pessimism and disenchantment and transform the latter into reasons for existence (pp. 166–170).

So we should not scoff at the idea that goodness is the indispensable foundation of moral progress, and we should also take note of the fact that it is increasing before our very eyes. He cites the physicians who brave death to enrich science with their biomedical discoveries, the aeronauts who expose themselves to unspeakable danger, the revolutionaries who give their lives for the sake of future societies, the workers who join strikes—these and many others are laboring for the benefit of generations that exist only in their imagination. He asks: Is this solidarity not an ideal expression of goodness that has been emancipated from the narrow bonds of blood ties and visible interests? If we fail to take note of the goodness all around us, this is in part because it has become more complex in form and expression. But the fact that it remains indiscernible does not prevent it from growing (pp. 172–174).

THE AFFECTIONS AS SOURCES OF HAPPINESS

In his discussion of the affections as sources of happiness, Finot focuses primarily on the family and friendships. He acknowledges that the family is often the source or cause of unhappiness. Although it can be the source of varied delights, it is also the locus of annoyances, disappointments, and sorrows. It has been said that a family is often only a group of members whose interests are frequently opposed. And examples of unhappy family relationships are all too easy to cite. But precisely because we are becoming more aware of the beneficent virtues of family life, efforts are being made to perfect the family. Marriage is being reformed and efforts are being made to establish stronger fraternal bonds among the family members through equality and liberty. Also, as parents take increasing advantage of child psychology, they rear their little ones in the sanctuary of love that the family of the future will become (pp. 176–179). Moreover, the child is often the very incarnation of happiness. As Victor Hugo says, the child "is joy wandering among us" (quoted in Finot 1914, p. 179).

Regarding friendship, Finot points out that the feeling of friendship makes us grow morally, and such growth occurs even in cases where one's feelings have been exploited. In friendship, as in love, what is important is the joy we have derived from the feeling of friendship, for even if we have been betrayed, no one can deprive us of the emotions we have enjoyed. After all, we discovered that we possessed an open heart, and we can be happy for this self-discovery (p. 184).

Closely related to feelings of friendship are feelings of admiration for others. Finot suggests that we might even speak of the *delight* of admiration, and he suggests that those who can maintain admiration in all its fullness are the happier for it. To be sure, the day may come when our admiration vanishes—when we realize, for example, that we have bestowed it on those who are unworthy of it. Yet, here again, we need to console ourselves, for no one can deprive us of the benefit of having admired, as the joys stored in the depths of our souls are ours to keep (p. 187).

Finally, Finot advises us to look within ourselves. When we do, we discover a rich spectacle of unexpected sensations. We are not, after all, a single and indivisible being, but we are, rather, "multiple beings," and during the course of our existence, numerous persons have lived and died in every one of us. When we are on the threshold of death and cast a glance backward, we are astonished to see that our moral and intellectual life has been only a successive passage of beings born within ourselves, and each of these beings were all dear to us because they formed a portion of our successive personality (pp. 220–224).

Of course, viewing these multiple beings can be disconcerting, especially as we watch them elbow one another, or, even more disturbing, when we witness the conflict between our passionate self and our moral self. Yet, if we observe more closely, we can see beneath the conflicts between two or three of these entities the formation of the guiding principles of our lives. Addressing readers who smile at this claim, Finot suggests that they should enter their own personalities and witness the drama that is being played out there as disinterested spectators. By repeating this experiment 10, 15, or 20 times, the day will come when these skeptical readers will be rapturously interested in the scenes of the life kindling or dying in the home of their own "ego" (p. 226).

HAPPINESS THROUGH FAITH

In his discussion of religion and religiousness, Finot focuses on the theme of "happiness through faith," in which he claims that faith is a supreme benefit to souls, for without it, life becomes colorless, if not sad, and its interest vanishes. Indifference and weariness invade our consciousness and provide a favorable soil for the growth of dissatisfaction. Life becomes a burden. We feel unhappy as a person would be who was condemned to remain in darkness. It is faith that triumphs over our troubles, our discouragements, and our weaknesses. Faith adorns life by giving it an ideal and it strengthens life by giving it a purpose. Whatever its object may be—God, native land, family, science, or humanity—it lends to life an intoxicating fragrance (p. 230).

But faith has been attacked from various sides. Some have argued, for example, that faith is opposed to the interests of real life. Others have claimed that it is not in harmony with scientific methods. Still others detach themselves from it because it is so closely identified with religion, and they are unwilling to walk in the ruts assigned by the churches. Ironically, the religions themselves suffer from its absence, for instead of true believers animated by faith, their followers are often only calculators who accept religions as social necessities or political possibilities. In his judgment, though, faith is one of the most living and dazzling sources of happiness. This being the case, we must, in the name of happiness, emancipate faith from the guardianship of its enemies. Furthermore, it is a mistake to view faith as a noncompanion of religion for even as religion is impossible without faith, so all sincere faith is equivalent to a religion. While their objects may vary and differ, their essence is the same (pp. 231–232).

Finot contends, however, that we need to distinguish between religions and religiousness, for religiousness, the domain of unutterable aspirations, is the divine essence of all religions while religions tend to develop dogmas and creeds, resulting in the diminution of the religiousness that gave birth to them in the first place. On the other hand, it would be unfair to regard all the dogmatic religions as foes of our happiness for when they do not lower the minds of believers by a degrading fanaticism, they exert a beneficial influence. Thus, as long as the spirit of tolerance and human understanding prevails in the religious domain, religion will be a source of serenity and happiness (pp. 240–241).

A FEW CATECHISMS OF HAPPINESS

In chapter 6, Finot employs the religious concept of the catechism to present the science of happiness in a very condensed form. Some readers will reject this effort because they assume that the roads of happiness are very long and complex, but Finot suggests that we know of persons who go there by the simplest means, and, in his view, the road they pursue is the best one. He suggests that we imitate these candid souls by identifying some of the articles of a catechism of happiness (p. 277).

He offers 11 such articles: (1) To be happy, one must wish to be so; (2) To enjoy our individual happiness, it must be seized when it occurs; (3) A harmonious life is one that embraces the past, present, and future; (4) Avoid anger; (5) Possess the consciousness of human dignity; (6) Happiness depends on our ability to love; (7) One should embrace effort, labor, action; (8) Be courteous to others, as this is the basis of success; (9) Avoid excess in food; (10) Harmonize your mental and physical activity; and (11) Respect your health. He acknowledges that these articles may not be entirely convincing, but he asks his readers to put them to the test. He also advises composing a sort of breviary based on one's own observations. To understand its advantages more readily, he suggests beginning with physical health because its effects are more prompt, and, for that very reason, more convincing (pp. 277–291).

THE MORALITY OF HAPPINESS

Finot begins chapter 7, "The Morality of Happiness," with the observation that we base moralities on principles of duty, justice, love, or the fear of heaven and of hell. But if we strip these principles of their artifices, we find that the true motive of life is the search for happiness. Therefore, we should openly grant happiness the dominant place, since, victorious, it has resisted and is resisting all the attempts to stifle it (pp. 294–295). The happiness of the individual, he notes, depends on the happiness of the community, but the individual also contributes to the happiness of the community by acting in ways that promote his or her own true happiness. On the other hand, the happiness of the individual must be subordinate to justice, which, as the vigilant guardian of the happiness of the community, remains the determining factor of individual happiness (p. 309).

No doubt, an involuntary distrust is aroused within us when we consider a morality founded on happiness. We fear that this will unchain all the passions and appetites that are harmful to the individual and to the community and will lead, in the end, to even greater unhappiness. He admits that this is possible, but for this very reason, we need to develop a human race that understands its real interests and that possesses a rational comprehension of happiness. And for this to occur, we need to educate the young in the development of the virtue of goodness. In addition, we need to become our own educators, teaching ourselves how to regulate our *own* lives and to bring them into harmony with our *own* happiness, in order that the happiness of others may be secured. At the very least, a morality based on happiness as its object is more elevated than a morality based on fear. It is more dignified, more generous, and especially more human (p. 310).

WHAT IS HAPPINESS?

Finot begins his concluding chapter—"What Is Happiness?"—by noting that definitions of happiness are not only numerous but also contradictory. We feel true happiness when we see happy people, but we are quite perplexed when the attempt is made to define their happiness. He suggests, therefore, that we try to derive from the different causes of happiness the conditions that create it and enable it to endure. As we do so, we must keep in mind that happiness assumes many different forms, for it is fashioned according to our souls and therefore infinitely variable (pp. 312–313).

On the other hand, he suggests that the primary attributes of ideal happiness are that it is *elevated* and *permanent*. By elevated, he means that it is based on motives that are good and true, not base and false; and to explain what he means by permanency, he distinguishes between happiness viewed as *pleasure* and happiness viewed as *felicity*. Pleasure suggests a momentary experience, event, or pleasant fact, while felicity presupposes a condition that is stable and enduring. Thus, when happiness strikes its roots into our inward life, it is transformed into a felicity, and it becomes an almost permanent condition. It secures the balance of our soul and guarantees to it a harmony that is difficult to find and still more difficult to destroy. But this does not mean that pleasures are to be rejected or despised. Rather, happiness adopts pleasure, but pleasure is not happiness. Or, to put it another way, we must be happy in order to feel pleasure, not enjoy pleasures in order to be happy (pp. 314–324).

Finally, in a concluding section of the chapter, he makes four brief points. The first is that life imposes upon us duties, but life also gives us rights. He thinks that too much has been said about the former, while the latter has been overlooked. As a result, we have not understood that by harmonizing the burdens and the pleasures of life, we render the former easier and the latter more permanent. Happiness, then, is the fruit of the union between the commands and caresses of life (p. 326).

Second, the more we reflect on our own experience, the more we are likely to find that happiness is a product of living a moral life. Material conditions undoubtedly contribute to it, but happiness is first of all in accord with morality, for it finds itself in complete harmony with the noblest social aspirations. It may appear that our personal interests and the interests of society are in conflict with one another, but this is due to our incapacity to comprehend our real interest. Personal happiness is never in conflict with social happiness as long as it allows itself to be guided by the true value of the principles of life. It is the conventional conception regarding wealth, envy, the pleasures, or the domination of others that causes us to seek objects that are contrary to the best interests of society (p. 327).

His third point is that everything warrants the belief that the human species is moving toward a more just appreciation of the object and the essence of life itself. The problem is that we all have within us the sense of happiness, but it is closely hidden in the depths of our being and is distorted and covered by a deposit of artificial feelings. We must therefore try to release it from these artificial feelings and restore it to its proper position by destroying the prejudices that stifle and prevent its manifestation. Above all, we need to educate it so that, one day, the sense of happiness, bursting forth in "the plenitude of its powers," will transform the moral universe (p. 331).

His fourth and final point is that we need not despair of realizing both individual and collective happiness, because both have extremely deep roots. Furthermore, they are beginning to flower. Brutal conquests are daily becoming more repugnant to us, and we are daily more respectful toward one another. Our dignity is ascending step by step, as well as our sentiments of justice and of truth. There is more joy and more sympathy on our planet. Sorrow seems to be weaker. Some day humankind will shelter in its bosom the children of every color and of every creed, loving them all with the same love. He also notes that half the human race, namely women, are profiting by more equity. So with these and other emerging developments, the hope of earthly salvation fills our hearts, a hope resting mainly on Solidarity and her companion Goodness, which some day will take possession of our planet. As for the science of happiness and its future, he anticipates that others will succeed far better than he has in achieving its triumph. He would only want to add, however, that they will not be capable of loving it more ardently than he does (pp. 332–333).

CHAPTER 4

The Conquest of Happiness

The fourth book we have chosen to review is Bertrand Russell's *The Conquest of Happiness* (1958). It was originally published in 1930. As noted in the introduction, Russell was a well-known British philosopher, mathematician, and social critic. Aware that he would be known to the American public as a philosopher, Russell states in the preface that the book is not addressed to elites or highly educated persons ("highbrows"), or to those who regard a practical problem merely as something to be talked about. The book, he notes, will not contain any profound philosophy or deep erudition. His only aim is to put together some remarks that are inspired, he hopes, by common sense. The only claim he wants to make for "the recipes" he offers to his readers is that they are confirmed by his own experience and observation, and that they have increased his own happiness whenever he has acted in accordance with them. The book itself is divided into two parts: the causes of unhappiness and the causes of happiness.

THE CAUSES OF UNHAPPINESS

Part 1 on the causes of unhappiness consists of nine chapters. The first two chapters—on what makes people unhappy and on Byronic unhappiness—consider the general topic of unhappiness. They are then followed by chapters on specific causes of unhappiness, including competition, boredom and excitement, fatigue, envy, the sense of sin, persecution mania, and fear of public opinion.

What Makes People Unhappy?

In chapter 1, "What Makes People Unhappy," Russell notes that he will not focus on the larger causes of unhappiness—such as war, economic exploitation, and education in cruelty and fear—or on those who are subject to extreme causes of outward misery. Instead, he will assume a sufficient income to secure food and shelter as well as sufficient health to make ordinary bodily activities possible. He also notes that he will not consider great catastrophes, such as the loss of one's children or some kind of a public disgrace. Rather, his purpose is simply to suggest a cure for the ordinary day-to-day unhappiness from which most people in civilized countries suffer and which is all the more unbearable because, having no obvious external cause, it appears inescapable (p. 5).

He believes that this unhappiness is largely due to mistaken views of the world, mistaken ethics, and mistaken habits of life that lead to the destruction of the natural zest and appetite for possible things on which all happiness, whether of humans or animals, ultimately depends. These are matters that lie within the power of the individual, and the book will propose strategies for change by which the individual's happiness may be achieved (p. 5).

Having stated the focus of the book, he provides a few autobiographical facts as an introduction to the philosophy for which he wants to advocate, beginning with his childhood. He notes that he was unhappy as a child, and that his favorite hymn was "Weary of Earth and Laden with My Sin."[1] When he was five, he calculated that if he were to live to 70, he had only endured one-fourteenth of his life so far, and the thought of the long-spread-out boredom ahead of him was almost unbearable. In adolescence, he hated life and was continually on the verge of suicide, from which he was restrained by the desire to know more mathematics. But now, in his late 50s, he enjoys life, and he can almost say that his enjoyment increases with each passing year. This is due in part to the fact that he has discovered the things that he most desires and has gradually acquired many of them. However, it is also because he has successfully dismissed certain objects of desire as more or less unattainable. But, most of all, it is due to a diminishing preoccupation with himself. The problem, in other words, was that he was too self-absorbed when he was younger (p. 6).

Self-absorption comes in various forms, but the sinner, narcissist, and megalomaniac are three very common types. The sinner, that is, the person who is absorbed in the consciousness of sin, is perpetually incurring his own disapproval that, if he is religious, he interprets as the disapproval of God. Perhaps because his own sense of being a reprobate was established in early childhood, Russell believes that liberation from this form of self-absorption comes mainly from throwing over the ridiculous ethical code that one was taught in childhood (i.e., that swearing, drinking, ordinary business shrewd-ness, and all forms of sex are wicked) (p. 7).

The narcissist is the converse of the sinner. This person is absorbed in the habit of admiring himself or herself and wishing to be admired by others. Some narcissists want to be admired for their own selves or for their own sake, while others seek admiration through what they produce or perform. But because the production or performance is a mere means to an end and not of interest in and of itself, the work is usually of inferior quality, so one is unlikely to achieve one's desire of being the object of admiration. The cure in this case lies in the growth of self-respect, which is only to be gained by successful activity inspired by objective interests (p. 9).

The megalomaniac differs from the narcissist in the sense that he or she wants to be powerful rather than charming, and to be feared rather than loved. Since no one can be omnipotent, a life dominated wholly by love of power will be confronted, sooner or later, by obstacles that cannot be overcome. Unfortu-nately, the sheer drive for power may prevent the knowledge that this is the case from entering the megalomaniac's consciousness. Moreover, if one does possess absolute power in the political sense, one can dismiss, imprison, or even execute anyone who has the temerity to point out this truth about the inevitable limits of power. Thus, repressions in the political and in the psy-choanalytic sense go hand in hand, and wherever psychoanalytic repression takes place, there is no genuine happiness (p. 10).

Russell concludes that the psychological causes of unhappiness are many and various, but they all have something in common: The typical unhappy person is one who, having been deprived in youth of some normal satisfaction, has come to value this particular satisfaction more than any other. As a result, his or her life has taken a one-sided direction, together with an excessive emphasis on the achievements instead of the activities connected with it. He suggests, however, that there is a further development that is very common in the present day, namely, that one may feel so completely thwarted in regard to this satisfaction that one does not seek any form of satisfaction—just dis-traction and oblivion. Such persons seek to make life bearable by becoming less alive; they have given up all hope of finding or experiencing happiness. Russell believes that very few persons will deliberately choose unhappiness if they see a way of being happy, and he assumes that his reader would rather be happy than unhappy. He doesn't know if he can help his reader realize this wish, but the attempt, at any rate, won't do any harm (pp. 10–11).

We will not attempt to discuss all of the succeeding chapters on unhap-piness and its causes, but, instead, we will focus on the ones that seem to be the most germane to Russell's concern to offer a cure for unhappiness. These are the chapters on competition, boredom and excitement, fatigue, envy, and the sense of sin.

Competition

In chapter 3, "Competition," Russell observes that if you ask any American man what most interferes with his enjoyment of life, he will say, "The struggle for life." Although he believes that they are sincere in this response, he thinks that what they really mean, but are reluctant to admit, is that the "struggle for success" interferes with their enjoyment of life. What people fear when they engage in the struggle is not that they will fail to get their breakfast the next morning but that they will fail to outshine their neighbors. Furthermore, success in America is measured by income, or money. This being the case, the American male needs to change his "religion" (i.e., his belief that it is his duty to pursue success and that a man who does not do so is a poor creature) in order to become happier. Russell cites, for example, financial investments, noting that many Americans would rather get 8 percent from a risky investment than 4 percent from a safe one. The consequence is that there are frequent losses of money and continual anxiety. Mere financial security, though, is not enough. Rather, what the typical modern man desires to get with it is more money, with a view to ostentation, splendor, and the outshining of those who have hitherto been his equals. Moreover, the money one makes is the accepted measure of intelligence, so a man who makes a lot of money is considered an intelligent person but a man who does not is considered unintelligent (pp. 26–29).

In Russell's view, the problem does not lie simply with the individual but, rather, arises from the all-too-prevailing philosophy of life that holds that life is a contest—a competition—in which the "winner" gains the respect of others. He concludes that when competition is the main thing in one's life and becomes grim and tenacious, the cure lies in allowing into one's life the sane and quiet enjoyment of life, thus achieving a more balanced life (p. 34).

Boredom and Excitement

Russell begins chapter 4, "Boredom and Excitement," with the observation that boredom, as a factor in human behavior, has received far less attention than it deserves. One essential component of boredom is the contrast between one's present circumstances and some other more agreeable circumstances that force themselves on one's imagination. Another is that one's faculties, both mental and physical, are not fully occupied. Running from enemies who are threatening one's life may be unpleasant but it certainly is not boring. Boredom, then, is essentially a thwarted desire for events, not necessarily pleasant ones, but simply occurrences that will enable the victim of ennui to know one day from another. Thus, the opposite of boredom is not pleasure but excitement. However, a life that is *too* full of excitement is an exhausting life, especially when one needs continually stronger stimuli to experience the thrill of excitement. Thus, too little excitement may produce morbid cravings, but too much will produce exhaustion. Thus, a certain capacity to endure boredom is essential to a happy life (pp. 34–39).

Russell concludes this chapter with the observation that all great books contain boring portions (he cites the Bible as an example), that all great lives contain uninteresting stretches, that rest is as essential as motion, and that we have much to learn about life by observing the rhythm of the earth, which can be slow and methodical. After all, fall and winter are as important to the earth as spring and summer. He believes that the special kind of boredom from which modern urban populations suffer is intimately bound up with their separation from the life of earth itself, and that in flying from the beneficial kind of boredom, they fall prey to the other far worse kind. In short, a happy life must be to a great extent a quiet life, for it is only in an atmosphere of quiet that true joy can live (p. 43).

Fatigue

In chapter 5, "Fatigue," Russell differentiates physical and nervous fatigue. If not excessive, physical fatigue tends, if anything, to be a cause of happiness, while, in contrast, nervous fatigue is often a cause of unhappiness. In advanced societies, nervous fatigue is most pronounced among the affluent, and tends to be much less so among the working class than among the business class. He notes that it is very difficult to escape from nervous fatigue in modern life. For one thing, the urban worker is exposed to a great deal of noise. Even though one may learn not to hear it consciously, it wears one out all the more due to the subconscious effort involved in *not* hearing it. For another, there is the constant presence of strangers. Our natural instinct, shared with other animals, is to investigate every stranger of one's species to determine whether to behave toward this stranger in a friendly or a hostile manner. This instinct has to be restrained by those who travel in the subway during the rush hour, and the result is that one feels a general diffused rage against all the strangers with whom one is brought into this involuntary contact. A third cause of nervous fatigue is the hurry to catch the morning train. By the time one reaches the office, one already has frayed nerves and a tendency to view others as a nuisance. One's employer arrives in a similar mood, which does nothing to dissipate it in the employee. Then there is the fear of being fired. This fear compels respectful behavior, but this unnatural conduct only adds to the nervous strain (pp. 44–45).

In Russell's view, the dominant cause of nervous fatigue is worry, and this, he believes, could be prevented by a better philosophy of life and a little more mental discipline. He suggests that most men and women are very deficient in controlling their thoughts. They seem unable to cease thinking about worrisome topics when no action can be taken in regard to them. Men take their business worries to bed with them, and during the night, when they should be resting in order to cope with tomorrow's troubles, they dwell on problems they can do nothing about at the moment, and they think about them, not in a way that would produce a sound line of conduct the next day, but in that half-insane way that characterizes the troubled meditations of insomnia. Something of this midnight madness still clings to them in the morning and more or less makes the problems worse throughout the day (p. 46).

Thus, it is the wise person who thinks about one's troubles only when there is some purpose in doing so, and at other times, one should think about other things or, if at night, about nothing at all. There are, of course, times of crisis when it is impossible to shut out the trouble at moments when nothing can be done about it. But it *is* possible to shut out the ordinary troubles of regular days, except while they have to be dealt with, and Russell observes that it is quite amazing how much happiness and efficiency can be increased by the cultivation of an orderly mind, which thinks about a matter adequately at the right time rather than inadequately at all times (pp. 46–47).

To illustrate the fact that a great many worries can be diminished by appreciating the unimportance of the matter that is causing the anxiety, Russell tells about his experiences of public speaking. At first, every audience terrified him, and his nervousness caused him to speak very poorly. He dreaded the ordeal so much that he hoped he would break his leg before he had to give a talk, and, when it was over, he found that he was exhausted from the nervous strain. Gradually, though, he taught himself to feel that it did not matter whether he spoke well or poorly. After all, the universe would remain the same in either case. He found that the *less* he cared whether he spoke well, the less poorly he spoke, and gradually the nervous strain diminished almost completely. This example illustrates the fact that most things we do in life are not as important as we assume them to be. Our successes and failures do not matter all that much in the end. And even great sorrows can be survived. Troubles that seem as though they must put an end to happiness for life fade with the lapse of time until it becomes almost impossible to remember why they had their poignancy. But over and above these self-centered considerations is the fact that one's ego is not a very large part of the world, so the person who can center his or her thoughts and hopes upon something transcending self can find a certain peace in the ordinary troubles of life, an achievement that is impossible for the pure egoist (pp. 47–48).

Russell concludes the chapter with a discussion of the fact that the hygiene of the nerves has not been studied enough. He notes that in studies of fatigue among adults, psychologists have mainly focused on muscular fatigue. However, in his view, the most important type of fatigue in modern life is emotional, and it is often the case that fatigue from overwork is due to the fact that work is an escape from unrelated emotional troubles in one's life. He acknowledges that the psychology of worry is by no means simple, but he believes that there are methods by which one can minimize nervous fatigue. Thinking of things at the right time is one such method. But this method does not touch the unconscious. So when the difficulty or problem is a very serious one, an effective method needs to take account of the unconscious mind. Although psychologists have made extensive studies of the effect of the unconscious mind on the conscious mind, they have not done nearly as much on the operation of the conscious mind on the unconscious mind, especially with regard to ways in which rational convictions may overcome the worries that fester in the unconscious mind. It is easy enough to tell oneself that a given misfortune would not be so very terrible if it happened, but as long as this remains merely a conscious conviction, it will not operate during the night or prevent the occurrence of nightmares. If, however, enough vigor and intensity is put into it, a conscious thought can be planted in the unconscious (p. 49).

Russell proposes this method: When some misfortune threatens, consider seriously and deliberately what is the absolute worst thing that could possibly happen. Having looked this possible misfortune in the face, give yourself sound reasons for thinking that it would not be so bad after all. Such reasons always exist, since the worst that can happen to oneself does not have any cosmic importance. When you have considered the worst possibility and have said to yourself with real conviction, "Well, after all, that would not matter so very much," you will find that your worry is significantly diminished. He also adds that it may be necessary to repeat the process a few times, but in the end, if you have shirked nothing in facing the worst possible issue, you will find that your worry usually disappears altogether and is even replaced with a kind of exhilaration (p. 50).

He suggests that this method of challenging one's worries is part of a more general technique for the avoidance of fear. Worry, in fact, is a form of fear, and all forms of fear produce fatigue. The person who has learned not to feel fear will find the fatigue of daily life enormously diminished. The problem is that most people use the wrong technique for dealing with fear because whenever it comes into their minds, they try to think of something else. But every kind of fear gets *worse* by not looking at it, so the proper course is to think about it rationally and calmly, but with great concentration, until it has become completely familiar. When the fear has become familiar, it diminishes and even disappears (pp. 50–51).

Finally, Russell notes that one of the worst features of nervous fatigue is that it acts as a screen between oneself and the outside world. Impressions reach us in a muffled and muted form. We no longer notice others except to be irritated by their mannerisms. We derive no pleasure from eating or from sunshine, but instead become tensely concentrated on a few objects and indifferent to all the rest. This state of affairs makes it impossible to rest, and the fatigue continually rises until it reaches a point where medical treatment is needed. In effect, this is the penalty for having lost contact with the earth, and the culprit behind this loss is urban population growth (p. 53).

Envy

In chapter 6, titled "Envy," Russell observes that, next to worry, envy is one of the most potent causes of unhappiness. Unfortunately, it is also one of the most universal and deep seated of human passions. It is very noticeable in young children, but it is no less evident among adults. He is especially concerned in this chapter with envy of others in one's own profession. He asks readers whether they have ever been so imprudent as to have praised an artist to another artist, a politician to another politician, or an Egyptologist to another Egyptologist. If you have, it is 100 to 1 that you will have produced a jealous reaction. Russell cites the correspondence between Leibniz and Huygens in which they "lamented" the supposed fact that Newton had become insane. Despite their own eminence, they wept crocodile tears with obvious relish. What especially concerns Russell is the effect of envy on humanity itself, for if this passion is allowed to run wild it becomes fatal to all excellence, and even to the most useful exercise of exceptional skill. Fortunately, though, human nature possesses a compensating passion—that of admiration—and whoever wants to increase human happiness must want to increase admiration and to diminish envy (pp. 54–56).

Is there a cure for envy? Russell believes that happiness is the cure for envy, but the problem is that envy is itself a terrible obstacle to happiness, and, moreover, envy is deeply rooted in misfortunes in childhood and is therefore difficult to eradicate because it has become so much a part of oneself. If, for example, I find that a brother or sister is loved more than I am, I will acquire the habit of envy, and then, when I go out into the world as an adult, I will look for injustices of which I am the victim, perceiving them immediately if they actually occur and imagining them if they do not. Such a person is inevitably unhappy, and becomes a nuisance to friends. Having begun by believing that no one likes me, my behavior confirms my belief. Another childhood misfortune that has the same result is to have parents who do not express much feeling. In this case, I compare myself to children in other families who are more loved by their parents than I am loved by my own (p. 57).

Russell anticipates the envious person's objection: "What is the good of telling me that the cure for envy is happiness? I cannot find happiness while I continue to feel envy, yet you tell me that I cannot cease being envious until I find happiness." The weakness of this objection is that real life is not as logical as this. In fact, simply recognizing the causes of one's envious feelings is to take a long step toward curing them. Also, a useful technique for overcoming envy is to break the habit of thinking in terms of comparisons. When anything pleasant occurs, it should be enjoyed to the full, without thinking about the pleasant things that may be happening to someone else (p. 57).

Envy, then, is a vice, partly moral and partly intellectual, which consists in not seeing things in themselves but only in their relations. Suppose, for example, that a man considers the woman in his life to be attractive but then thinks of the Queen of Sheba who, he assumes, was more attractive, and this leads him to envy King Solomon and his opportunities. Or consider employed persons who are earning a salary that is sufficient for their needs, but then hear that someone else whom they believe to be in no way their superior has a salary twice what they are earning. If they have an envious disposition, the satisfactions they would otherwise derive from what they have are diminished, and they become obsessed with a sense of injustice. The cure for such envy is mental discipline, the habit of not thinking profitless thoughts. After all, what is more enviable than happiness? So, if I can cure myself of envy, I can acquire happiness and become the envy of others! (p. 58).

The Sense of Sin

This brings us to chapter 7 titled "The Sense of Sin." Russell considers this to be one of the most important of the underlying causes of unhappiness in adult life. He believes that the orthodox view of sin has been largely rejected, even by those who consider themselves to be orthodox in their religious beliefs. This is the view that one's conscience reveals when an act to which one is tempted is sinful with the result that one feels painful feelings of remorse, which lead to repentance, thereby wiping out one's feelings of guilt. He thinks it is far more likely that fear of being found out, and consequently ostracized, especially if the act was committed by an otherwise respectable person (e.g., a banker who embezzles funds or a clergyman who has engaged in some sexual irregularity), will produce the painful feelings previously ascribed to a guilty conscience (pp. 63–64).

This change does not mean, however, that the sense of sin is no longer a cause of unhappiness, for the sense of sin in its most important forms is something that goes deeper than the fear of other people's disapproval. Although the sense of sin is no longer as strongly attached to a guilty conscience, it continues to manifest itself in the unconscious mind, especially in the realm of sex. Russell faults traditional sex education, which makes an association between sin and the sex organs, for this. And he suggests that the sense of sin in this regard is especially prominent when the conscious will is weakened by fatigue, illness, alcohol, or some other cause. In such moments, one is more likely to feel guilty of wrongdoing. But why should one believe that moments of weakness afford more insight than moments of strength? (p. 68).

Russell devotes much of this chapter to techniques designed to overcome infantile suggestions of the unconscious relating to sin and wrongdoing. He suggests, for example, that whenever we begin to feel remorse for an act that our reason tells us is not immoral, we should examine the causes of our feelings of remorse, and we should convince ourselves in detail of their absurdity. He stresses that it is important that we not vacillate between rationality and irrationality. One reason we do so is that we are swayed by the reverence we feel toward the persons who controlled our childhoods. An effective way to address these alleged wrongdoings is to view them in light of the really harmful acts to which the average person is tempted, such as sharp and shrewd business practices of the sort not punished by law, harshness and meanness toward employees, cruelty and abuse toward wife and children, malevolence and wickedness toward competitors, and vicious language and behavior in political conflicts and public affairs. These are the really harmful sins that are common among otherwise respectable citizens, and by means of them they spread misery in their immediate circle and undermine civilization itself (p. 70).

He also cautions against the assumption that we have thrown off the superstitions of our childhood. We often fail to realize that these superstitions have simply gone underground. So, when a rational conviction has been arrived at, we need to dwell on it, to follow out its consequences, and to search out in ourselves whatever beliefs inconsistent with the new conviction might otherwise survive; and when the sense of sin grows strong, as it occasionally will, we need to treat it not as a revelation and a call to higher things but as a disease and a weakness, unless, of course, it is caused by some act that a rational ethic would condemn (p. 70).

Russell concludes that the sense of sin tends to make us unhappy, and because we are unhappy, we are likely to make claims on other people that are excessive and that prevent us from enjoying happiness in our personal relations. In contrast, an expansive and generous attitude toward other people gives happiness to others, and is also a great source of personal happiness, because others generally will like us on account of our generosity toward them. But such an attitude is hardly possible to the person haunted by a sense of sin. Rather, it is the outcome of poise and self-reliance, and it requires mental integration, or a harmonious working together of the various layers of our nature—conscious, subconscious, and unconscious (p. 71).

Ordinarily, such harmony is the product of wise education, but where such education is lacking, a more difficult process (for example, psychoanalysis) may be required. In any event, since nothing so much diminishes happiness as a divided personality, the time spent in producing harmony between the different parts of one's personality is time usefully employed. On the other hand, we should avoid devoting too much time to such self-examination lest we become self-absorbed, which is part of the disease to be cured and, as noted earlier, is one of the psychological causes of unhappiness. The important thing is to make up our minds as to what we rationally believe and not allow contrary irrational beliefs to pass unchallenged or to obtain a hold over ourselves for any period of time. Moreover, we should not fear that by making ourselves rational, we will thereby forego our emotions and passions, for there is nothing irrational in the passions as such. So, in passionate love, in parental affection, in friendship, in benevolence, in devotion to science or art, there is nothing that reason should wish to diminish (pp. 71–73).

THE CAUSES OF HAPPINESS

The second part of the book on the causes of happiness consists of eight chapters. The introductory chapter on the subject of whether happiness is still possible is followed by chapters on zest, affection, the family, work, impersonal interests, effort and resignation, and the happy individual. We will focus here on Russell's reflections on zest, affection, and effort and resignation because they emphasize positive dispositions and conditions that counter the negative dispositions and conditions of competition, boredom, fatigue, envy, and the sense of sin.

Is Happiness Still Possible?

In the introductory chapter, Russell notes that from personal conversations and books written by some of his friends, he has almost been led to conclude that happiness in the modern world is no longer possible. However, he finds that this conclusion is greatly diminished when he engages in introspection, foreign travel, and conversations with his gardener. Thus, in this chapter, he wishes to make a survey of the happy people that he has come across in the course of his life (p. 101).

He proposes that happiness is of two sorts with intermediate degrees between them. They might be distinguished as plain and fancy or as animal and spiritual, or of the heart and the head. The designation chosen among these alternatives depends on the thesis one wishes to prove, but the basic difference between the two sorts of happiness is that one is open to any human being, while the other is open only to those who can read and write. The happiness of his gardener is of the former type. This man wages a perennial war against rabbits and considers them dark, designing, and ferocious, and he is of the opinion that they can only be met by means of a cunning equal to theirs. Although he is over 70 years old, works all day, and bicycles 16 hilly miles to and from his work, his fount of joy is inexhaustible because his war against the rabbits supplies infinite pleasures (p. 102).

Russell contends that pleasures exactly similar to those of his gardener are open to the most highly educated people. The difference is only in regard to the activities by which these pleasures are to be obtained. Among the more highly educated, he believes that scientists are the happiest because they have an activity that utilizes their abilities to the fullest and achieves results that appear important not only to themselves but also to the general public, even when the general public cannot understand these results. The scientist is more fortunate in this respect than the artist, for when the public fails to understand a picture or a poem, it concludes that it is a bad picture or a bad poem—a conclusion that it seldom makes when it does not understand science (pp. 103–104).

On the other hand, the scientist is not the only one who can derive pleasure from work. On the contrary, the pleasure of work is open to anyone who can develop some specialized skill, provided that one is able to gain satisfaction from the exercise of one's skill without demanding universal applause. He cites the example of a man who lost the use of both legs in early youth but remained serenely happy throughout a long life, having achieved this happiness by writing a five-volume work on rose blight, a topic on which he was the leading expert. He also cites the case of a man who was the best typesetter in the world and was sought out by those who devoted themselves to inventing artistic forms. This man derived joy, not so much from the genuine respect in which he was held by others as from the actual delight in the exercise of his craft, a delight not wholly unlike that which good dancers derive from dancing. Citing these and several other cases, Russell rejects the idea that there is less room than formerly for the craftsperson's joy in skilled work (p. 106).

Another source of happiness is devotion to a worthy social cause, especially if one's interest in the cause is genuine, and the cause itself is based on rational convictions or beliefs. Hobbies are yet another source of pleasure, and Russell cites in this case the eminent mathematician who divides his time equally between mathematics and stamp collecting. Collecting stamps undoubtedly affords consolation at the moments when progress on a mathematical problem stalls. On the other hand, hobbies that serve as a means of escape from reality are unlikely to be a source of fundamental happiness, for fundamental happiness depends more than anything else on what may be called a friendly interest in persons and things. A friendly interest in persons is a form of affection, but not in a grasping or possessive way, which is very often a source of unhappiness. Rather, the interest that makes for happiness is the kind that finds pleasure in the individual traits of others and affirms their interests and pleasures without trying to control them or to procure their admiration (pp. 108–110).

The idea that one might also take a friendly interest in things may seem rather forced, but there is something analogous to friendliness in the kind of interest that a geologist takes in rocks or an archeologist in ruins, and this interest ought to be an element in our attitude toward individuals and societies. An interest in impersonal things may be less valuable as an ingredient in everyday happiness than a friendly attitude toward other persons, but it is very important, for the world is vast, and our own powers are limited. If all our happiness is bound up entirely in our personal circumstances, it is difficult not to demand of life more than it has to give, and to demand too much is the surest way of getting even less than is possible. Those who are able to forget their worries by means of a genuine interest in impersonal things—for example, by taking an interest in the life history of stars—will find that when they return from their excursion into the impersonal world they have acquired a poise and calm that enables them to deal with their worries in the best way, and in the meantime they will have experienced a genuine, even if temporary, happiness. In short, the secret of happiness is this: let your interests be as wide as possible, and also let your reactions to the things and persons that interest you be friendly rather than hostile (p. 111).

Zest

In chapter 11 titled "Zest," Russell claims that zest is the most universal and distinctive mark of happy individuals. He suggests that the best way to understand what is meant by zest is to consider the different ways in which persons behave when they sit down to a meal. Eating a meal may be a boring convention, a duty prescribed by a doctor, a disappointment because nothing tastes as good as one had hoped, or "a rapacious act of gorging," followed by dull and lethargic feelings. On the other hand, some eaters begin with a sound appetite, are glad for the food, eat until they have had enough, and then stop. Russell observes that those who sit down before the feast of life have similar attitudes toward the good things that life offers, and suggests that the happy person corresponds to those eaters who begin with a sound appetite, appreciate their food, and eat until they have had enough (pp. 112–113).

Yet, with the possible exception of the rapacious eater, the others tend to despise persons of healthy appetite and consider themselves their superior. It seems vulgar to them to enjoy food because one is hungry or to enjoy life because it offers a variety of interesting spectacles and surprising experiences. From the height of their disillusionment, they look down upon those whom they denigrate as simple souls. Russell, however, says that he has no sympathy with this outlook, because we need to take interest in life, and we need enough interests so that if we lose one thing we can fall back on another. Life is too short to be interested in everything, but we should be interested in as many things as are necessary to fill the days. To be sure, we are all susceptible to the malady of the self-absorbed who turn away from the manifold spectacle of the world around them and gaze only upon the emptiness within. But we should not imagine that there is anything grand about the unhappiness that such self-absorption produces and reflects (pp. 113–114).

In Russell's view, genuine zest is part of the natural makeup of human beings. After all, young children are interested in almost everything that they see and hear. The world is full of surprises to them, and they are perpetually engaged with ardor in the pursuit of knowledge, especially of the kind that involves acquiring familiarity with the objects that attract their attention (p. 121).

The loss of this natural zest for life in civilized society is largely due to the restrictions on liberty that are essential to our way of life. Yet some persons retain their zest in spite of the handicaps of civilized life, and others could do so if they were free from the inner psychological conflicts on which a great part of their energy is expended. Zest requires energy that is more than sufficient for the necessary work that life in civilized society requires of us, and this in turn requires "the smooth working of the psychological machine" (p.123).

Affection

In chapter 12 titled "Affection," Russell notes that a chief cause of the lack of zest is the feeling that one is unloved. Conversely, the feeling of being loved promotes zest more than anything else does. He suggests that genuine affection provides a feeling of security that enables us to engage the world with confidence, and that the best type of affection is reciprocally life giving, wherein each person receives affection with joy and gives it without effort, and each finds the whole world more interesting because of the existence of this reciprocal happiness. Unlike relationships in which one person sucks the vitality of the other, affection in the sense of a genuine reciprocal interest of two persons in one another is one of the most important elements of real happiness. He also suggests that, in terms of work, his advice would be to pursue occupations and environments in which one can find companionship, even if this means receiving a lower wage or salary (pp. 130–131).

Effort and Resignation

In chapter 16 titled "Effort and Resignation," Russell notes that happiness is not something that drops into one's mouth, like a ripe fruit, by mere chance or good luck. In fact, this is why he titled the book *The Conquest of Happiness*, for in a world so full of avoidable and unavoidable misfortunes, of illness and psychological tangles, of struggle and poverty and ill will, the person who desires to be happy must find ways of coping with the many causes of unhappiness by which each individual is assaulted. Effort is essential in this regard for happiness is an achievement rather than a gift of the gods, and in this achievement effort, both inward and outward, plays a major part (pp. 167–168).

He discusses such efforts as occupation, marriage, and raising children, but most of the chapter is devoted to resignation, which also has its part to play in the conquest of happiness and is just as essential as effort. Wise individuals use effort against preventable misfortunes, but they will not waste time and emotion on unavoidable misfortunes. Nor will they devote time and energy on misfortunes that are avoidable if the time and labor required to avoid them would interfere with the pursuit of some more important object, one more likely to yield happiness. Many people get irritated or upset over every little thing that goes wrong, and in doing so, they waste a great deal of energy that might be more usefully employed. But even in the pursuit of really important objects, it is unwise to become so deeply involved emotionally that the thought of possible failure becomes a constant threat to one's peace of mind. Christianity taught submission to the will of God, and even for those who cannot accept this phraseology, they would do well to cultivate something of the same kind of spirit in all of their activities (pp. 170–171).

On the other hand, there are two types of resignation: one rooted in despair, the other in unconquerable hope. Those who have suffered such fundamental defeat that they have given up hope of serious achievement may learn the resignation of despair and, as a result, abandon all activity. They may camouflage their despair with religious phrases or by the doctrine that contemplation is the true end of humankind. But whatever disguise they may adopt to conceal their inward defeat, they will remain essentially useless and fundamentally unhappy (p. 171).

Resignation based on unconquerable hope is very different from this. For one thing, to be unconquerable, the hope needs to be large and impersonal. One can be defeated by diseases, enemies, an unwise course that cannot lead to success, and by death itself. If one thinks only in terms of one's purely personal aims and aspirations, one can easily lose hope. But if one's personal aims and aspirations are part of the larger aims and aspirations for humanity, there is not the same sense of utter defeat when failure comes. Humor may also help one maintain a hopeful outlook. It can be especially useful in cases of relatively minor misfortunes, the sorts of misfortunes that cause irritation and frustration. If, for example, one is interrupted in a proposal of marriage by the visit of a tedious neighbor, one may consider the fact that all humankind has been vulnerable to this very disaster except Adam, and that even Adam had his troubles (pp. 171–173).

In conclusion, Russell notes that many active persons believe that the slightest grain of resignation and the faintest gleam of humor may destroy the energy with which they do their work and the determination by means of which they achieve success. He disagrees, for work that is worth doing can be done even by those who do not deceive themselves either as to its importance or as to the ease with which it can be done. Furthermore, it is better to do nothing than to do harm, and much of the useful work in the world consists of combating the harmful work. Moreover, much of the harmful work is done by those who need a continual inflation of their ego as a stimulant to their energy. Thus, a certain kind of resignation is involved in a willingness to face the truth about ourselves. While this may involve pain at first, it ultimately affords protection, the only possible protection, against the disappointments and disillusionments to which the self-deceiver is liable. Russell points out that nothing is more fatiguing or more exasperating in the long run than the daily effort to believe things that daily become more unbelievable, and that to be done with this effort is an indispensable condition of secure and lasting happiness (p. 174).

The Happy Individual

The Conquest of Happiness ends with a brief chapter on the happy individual. This chapter highlights some of the points and the themes discussed in earlier chapters. Here, Russell emphasizes that the book has focused on what one can do oneself to realize happiness, and not on the external circumstances that also contribute to happiness. With this focus in mind, he concludes that as far as this aspect of realizing happiness is concerned, the recipe for happiness is a very simple one. Many people think that happiness is impossible without a creed of a more or less religious kind, and many persons who are themselves unhappy think that their sorrows have complicated and highly intellectualized sources. He disagrees. In his view, such things are not genuine causes of either happiness or unhappiness. At most, they are only symptoms (p. 175).

He returns to the issue with which he began—that of self-absorption—and claims that if outward circumstances are not definitely or overwhelmingly unfortunate, one should be able to achieve happiness, provided that one's passions and interests are directed outward, not inward. Thus, the happy individual is the one who lives objectively; who has free affections and wide interests; who realizes personal happiness through these interests and affections that, in turn, make oneself an object of interest and affection to others (pp. 176–177).

As for what those who are unhappy can do for themselves, the first thing they should do is to cease thinking about the causes of their unhappiness, because, in so doing, they continue to be self-absorbed and therefore fail to get outside the vicious circle. To get outside of it, to make a conquest of happiness, they need to acquire or to develop genuine, not simulated, interests. What these interests may be should not be prescribed in advance, for when a person has overcome the disease of self-absorption, these genuine interests will arise out of the spontaneous workings of one's nature and also of one's external circumstances—for the world, after all, is filled with happy surprises (pp. 176–177).[2]

PART II

Some Findings about Happiness

CHAPTER 5

THE PURSUIT OF HAPPINESS

The fifth book we have chosen to review is David G. Myers's *The Pursuit of Happiness* (1992). As noted in the introduction, Myers is a psychology professor at Hope College. His book consists of a brief introduction, an epilogue, and 10 chapters on what is well-being; wealth and well-being; the satisfied mind; the demography of happiness; reprogramming the mind; the traits of happy people; "flow" in work and play; the friendship factor; love and marriage; and faith, hope, and joy.

WELL-BEING, HAPPINESS, AND LIFE SATISFACTION

As the topics of the first two chapters indicate, Myers frequently uses the word "well-being" as the larger frame of which "happiness" is a constituent part. Although well-being is a state of mind, and is, therefore, not easily measured, it can be described as "a pervasive sense that life is good." It outlasts yesterday's moment of elation, today's buoyant mood, and tomorrow's hard time. In other words, it is an ongoing perception that this moment of one's life, or even one's life as a whole, is fulfilling, meaningful, and pleasant. It is what some people experience as joy in the sense that despite the day's problems, all is, or will be, well (pp. 23–24).

To probe people's sense of well-being, researchers ask them to report their feelings of happiness or unhappiness along with their thoughts about how satisfying their lives are. Although happiness and life satisfaction are subtly different, they share much in common. In fact, people who *feel* happy also tend to *think* that their lives are satisfying. Thus, at the risk of oversimplifying, we can say that happiness is the emotional (or temperamental) aspect of well-being, while life satisfaction is its cognitive aspect (p. 24).

The view that happiness is emotional is reflected by Myers's observation in the introduction that psychological studies of negative emotions such as depression, anxiety, and stress have greatly overshadowed studies of positive emotions. As a result, textbooks in psychology, his own included, have far more to say about suffering than about joy. However, this is now changing. In *Psychological Abstracts*, the number of articles pertaining to happiness, life satisfaction, or well-being grew from 150 articles in 1979 to 780 in 1989. Drawing on these studies, *The Pursuit of Happiness* reports what has been learned so far, and although the new research offers no easy how-to-be-happy formula, the findings are instructive (pp. 15–16).

Basically, this research has found that happy people are less self-focused than unhappy people; that they are more energetic, decisive, flexible, creative, and sociable; that they tolerate more frustration; that they are more willing to help those in need; and that our body's immune system fights disease more effectively when we are happy than when we are sad. One important consequence of these studies is that some of our culture's deeply held values are thereby affirmed, while others are challenged or questioned. Myers views this as a positive contribution because it can help us reassess our priorities and may also assist our quest to recover a sense of shared values (pp. 20–21).

Myers also notes that although the book's distinctiveness lies in its revelations based on research, he will connect its conclusions to the lives of real people. Thus, when discovering answers to the happiness question—who is happy, and why?—he will pause to ponder what the answers might mean for our everyday lives (p. 22).

In chapter 1 titled "What is Well-being?" Myers cites the finding presented in recent books on happiness (Hart 1988; Powell 1989; Wholey 1986) that only 10–20 percent of Americans think they are "truly happy." But when Americans are asked in national surveys about their happiness, a more positive picture emerges, for one-third say they are *very happy*, one-tenth are *not too happy*, and the remainder are *pretty happy*. He also cites a study in which researchers asked Americans to express their feelings about their life as a whole, and they do so nonverbally by means of choosing one of seven faces ranging from a broad smile to a deep frown. Only 2 percent identified with the frowning faces, and 20 percent identified with the face with the happiest smile. Myers agrees with critics of these research findings that these percentages may be inflated, because, after all, there are many other research studies on other topics where people generally color the truth toward the positive or optimistic side. Yet, even if we assume some inflation of the degree of happiness, the happy are clearly in the majority (pp. 25–26).

Myers also takes up the issue of whether people's current mood affects their responses, thus making these responses unreliable because external circumstances play a major role in mood changes. He concludes that when asked at various points in time to assess their happiness and life satisfaction, people's reports retain a respectable consistency. He also notes that people who *say* that they are happy give every indication of actually being so—for example, they smile and laugh during interviews; they have happier memories; they report more joy when their experience is sampled daily; and their friends and family are more likely to see them as happy individuals (p. 29).

WEALTH AND HAPPINESS

In chapter 2 titled "Wealth and Well-being," Myers addresses three questions relating to wealth and happiness: Are people who live in affluent countries happier than those who do not? Within any single country, are the richest people the happiest? And does happiness rise with affluence? Regarding the first question, Myers cites an extensive cross-national survey conducted in the 1980s of Western European countries that consistently found the Danes, Swiss, Irish, and Dutch feel happier and more satisfied with life than do the French, Greeks, Italians, and West Germans. The national differences correlate modestly with national affluence, as those living in the Scandinavian countries (Denmark, Sweden, and Norway) and in Switzerland are generally both prosperous and happy. But the relationship between national affluence and well-being is not consistent—for example, West Germans averaged more than double the incomes of the Irish, but the Irish were happier. Myers cites another study that suggests a positive correlation between countries with stable democratic governments and the sense of well-being of the people, and he concludes that it may not be the wealth of the Scandinavians and the Swiss that matters so much as the trust engendered by their history of freedom (pp. 34–36).

Concerning the question whether the richest people in any country are the happiest, Myers cites research evidence that people who have basic necessities in terms of food, rest, warmth, and social contact are happier than persons who are impoverished, but having more than enough provides little additional boost to well-being. The national surveys noted above also indicate that actual income doesn't much influence happiness but how *satisfied* we are with our income does, so if we are content with our income, regardless of how much it is, we tend to be happier. On the other hand, people who make lots of money are only slightly more satisfied with what they make, and it is also striking that our income level does not noticeably influence satisfaction with marriage, family, friendship, or ourselves (pp. 37–39).

Regarding the question whether our happiness rises as our affluence increases, Myers reports that in the United States as a whole, the answer is clearly no. He compares the findings of the National Opinion Research Center in 1957 and 1990, a period in which the nation's buying power had doubled, and observes that the same percentage of Americans (one in three) said that they were "very happy" (p. 41).

Myers concludes that the findings from the research relating to wealth and happiness are liberating in two ways: They liberate us from envying the rich and famous; and they liberate us to invest ourselves in cultivating traits, attitudes, relationships, activities, environments, and spiritual resources that will promote our own and others' well-being (p. 46).

THE SATISFIED MIND

In chapter 3 titled "A Satisfied Mind," Myers cites the observation of the late New Zealand researcher Richard Kammann (1983) that objective life circumstances have a negligible role to play in a theory of happiness. This is not to say that the events of our lives have no influence on our emotions—they do—but the influence is only temporary. Bad events—such as an argument, a rejection, a headache—put us in the dumps; and good events—a pay raise, winning a game, getting an A on a test, a first passionate kiss—increase our happiness for a while. But within a day or two, our moods usually return to where they were before (pp. 47–48).

How to explain the fact that objective life circumstances play a negligible role in our personal happiness? The simple answer is that happiness is relative. Myers presents two psychological principles that help to explain this. Based on adaptation levels, the first principle states that happiness is relative to our prior experience, so if, for example, we receive a pay raise, or if we receive an improved test grade, we feel an initial surge of pleasure. But if these new realities continue, we get used to them, and they no longer afford their initial pleasure. Thus, every desirable experience is transitory, and this means that the only way that life could be an unending pleasure cruise is if it were a series of highs followed by higher highs. In practical terms, this principle suggests that, as far as happiness is concerned, a steadily rising income is better than a higher income that is permanently fixed (pp. 51–55).

Based on social comparison, the second principle is that happiness is relative to what others, especially those closest to us, have. In other words, we are always comparing ourselves to others, and we feel good or bad depending on to whom we compare ourselves. When we compare ourselves with those above us, especially those *immediately* above us, we tend to feel less satisfied with our lives because we can imagine ourselves in their position. Myers mentions in this connection Bertrand Russell's observation in *The Conquest of Happiness* that you cannot get away from envy by means of success alone, for there will always be in history or legend some person even more successful than you are.[1] On the other hand, when we are demoralized or feeling threatened, we more often than not compare ourselves with those less fortunate. He cites several examples of the uplifting effects of comparing downward, such as the case of an older woman who was diagnosed with breast cancer feeling sorry for younger women diagnosed with breast cancer: "I'm seventy-three. What do I need a breast for?" (pp. 56–62).

To be sure, comparing downward can have certain negative effects or outcomes. In experiments, subjects who have just experienced failure or have been made to feel insecure in some way will often alleviate their self-doubts by disparaging a rival group or person. On the other hand, and more positively, people often tend to look on the brighter side of life. The processes of adaptation and social comparison reassure us that if forced to adjust our living standard downward, we could regain our sense of well-being. Thus, Myers says that he takes personal comfort in the resilience of well-being in the face of downward, as well as upward, adaptation; and he cites in this regard his own hearing loss, which is on a trajectory leading eventually to total deafness. Although he wishes his hearing were more acute, the prospect of deafness neither frightens nor depresses him. He does not want to delude himself into thinking that his sensory disability will be fully compensated for in other ways, but he is optimistic that he will adapt, that he will develop new sensitivities, and that he will experience other sources of continuing joy. He notes that others have experienced life enhancements as a result of their deafness, such as improved concentration in their work and being able to sleep more soundly (pp. 60–62).

Myers concludes this chapter on the satisfied mind with a brief discussion of the need to manage our expectations and comparisons. One way to do so, he suggests, is to avoid thinking about past experiences of happiness. While there may be truth in the old saying that "we are always happier for having been happy," this does not mean that we should dwell on our happiest times from the past, because both theory and evidence suggest that dwelling on these happy memories makes the present seem rather pedestrian. In one experiment, German adults were asked to recall and to write down a significant low moment in their lives. The study found that they felt better about their present life if they recalled an earlier low moment in their lives than if they recalled an earlier high moment in their lives. Thus, if we use our happiest memories as our yardstick for assessing the present, we doom ourselves to disappointment. The memories may be pleasant ones, but these studies suggest that nostalgia can negatively affect our life satisfaction (pp. 62–63).

Another way to manage our expectations and comparisons is to recognize that ever-rising desires mean never-ending dissatisfaction, and, this being the case, we should strive to make our goals short term and sensible. Various studies suggest that it is better to fulfill a succession of modest goals and to

enjoy the sense of competence that these achievements provide rather than
to reach for a higher long-term goal and to fail. In fact, although Myers does
not say this in so many words, the evidence presented earlier in the chapter
would suggest that fulfilling a succession of modest, short-term goals is far
better than reaching for a higher long-term goal and *succeeding*. The happiness gained in the former case would be incremental while the happiness
gained in the latter case would be momentary and transient (p. 65).

In short, if a satisfied mind is our goal, we should restrain our unrealistic
expectations, go out of our way to experience reminders of our blessings,
make our goals short term and sensible, and choose comparisons that inspire
gratitude rather than envy (p. 67).

THE DEMOGRAPHY OF HAPPINESS

In chapter 4 titled "The Demography of Happiness," Myers focuses on
demographic factors besides those discussed earlier (i.e., income levels and
nationality). He gives particular attention to age and gender. Regarding the
association of happiness and age, he notes that our beliefs are generally inaccurate. When people are asked which age cohorts they think are the least
rewarding, they often say that adolescents and the elderly are the unhappiest.
But he cites a meta-analysis of more than 100 studies that showed that less
than 1 percent of the variation in well-being is related to age. Does happiness
align itself to a greater extent with any particular age group? The answer
is no (p. 69).

On the other hand, he points out that the stability of well-being across the
life span obscures some interesting age-related emotional differences. Research studies show that as the years go by, our feelings mellow: our highs
are less high and our lows less low. So, although with age our *average* feeling
level remains stable, we find ourselves less often feeling excited, intensely
proud, elated, and so forth, but we also feel depressed less often. The stability of well-being across the life span also obscures how feelings change
concerning specific domains of our lives. For example, older people report
feeling slightly more satisfied with their work, their marriage, their standard
of living, their housing, and their community than younger adults. On the
other hand, while older persons also experience less stress, Myers points out
that they often feel lonelier and less satisfied with their health and physical
attractiveness (pp. 73–74).

Another consistent finding is that at any age, the aspects of our lives that
most preoccupy us are the ones that best predict our well-being. For example, older persons are less occupied with work and they are more involved in
leisure activities and social relations; and in comparison with younger adults,
their work satisfaction is a less important predictor of their well-being than
satisfaction with leisure activities and social relationships. This, of course,

may present problems for those individuals for whom work has been a major source of personal happiness (p. 75).

Myers discusses a variety of other factors that are positively associated with happiness, regardless of age. Among these, physical health is especially noteworthy. He reports that more than 100 studies confirm that for adults of all ages, and certainly for older adults, one predictor of happiness is health and physical fitness. Moreover, persons of all ages tend to be more upset by illness than delighted by health, and so health is like wealth: Their absence can breed misery, but their presence is no guarantee of happiness (p. 76).

With regard to the association of happiness and gender, research studies report results similar to those that focus on age. One literature review of 146 studies found that gender accounted for less than 1 percent of people's differences in well-being, and another review found that women expressed only "slightly greater happiness" than men—thus, men and women are equally likely to report being "very happy" and "satisfied or very satisfied" with life (p. 79).

But, Myers asks, do these similarities between genders obscure important differences within genders? For example, what about employed women as compared with women who do not work for pay? He points out that various studies show that employed married women are only slightly more likely than unemployed married women to say that they are "very happy" and "fully satisfied" with their lives. He also cites a study of middle-class housewives that found that those who feel *less* free—that is, those who have *more* obligations—express *greater* feelings of happiness and fulfillment. On the other hand, national surveys suggest that the combined stresses of motherhood and employment do, in fact, erode some women's sense of well-being. By and large, however, whether a woman has children or not makes little predictable difference in her sense of well-being (pp. 80–85).

Myers also discusses the fact that although men and women are similar in their average well-being, they are surprisingly different in their experiences of misery. Studies conducted in the United States and Europe show that women are twice as likely as men to suffer a prolonged bout of depression. Under good circumstances, women more often report intense joy (or highs) in comparison with men, but, under bad circumstances, women also report more intense sadness (or lows) in comparison with men. This helps to explain why women's average happiness is often found to be equal to men's *and* why women are twice as likely to suffer from depression (pp. 82–83).

Myers concludes his discussion of age and gender with the observation that it is quite astonishing that such profound differences in our lives—between being old or young, being a woman or a man, being employed or a homemaker—should have such miniscule effects on overall well-being. He notes that this is also true for whether one lives in a rural area, town, suburb, or city. Also, according to the studies noted above, race and education account for less than 2 percent of the person-to-person variations in well-being.

Noting that self-esteem is an important factor in a person's sense of well-being, he cites Jennifer Crocker and Brenda Major's (1989) observation that a host of studies conclude that blacks have levels of self-esteem equal to or higher than that of whites. They attribute this finding to three factors: blacks value the things at which they excel, they often attribute their problems to prejudice, and they tend to compare themselves to others in their own group. The latter especially helps us to understand why individual members of all groups report comparable levels of happiness: there is always someone whom one perceives to be less fortunate than oneself—that is, it is always possible to compare downwards (pp. 85–86).

REPROGRAMMING THE MIND

In chapter 5 titled "Reprogramming the Mind," Myers discusses historical and contemporary advocates of "mind power" in order to answer the question: Can the mind really precipitate health and happiness? Acknowledging his earlier skepticism regarding the claims of the "positive thinking" proponents of an earlier era, as well his skepticism toward contemporary "possibility thinking" advocates, he now believes on the basis of a decade of "hard-nosed" research that "certain claims of the mental power movement seem valid" (p. 89).

He notes, for example, that Norman Vincent Peale foresaw what recent research shows, namely, that objective life circumstances have little effect on well-being (pp. 89–90).[2] Moreover, there is no longer any doubt that our appraisal of challenging situations affects our blood pressure; that chronic anger triggers the release of hormones that accelerate the buildup of deposits on the heart's vessels; and that persistent psychological stress depresses the immune system. He cites Michael Scheier and Charles Carver's (1987) finding in their study of dispositional optimism and physical health that positive thinkers—people who agree with statements such as "in uncertain times, I usually expect the best"—cope more successfully with stressful events and enjoy better health than do pessimists (p. 90).

This evidence raises the following questions: Precisely how, and to what extent, do inner mental states affect our sense of joy and happiness? Where in the claims for positive mental power can we separate fact from fiction? And how might one strengthen those traits and attitudes that engender joy rather than dejection? Noting that these are the questions he will consider in the following chapter on the traits of happy people, Myers presents three popular techniques for reprogramming unhappy minds: fire walking (i.e., walking on red-hot coals without pain or burn), listening to subliminal tape messages (i.e., the embedding of positive messages in one's mind below the level of conscious awareness), and hypnosis. The purpose of these illustrations is to assist readers in distinguishing between techniques and methods that make false or misleading claims and those that have been proven to be effective (p. 90).

The first two illustrations (fire walking and subliminal tapes) fall into the first category of making false or misleading claims, while the third (hypnosis) belongs to the second category. Research studies have shown that despite misconceptions and exaggerated claims, hypnosis has two therapeutic uses that reveal the mind's healing power. One is that it helps relieve physical pain. The other is that it helps individuals harness their own healing powers, especially in cases of psychophysiological disorders (strikingly, hypnosis has proven to be an effective treatment for warts). Myers concludes that positive, focused, believing attitudes make a difference. This being so, the question is what sorts of people characteristically have such attitudes? He takes up this question in chapter 6 (pp. 102–104).

THE TRAITS OF HAPPY PEOPLE

In chapter 6 titled "The Traits of Happy People," Myers identifies four personal traits that are characteristic of happy people. The first trait is *self-esteem*—people who are happy like themselves. The University of Michigan studies of well-being in America (Campbell 1981) showed that the best predictor of general life satisfaction is not satisfaction with family life, friendships, or income, but satisfaction with self (p. 109). This is true in other parts of the world as well. Studies in other countries have shown that people who like and accept themselves feel good about life in general. To be sure, there is also much evidence of "self-serving bias," or the tendency to think better of oneself than the facts support. After all, we tend to remember and justify our past actions in self-enhancing ways, to exhibit an inflated confidence in the accuracy of our beliefs and judgments, and to overestimate how desirably we would act in situations where most people behave less than admirably. Moreover, our self-disparaging or self-deprecating statements are often subtly strategic, as they are expressed in such a way as to elicit reassuring responses—fishing for a compliment, as it were. And, of course, no one is immune to feelings of inferiority, especially when comparing oneself with those who are a step or two higher on the ladder of status, physical appearance, income, or agility (pp. 109–112).

However, in general, Myers concludes from the research studies that most people have a *reasonably* high opinion of themselves, and this fact goes a long way toward explaining why most of us are reasonably happy and satisfied with our lives. He notes that this is especially the case with those whose self-esteem is "healthy" rather than "defensive," for whereas defensive people maintain self-esteem by managing the impressions they create and denying threats and pain, a healthy self-esteem is positive yet realistic. Precisely because it is based on the genuine achievement of realistic ideals, and on feeling accepted for what one is—skewed perhaps by the positive biases that pervade happy outlooks—healthy self-esteem provides a foundation for lasting joy (pp. 112–113).

The second trait is *personal control*—happy people believe they choose their destinies. Persons who agree with the statement "What happens to me is my own doing" and disagree with the statement "I don't have enough control over the direction of my life" are more likely to achieve more in school or work, cope better with stress, and live more happily. Also, increasing people's control can noticeably improve their health, morale, and happiness. Myers cites in this regard a study by Judith Rodin (1986) in which nursing home patients were encouraged to exert more control, such as making choices about their environment and weighing in on the policies of the nursing home. As a result, 93 percent became more alert, active, and happy. Similar results have been observed when workers have been included in decision making and prisoners have been given more control over their environments (pp. 113–115).

Myers gives particular attention to the relationship between happiness and the sense of control that comes with effective time management. According to Michael Argyle, author of *The Psychology of Happiness* (1986), for happy people, time is filled and planned, and they are punctual and efficient; but for unhappy people, time is unfilled, open and uncommitted, and they postpone things and are inefficient (p. 116).

The third trait is *optimism*—happy people are hopeful. Myers points to the research studies by Martin Seligman (e.g., Seligman and Schulman 1986) and others that confirm what positive thinking advocates, such as Norman Vincent Peale (Peale 1952), were claiming several decades earlier, namely, that a person who approaches life with an attitude that often says "Yes!" to people and possibilities lives with far more joy and zest than do habitual naysayers. On the other hand, Myers cautions against the perils of unrealism, for excessive optimism can produce a sense of invulnerability, resulting in the failure to protect oneself against diseases; can cause one to endanger oneself and others on the road; and can prevent oneself from preparing for contingencies, including those that could well be predicted on the basis of available information (such as the effect of birthrates on college enrollments). He concludes that the recipe for well-being requires neither positive nor negative thinking alone, but a mix of *ample optimism* to provide hope, a *dash of pessimism* to prevent complacency, and enough *realism* to discriminate those things that we can control from those that we cannot (pp. 118–119).

The fourth trait is *extraversion*—happy people are outgoing. Myers notes that in study after study, extraverts—sociable, outgoing people—report greater happiness and satisfaction with life than do introverts. The explanation seems to be partly temperamental. Extraverts, various studies suggest, are simply more cheerful than introverts, and they tend to be more accepting of themselves. Because they like themselves, they are confident that others will like them too, and such attitudes tend to be self-fulfilling, leading extraverts to have more positive experiences. Also, their daily mood level is higher than that of introverts. Because they are more involved with people, have a larger circle of friends, engage in more rewarding social activities, experience more affection, and enjoy greater social support, they have a greater sense of well-being, happiness, and life satisfaction (pp. 120–121).

Myers concludes this chapter with a discussion of how we may strengthen the four traits that contribute to happiness. This raises the question of how "malleable" we are, that is, to what extent is change possible when it comes to happiness? On the one hand, he cites studies showing that there is, in fact, an underlying consistency of personality. For example, a longitudinal study of Swedish 13-year old boys showed that traits such as outgoingness, emotional stability, openness, agreeableness, and conscientiousness persisted into young adulthood, and it also revealed that trouble-prone and hyperaggressive boys often have problems with the law and with alcohol as adults. Given this consistency of personality, one might be tempted to conclude that little change is possible, and that unhappy persons are thus doomed to remain unhappy. On the other hand, social psychologists have proven over the last 30 years that the actions we elect—that is, our behaviors—do leave a residue inside us. Every time we act, we reinforce an underlying idea or tendency. Most people assume that our traits and attitudes affect our behavior, and while there is some truth to this, it is less so than is commonly supposed because it is also true that our traits and attitudes are shaped by our behavior (pp. 122–123).

So, if we want to change ourselves in some important way—for example, to develop one or more of the traits that are characteristic of happy people—a potent strategy is to get up and start doing that very thing. But what if we don't really feel like it? What if "acting happy" or behaving as if one is happy by adopting the traits of happy people feels forced or phony? This should not deter us. Myers cites experiments in which people have been asked to write essays or present themselves to an interviewer either in self-enhancing or in self-deprecating ways. One study found that those who act *as if* they are very intelligent, caring, and sensitive persons later express higher self-esteem when describing themselves to a different researcher in private. He also notes that when we step into a new role, such as a parent, salesperson, or a teacher, we notice that the feeling of phoniness gradually subsides, and that we no longer feel that we are pretending to be something or someone that we are not. He cites William James (1884) in support: "If we wish to conquer undesirable emotional tendencies in ourselves, we must assiduously, and in the first instance cold-bloodedly, go through the *outward* motions of those contrary dispositions we prefer to cultivate." In effect, Myers is advising us to begin with the second trait of happy people—*personal control*—or the belief that we can control our destinies. But as we take these first behavioral steps toward the development of a happier self, it also helps to have a certain amount of the third trait of happy people—*optimism*—or a sense of hope based on the belief that some things, at least, are in our own power to change for the better (pp. 124–126).

"FLOW" IN WORK AND PLAY

In chapter 7 titled "Flow in Work and Play," Myers first focuses on the relationship of work to well-being. He discusses the fact that although work is considered both bane and blessing, it is more a blessing to those who are not unemployed. He cites Ronald Inglehart's study (1990) of persons from 16 nations, which reports that 83 percent of white-collar workers, 78 percent of manual laborers, and 61 percent of unemployed persons said they were "satisfied with life." He also cites job satisfaction studies showing that most satisfied workers often have higher-status positions within a field, and he adds that higher-status jobs also provide more of the important happiness factor of the sense of *personal control*. Thus, when workers have more control (i.e., when they can set or at least help to define their own goals, when they have some control over their time, and when they can participate in decision making) their job satisfaction rises (pp. 128–130).

On the other hand, work is often unsatisfying, and this is for one of two reasons: either one is overwhelmed (when challenges exceed our available time and skills) or underwhelmed (when challenges do not engage our time and skills). The former creates anxiety, the latter boredom. There is a middle ground or zone in which we experience what Mihaly Csikszentmihalyi (1988) terms "flow," a concept he formulated after studying artists who would spend many hours painting or sculpting with great concentration. The flow model consists of four quadrants: (1) high challenge/low skills makes for *anxiety*, (2) low challenge/low skills makes for *apathy*, (3) high skills/low challenge makes for *boredom*, and (4) high challenge/high skills makes for *flow*. Thus, when challenges engage our skills, we often become so absorbed in the flow of an activity that we lose awareness of self and time. In support of Csikszentmihalyi's model, various studies confirm that a key ingredient of satisfying work is whether or not it is challenging; the most satisfied workers find their skills tested, their work varied, and their tasks significant (pp. 132–133).

In addition to the steps that Csikszentmihalyi recommends (set goals, immerse yourself in the activity, pay attention to what is happening, and enjoy the immediate experience), Myers suggests that we can put more flow into our lives by living more intentionally (i.e., by saying yes to the things that we do best and find most meaningful, and no to time-wasting demands). But we should also use our leisure time intentionally. Csikszentmihalyi found that people are unhappiest when they are alone and no specific task requires their attention. Thus, Myers recommends leisure *activities* because well-being resides not in mindless passivity but in mindful engagement. At the same time, happy people not only live full, active, industrious lives, but they also reserve time for renewing solitude and rest. Sleep studies show that subjects deprived of sleep often feel a general malaise, and that those persons who sleep seven to eight hours a night were 50 percent less likely to be depressed than those who slept less than, or more than, seven to eight hours. Thus, to experience well-being, a balance of activity and rest is particularly desirable (pp. 137–141).

FRIENDSHIP, LOVE, AND MARRIAGE

Chapter 8 titled "The Friendship Factor" is the first of two chapters on the role that close relationships play in personal happiness. Myers cites several studies that collectively show that close relationships with friends and family members promote health and help persons cope better with various stresses, including bereavement, rape, job loss, and illness. This research also suggests that the negative effects of various traumatic experiences are reduced by having someone to confide in. The National Opinion Research Center posed this question to respondents: "Looking over the last six months, who are the people with whom you discussed matters important to you?" Myers notes that compared to those who could not identify anyone to whom they discussed important matters, those who named five or more such friends were 60 percent more likely to feel "very happy." In effect, the relationship between well-being and self-disclosure is two-way because happiness promotes intimacy and intimacy promotes happiness (pp. 149–154).

In chapter 9 titled "Love and Marriage," Myers discusses the relationship between marriage and well-being, and he notes that the consistent finding of many studies is that whether one is young or old, male or female, rich or poor, people in stable and loving relationships enjoy greater well-being. In the United States, less than 25 percent of unmarried but nearly 40 percent of married adults report being "very happy." But the quality of the marriage is even more important than the fact of being married. People who say their marriage is satisfying rarely report being unhappy, discontented with life, or depressed. And most married people report that their marriages are happy ones. In the United States, almost two-thirds say their marriage is "very happy," three out of four say their spouse is their best friend, and four out of five people say they would marry the same person again. Thus, the consequence of marital happiness is that most such people feel very happy with life as a whole (p. 156).

But why is this so? Why are married people generally happier? Are happy people more desirable as marriage partners? Research studies suggest that the answer is generally yes, that positive, happy people more readily form happy relationships. But the converse is true as well. Marriage also enhances happiness and for two reasons: (1) married people are more likely to enjoy an enduring, supportive, intimate relationship (and less likely to suffer loneliness); and (2) marriage offers the roles of spouse and parent, and these can provide additional sources of self-esteem because one can find meaning in these different roles (p. 157).

On the other hand, Myers cautions against an overly optimistic (or simplistic) view of marriage as conducive to happiness. He notes that in one survey after another, the National Opinion Research Center has found that nearly 6 in 10 Americans who rate their marriage as "very happy" also rate *life as a whole* as "very happy," but among those who are *not* in a very happy marriage, the proportion who are very happy with life as a whole plummets to 1 in 10. This is an even lower level of happiness than among the relatively unhappy separated and divorced. Also, noting the rising divorce rate from 1960 to 1990, Myers asks whether this indicates that the marriages that survive are happier than those that end in divorce. The answer is no. When compared with married persons when divorce was relatively uncommon, those in today's surviving marriages are actually *less* likely to describe their marriage as very happy. This suggests that despite the fact that married people are still considerably more likely to feel happy than unmarried people, in recent years the gap has lessened because (1) married women are not as happy as they once were; and (2) unmarried men and women are happier than before. In other words, individuals are more comfortable staying single, and the apparent contribution of marriage to happiness has weakened (pp. 158–161).

On the positive side, one literature review of 16 studies (Vemer et al. 1989) revealed that people in first marriages report greater satisfaction than those in second marriages. But the difference is miniscule. Also, although second marriages have a 25 percent greater risk of divorce, remarried people are basically as satisfied with their marriages as those in first marriages (p. 165).

Myers concludes from these and many other studies reported in this chapter that the psychological ingredients of marital happiness are kindred minds, sexual warmth, social intimacy, and equitable giving and receiving of emotional and material resources. We might also add that happy marriages foster the basic traits of happy people: self-esteem, personal control, optimism, and extraversion. The difference is that these traits are characteristic of a relationship involving two individuals (p. 174).

FAITH, HOPE, AND JOY

In chapter 10 titled "Faith, Hope, and Joy" Myers focuses on the relationship between faith and happiness. He notes that many studies across North America and Europe reveal that religious people more often report feeling happy and satisfied with life than nonreligious people do, and these findings challenge the presumption in much of the happiness literature that religion restricts happiness or is irrelevant to it. He cites the finding of a 1984 Gallup Organization study that found persons with high "spiritual commitment" were twice as likely as those with low "spiritual commitment" to say that they were "very happy." He also notes that studies have shown a positive relationship between religious faith and coping with a crisis. A 1988 National Opinion Research Center survey found that people who had recently suffered divorce, unemployment, bereavement, serious illness, or disability retained greater joy if they also had a strong faith. Other studies have shown that persons with a deep religious faith are less susceptible to depression (pp. 183–184).

While cautioning against viewing religious faith as a guarantee of happiness, Myers identifies the personal benefits of religious faith. These include being connected to a caring community; a sense of significance; the experience of humility and deep acceptance; a focus beyond ourselves; and a perspective on life's tragedies, especially death. He writes: "To take the leap into active faith is to bet one's life on a worldview that makes sense of the universe, gives meaning to life, offers hope in the face of adversity and death, and provides vision and courage for living in the present" (p. 204). He acknowledges that the tools of his empirical science cannot prove any faith true or false (or that one faith produces more joy than another), but he also notes that we marry in the *hope* of a happy life and choose a career *believing* that it will prove satisfying—so we are, in effect, no strangers to leaps of faith, whether we are religious or not. And, if we can develop traits of happiness by acting as if we already possessed them, there is no reason in principle why this would not also apply to the leap of active faith.

CONCLUSION

In the epilogue, Myers provides an extensive list of popular but mistaken ideas about happiness, including the following: (1) that few people are genuinely happy; (2) that wealth buys well-being; (3) that tragedies, such as disabling accidents, permanently erode happiness; (4) that happiness springs from the memories of intense, if rare, positive experiences (such as idyllic vacations, ecstatic romances, and joy-filled victories); (5) that one sex is happier than the other; (6) that opposites attract and continue to find each other fascinating; and (7) that religious faith suppresses happiness. He also provides the following list of the 10 things that enable or promote happiness: (1) fit and healthy bodies; (2) realistic goals and expectations; (3) positive self-esteem; (4) feelings of control; (5) optimism; (6) outgoingness; (7) supportive friendships that enable companionship and confiding; (8) a socially intimate, sexually warm, equitable marriage; (9) challenging work and active leisure, punctuated by adequate rest and retreat; and (10) a faith that entails communal support, purpose, acceptance, outward focus, and hope (p. 206).

Then, in conclusion, he notes that in writing this book, his purpose has been more to inform than to prescribe or advise. He compares his book to *Consumer Reports*, which doesn't tell us what to buy, because that depends on our personal needs and circumstances. But he also notes that we would be foolish to ignore its information when making purchasing decisions. In a similar way, we should not be so smug as to ignore new information about well-being in ways that could enhance our own. We can decide to exercise, to allow enough hours for sleep, to make comparisons that remind us of our blessings, to manage our time in ways that boost our sense of control, to begin acting as if we had the traits we would like to develop, to initiate relationships, to devote effort to maintaining love rather than taking it for granted, to plan involving rather than passive leisure activities, to take the leap into an active faith, and even to begin working at reshaping our culture in ways that will promote the well-being that fame and fortune cannot buy. Admittedly, for those of us who are not already doing at least a few of these things, this may sound rather daunting, but these are steps we can take if we wish to discover greater peace and joy (p. 207).

Myers ends on this note: "Well-being is found in the renewal of disciplined lifestyles, committed relationships, and the receiving and giving of acceptance. To experience deep well-being is to be self-confident yet unselfconscious, self-giving yet self-respecting, realistic yet hope filled" (p. 207). Thus, happiness is less a pursuit than a constituent of a state of mind characterized by a sense that life is good; a sense that this time of life, or even life as a whole, is fulfilling, meaningful, and pleasant; and a deep and abiding sense that all is—or will be—well with us.

CHAPTER 6

AUTHENTIC HAPPINESS

The sixth book that we have chosen to review here is Martin Seligman's *Authentic Happiness: Using the New Positive Psychology to Realize Your Potential for Lasting Fulfillment* (2002). As noted in the introduction, Seligman is a psychology professor at the University of Pennsylvania and the founder of the field of Positive Psychology. *Authentic Happiness* articulates Positive Psychology's central ideas and is written for the layperson.

Seligman points out in the preface that there has been a great deal of progress in treating mental illness during the last 50 years, but there has not been much progress in understanding happiness or what Aristotle called "the good life." One reason for this is that there is a bias in the scientific literature that suggests that happiness cannot be changed: that changing happiness, in other words, is like trying to lose weight—we can diet, but most of us probably won't change all that much. Another is the prevalent impression that happiness is inauthentic. In other words, there is a deep-seated view in Western culture that human beings are fundamentally bad, selfish, and sinful, and this view manifests itself in, for example, the doctrine of original sin in theology and in Freud's writings on sexuality and aggression in psychoanalysis. Seligman challenges both of these views in his book.

What is Positive Psychology? Seligman defines Positive Psychology by postulating its three "pillars": the study of positive emotion; the study of the positive traits (the foremost being strengths and virtues but also "abilities" such as intelligence and athleticism); and the study of positive institutions, such as democracy, strong families, and free inquiry that support the virtues, which in turn support the positive emotions. Positive Psychology, he suggests,

is a journey that leads one through "the country side" of pleasure and gratification, up into "the high country" of strength and virtue, and finally to "the
peaks" of lasting fulfillment: meaning and purpose (pp. xi–xii).

The book consists of three parts—"Positive Emotion," "Strength and Virtue," and "In the Mansions of Life." Part 1 has seven chapters on the following topics: positive feeling and character; how psychology lost its way, and he
(Seligman) found his; why one should bother to be happy; whether you can
make yourself happy in a lasting way; satisfaction about the past; optimism
about the future; and happiness in the present. Part 2 has two chapters on
the topics of renewing strength and virtue, and your signature strengths.
Part 3 has five chapters on the following topics: work and personal satisfaction, love, raising children, reprise and summary, and meaning and purpose.
We will comment on all the chapters with the exception of chapter 2 (which
focuses on Seligman's critique of psychological approaches that, in his view,
overemphasize human unhappiness).

POSITIVE FEELING AND POSITIVE CHARACTER

In chapter 1, titled "Positive Feeling and Positive Character," Seligman
asks: Is happiness good for your health? It is well known, he points out, that
people from Utah live longer than people from Nevada, but there are too
many variables—diet, drinking, smoking, gambling, Mormon values—to understand why this is the case. Studying longevity and health, no matter what
the variables, has its problems and complications. But one study of Roman
Catholic nuns seems to have isolated many of these variables because nuns
collectively tend to have the same diets, do not drink or smoke, have the same
reproductive and marital histories, are in the same economic and social class,
and have the same access to good medical care. What is striking about the
findings from this study is that nuns whose journals included positive emotion
were a strong predictor of health and longevity. Happiness, it seems, is good
for your health, or, as Seligman suggests, a happy nun lives a long life (p. 4).[1]

Pointing out that the study of happiness is new and that its conclusions
are uncertain at this point, Seligman's book is intended to serve as the flag-
ship book for Positive Psychology, which goes beyond "hedonics," which
is the study of positive emotion and pleasant experiences, or the study of
what feels good. More than positive emotion and pleasant experience, Positive Psychology is also about strengths and virtues, as well as meaning and
purpose. Eating chocolate or doing drugs, for example, can lead to positive
emotions and pleasant experiences, but these means to happiness, Seligman
suggests, are, by themselves, inauthentic—they are shortcuts. In contrast,
the positive feelings that arise from the exercise of various strengths and
virtues are authentic. To be sure, eating chocolate has its place because plea-

sure is a part of happiness, but what Seligman calls "gratification," such as the exercise of kindness, is really the key to happiness. Thus, our lives are authentically happy when our well-being derives from exercising our own personal strengths and personal virtues (p. 8).

Seligman notes that because psychology has focused on pathology for many years, psychologists have developed rigorous classifications for various mental illnesses, codified and refined in the *Diagnostic and Statistical Manual of Mental Disorders* (*DSM-IV-TR*) (American Psychiatric Association 2000). But he wants to develop a system that is intended to be the opposite of the DSM-IV-TR, one that classifies strengths and virtues. On the basis of his study of the world's religious and philosophical traditions, he identifies these six core virtues: (1) wisdom and knowledge, (2) courage, (3) love and humanity, (4) justice, (5) temperance, and (6) spirituality and transcendence. These core virtues can be broken down into subcategories. Wisdom, for example, may include the subcategories of curiosity, originality, and various others. He also suggests three criteria for the inclusion of strengths in his classification scheme: They must be valued in "almost all" cultures, they must be valued in their own right, and they must be malleable. Thus, kindness is a strength, but intelligence is not, because intelligence is not very learnable, while kindness, in contrast, is learnable (p. 11).

Seligman suggests that we should not spend much time developing strengths that we do not have. Rather, we should work on improving the strengths that we already have, especially our strongest areas, which he calls "signature strengths." He notes that the good life is using your signature strengths every day to produce authentic happiness, and that the well-being that using your signature strengths engenders is grounded in authenticity. But just as well-being needs to be grounded in strengths and virtues, these strengths and virtues must, in turn, be rooted in something larger, for even as the good life is beyond the pleasant life, so the meaningful life is beyond the good life (pp. 13–14).

Choosing not to put forward a definition of the meaningful life, he simply states that it is attachment to something larger. He notes that he has always had trouble with the idea of a supernatural God, and that in the final chapter of the book he will discuss the fact that Positive Psychology points the way toward a secular approach to "noble purpose" and "transcendent meaning" and toward a God who is not supernatural (pp. 13–14).

He closes the chapter by asking his readers to take a short survey: the Fordyce Emotions Questionnaire.[2] Recognizing that readers may have a question that has been bothering them as they read the chapter, namely, "What is happiness?" he points out that more has been written about defining happiness than about almost any other philosophical question, and notes that it is not his intention to add to this "clutter." Instead, he will use his own terms and present them in consistent and well-defined ways (pp. 15–16).[3]

WHAT MAKES US FEEL HAPPY?

In chapter 3 titled "Why Bother to Be Happy?" Seligman offers an evolutionary explanation of why human beings feel happy. He begins by noting that there is a broad consensus with regard to the evolutionary value of negative emotions. For example, fear, sadness, and anger help to buffer us against the threats of attack, loss, and trespass. All emotions, he notes, have feeling, sensory, thinking, and action components, and feelings such as disgust help us to move away from, say, vomit in the hallway.

He also notes a common distinction between phenomena and epiphenomena. When, for example, you press the gas pedal in your car, the car accelerates. The phenomenon of pressing the pedal causes the acceleration of the car. When you accelerate, the speedometer also rises, but the rising of the speedometer does not cause the car to accelerate; rather, it is the other way around—this is an epiphenomenon. In the early 20th century, some behaviorists, such as B. F. Skinner, argued that all mental life is epiphenomenal, that, in other words, when you flee from a bear your fear merely reflects the fact that you are running away (a behavior) with the subjective state frequently occurring *after* the behavior. Fear, that is to say, is not the engine of running away but, rather, the speedometer. Seligman accepts the distinction between phenomena and epiphenomena—these are descriptive terms—but he rejects the assumptions of behaviorism (p. 31).

His work on learned helplessness convinced him that behaviorism is misguided. Animals, he found, could discover complex relationships and come to the conclusion that nothing that they do matters. He discovered this by experimenting on various groups of dogs. He would give them painful electrical shocks from which they had no means of escaping. Later, however, when he gave them the same shocks, he found that they would not even try to escape when they easily could do so—in other words, they learned to be helpless. Ideas and feelings, he holds, do cause behavior—it is not simply the other way around.

Strikingly, when it came to positive emotions, he did not assume that they caused behavior (despite his earlier research), and he regarded them as epiphenomenal. However, he began to change his views after reading the work of Barbara Fredrickson (1998, 2001) who argued for the evolutionary significance of positive emotions. She claimed that they broaden our abiding resources (intellectual, physical, and social) by building up reserves that we can draw upon when a threat or opportunity presents itself. She also observed that when we are in a positive mood, people like us better—so friendship, love, and other such coalitions are more likely to form when we display positive emotions (p. 35).

The rest of the chapter is devoted to discussing various studies related to Fredrickson's point of view. He considers studies related to mood and thinking and notes that negative moods can cause one to be more of a critical thinker, while positive moods can help one to be more of a creative thinker. He also cites the happiness and health literature (which, we might point out, has striking similarities to the religion and health literature). It suggests that happiness is associated with healthy aging and longevity, and that happier people seem to have higher tolerances for pain. Happiness also seems to be associated with productivity, better friendships, and better romantic relationships. The upshot of this research is that feeling positive emotion is important, not just because it is pleasurable, but because it causes a much better "commerce" with the world. The next chapter discusses the possibility of how to go about doing so (p. 43).

THE HAPPINESS FORMULA

In chapter 4 titled "Can You Make Yourself Lastingly Happier?" Seligman focuses on his happiness formula: $H = S + C + V$. "H" stands for one's enduring level of happiness, as opposed to one's momentary happiness. "S" stands for one's set range for happiness and refers to one's genetic endowment with regard to one's capacity for and tendency toward negative and positive emotions. "C" stands for one's circumstances, such as whether one is unemployed or living in a war zone, and "V" stands for one's voluntary control. He notes that "V" is the most important variable in Positive Psychology, and he devotes chapters 5–7 to it (pp. 45–50).

The bulk of chapter 4 focuses on the conclusions of various studies related to "C," and, more specifically, on the relationship of happiness to one's circumstances in the following areas: money, marriage, social life, negative emotion, health, religion, education, climate, race, and gender. Money is important in that it provides for basic needs, but after these needs are met, it does not affect happiness all that much. Marriage seems to be related to happiness in some way, though it is unclear whether happy people get and stay married more easily, or whether success in marriage yields higher levels of happiness. Social life manifests the same uncertainties. It is unclear whether people who are more social tend to be happier, or whether happier people are more social (pp. 51–56).

With regard to negative emotion, he reports some striking findings: People who tend to experience more negative emotion also tend to experience more positive emotion. Many studies have shown that women tend to be more depressed than men, but, recently, women have also been found to experience higher levels of happiness. Seligman notes that there is much debate about these findings (women may simply be more likely to report their emotions), but they are striking nevertheless. With regard to age, life satisfaction tends to increase with age, while pleasant affect decreases slightly, and negative affect does not change. Moderate ill health does not seem to affect happiness, but severe ill health does. Education, climate (as in where one lives), and race do not seem to be related to happiness. Religion does seem to affect happiness. He postulates that this is due to the meaning that religion provides in people's lives. He returns to this topic later in the book (pp. 56–60).

Based on the conclusions of these various studies, Seligman offers this advice with regard to improving one's circumstances: (1) live in a wealthy democracy, (2) marry, (3) try to avoid negative events and negative emotions, (4) cultivate a rich social network, and (5) be religious. The other factors, such as making more money or moving to a sunny climate, won't make you much happier (p. 61).

SATISFACTION ABOUT THE PAST

As noted, Seligman devotes chapters 5–7 to the "V" or voluntary variables in his happiness equation. He does this by writing about what we can change about our past, our present, and our future. In chapter 5, "Satisfaction about the Past," he discusses three ways in which people can change their satisfaction with the past. The first involves "intellection," and the second and third are emotional. The intellection way is to dispense with theories that suggest we are determined by our past, because such theories are counterproductive and not supported by scientific research derived from cognitive psychology. He suggests that simply knowing the surprising fact that early past events exert little or no influence on adult lives is liberating. He cites several large-scale surveys of adult personality to support this view (p. 68).

The other two ways of changing one's satisfaction with the past are emotional. The first involves cultivating gratitude in one's life. There is some debate in psychology as to whether emotion drives thought (what psychoanalytic psychology stresses) or whether thought drives emotion (what cognitive psychology stresses). He states that there is evidence for both views, and that it is likely that both, at times, are true, and then goes on to discuss in some detail an exercise he uses in his Positive Psychology class in which he asks students to write a statement of gratitude about someone in their lives. Students then invite this person to the class, and they read their statements—or some other such means of expressing gratitude, such as singing a song—to the person. The person has no idea of the purpose of the class visit, and these experiences prove to be deeply emotional—some persons even indicate that this experience has been one of the most meaningful experiences of their lives (pp. 70–75).

The second emotional way of changing one's satisfaction about the past involves forgiving. It would be nice, Seligman suggests, if we could actively suppress or consciously forget unpleasant memories, but there are no known ways to do this. The best we can do, then, is to forgive. Although forgiving is difficult because it violates our sense of justice and our desire for revenge, one reason to incorporate it into our lives is that, as one large-scale study found, people who are more forgiving tend to have lower levels of stress and higher levels of optimism, and report better health. As to offering advice about how to forgive, Seligman commends Everett Worthington's REACH model (2001) of forgiveness, which stands for *recall* the hurt, *empathize* with the transgressor, extend forgiveness as an *altruistic* gift to the transgressor, *commit* to forgiving publicly, and *hold* onto forgiveness (pp. 75–81).

Seligman closes this chapter by advising readers to "weigh up" their life once a year, on January 1. One should especially look at one's life in terms of love, work, money, play, and friends, and look for patterns of past growth from previous years and opportunities for growth in the future. This advice serves as a transition, as the next chapter deals with the future (pp. 81–82).

OPTIMISM ABOUT THE FUTURE

Chapter 6, titled "Optimism about the Future," presents several tools for assessing one's own optimism as well as strategies for becoming more optimistic. Why should one want to be more optimistic? Because optimism and hope cause better resistance to depression when bad events occur, better performance at work, and better physical health (p. 83). Seligman introduces two crucial dimensions relating to optimism and pessimism: permanence (which is about time) and pervasiveness (which is about space). Concerning permanence, pessimists tend to see bad events in more permanent than temporary ways. Say, for example, that you are having problems with your diet. A pessimist is more likely to observe that diets never work (a permanent explanation), while an optimist is more likely to point out that diets don't work when you eat out (a temporary explanation). The reverse holds true for good events: optimists view them as permanent, whereas pessimists view them as temporary (pp. 88–90). Similarly, with regard to pervasiveness, a pessimist may, for example, view all professors as unfair, while an optimist may view a particular professor as unfair. The reverse also holds true with regard to positive events. After doing well on a math exam, an optimist might conclude that he or she is smart, while the pessimist might conclude that he or she is only smart at math. Seligman includes various self-assessment tools in the book to calculate one's optimism and pessimism in terms of pervasiveness and permanence, and suggests a way to calculate one's hope based on all of one's optimism and pessimism scores. The rest of the chapter focuses on strategies for increasing one's optimism and hope. These strategies are based on the ABCDE model, a model designed to help a person identify and challenge pessimistic thoughts. ABCDE is an acronym that stands for: A—Adversity (which deals with recognizing the event that evokes pessimistic thoughts; B—Belief (which deals with identifying one's beliefs in relation to the event); C—Consequences (which deals with identifying the consequences of the belief); D—Disputing (which involves disputing the belief); and E—Energization (which deals with the energy one gains from successfully disputing the belief) (pp. 90–95).

With regard to pessimistic thoughts, Seligman advises that it is essential to learn to argue with oneself. We often dismiss criticism from others, but we also need to be able to dismiss criticism when it comes from within. Seligman suggests asking these types of questions in learning how to dismiss the criticism that comes from within: What is the evidence for a particular belief? What are alternative explanations? What are the consequences of holding a negative belief? How likely, for example, is the worst-case scenario of a given belief? Asking these kinds of questions helps to put our negative thoughts in perspective and thereby decrease our pessimistic thoughts about the future and open the way for an optimistic perspective toward it (pp. 95–101).

HAPPINESS IN THE PRESENT

Chapter 7, titled "Happiness in the Present," focuses on pleasures and gratifications. Pleasures have bodily sensory components—such as having an orgasm, eating chocolate, sitting by a warm fire on a snowy day—while gratifications are characterized by a state of "flow," a state in which one is totally engaged—such as when one is reading a book, playing tennis, or rock climbing. Pleasures are fleeting, and they are subject to habituation (e.g., most of the time, only the first couple of mouthfuls of ice cream are truly delightful). So we should incorporate as many pleasures into our lives as possible but spread them out to maximize pleasure. Seligman also offers advice with regard to *savoring* pleasure, such as by sharing the experience with others, preserving memories through photographs or souvenirs, being willing to self-congratulate, sharpening one's perception during pleasurable activities, and allowing oneself to become totally absorbed (pp. 102–111).

Gratifications are more complex than pleasures. They are a part of the good life and beyond the pleasant life. Seligman notes that the good life cannot be attained from bodily pleasure, that it is not a state that can be chemically induced or by any other such shortcuts, and that it can only be had by activity that is grounded in "noble purpose." In this connection, he discusses Mihaly Csikszentmihalyi's concept of "flow," which, as discussed previously in this book, are experiences in which the task challenges us and requires skill, involves concentration, has clear goals, includes immediate feedback, induces a deep and effortless involvement, yields a sense of control, and provides a sense of the vanishing of the self as time stands still. More than increasing pleasures, cultivating these kinds of activities in our lives will help us to find happiness in the present (pp. 112–121). There are no shortcuts to happiness, Seligman suggests, and American culture, which emphasizes quick fixes and immediate gratifications, is likely to leave us more depressed than satisfied. The rest of the book is dedicated to helping readers discover how and where they might experience "flow."

VIRTUES AND STRENGTHS

Part 2 of *Authentic Happiness* on strength and virtue consists of two chapters. In chapter 8, "Renewing Strength and Virtue," Seligman makes the case for restoring the study of virtue and character in psychology. He wants to resurrect the idea of character in Positive Psychology and does so on the grounds that (1) personality and character seem, to some degree, to be inheritable traits; (2) science, while not being prescriptive, should give us information about what is possible in life in terms of ways of being; and (3) there are virtues that are ubiquitous in virtually every culture that transcend any particular worldview (pp. 125–129).

But how can one resurrect the study of character in psychology? In this chapter, Seligman relates the story about how a major portion of the Positive Psychology was launched. He notes that a large grant from the Mayerson Foundation enabled him to carry out research leading to the formulation of a taxonomy of strengths and virtues. The first step in the research involved reading the great religious and philosophical traditions, both East and West. Based on this reading, he and his colleagues posited the six ubiquitous (not universal) virtues noted earlier: wisdom and knowledge, courage, love and humanity, justice, temperance, and spirituality and transcendence. The next step in the research was to make these categories more measurable, which is the subject of the next chapter (pp. 129–133).

YOUR SIGNATURE STRENGTHS

In chapter 9, titled "Your Signature Strengths," Seligman focuses on how to identify one's signature strengths. He does so by utilizing the VIA Strengths Survey.[4] Unlike the six virtues in chapter 8, the strengths in this chapter are measurable and also learnable. The VIA Strengths Survey includes two items for each strength, and there are 24 strengths in all (pp. 137–140).

The six strengths that constitute the first virtue (wisdom and knowledge) include curiosity, love of learning, critical thinking, ingenuity, social and emotional intelligence, and perspective. They are listed from developmentally basic (curiosity) to developmentally mature (perspective) and are grounded in scoring responses to statements such as: "I like to think of new ways to do things." There are similar such grounding statements for each of the strengths. The strengths that constitute the second virtue (courage) include valor, perseverance, and integrity. The strengths for the third virtue (humanity and love) are kindness, loving, and allowing oneself to be loved. The strengths for the fourth virtue (justice) include duty and loyalty, fairness and equity, and leadership. The strengths for the fifth virtue (temperance) are self-control, prudence, and humility. There are seven strengths associated with the sixth virtue (spirituality and transcendence). Seligman intimates that this virtue has so many strengths associated with it because there is conceptual confusion around this term, so he is using it to identify a "cluster of strengths," both religious and nonreligious. They include appreciation of beauty and excellence, gratitude, hope and optimism, spirituality and faith, forgiveness and mercy, humor, and zest (pp. 140–160).

As noted, there are 24 strengths included in the VIA Strengths Survey. After taking the survey, the participant is invited to identify the five strengths that he or she has scored the highest on, and is then instructed to apply additional criteria (which are listed in his book) to these top five strengths to determine whether they are "authentic." For example, the participant is asked to consider whether he or she is excited when displaying one of these strengths and whether he or she has a sense of ownership of this strength. These criteria provide a kind of personal validation of the scores from the survey, and, if the results pass this test, the participant has found his or her "signature strengths." The result is a formula for the good life: One should use one's own signature strengths every day in the main realms of one's life to yield authentic happiness (pp. 160–161).

WORK AND PERSONAL SATISFACTION

The first three chapters of part 3 focus on the arenas in which happiness is experienced and fostered. In chapter 10 on "Work and Personal Satisfaction," Seligman begins by noting that in the wealthiest nations, money is losing its power. It is becoming increasingly obvious that money cannot buy happiness, so people are beginning to make choices about their work based on life satisfaction rather than on income. He acknowledges that these trends go up and down, but he has observed that the trend for two decades has been in favor of personal satisfaction (pp. 165–166).

He distinguishes among jobs (that are done for money), careers (that are done for recognition as well as for money), and callings (that are engaged in for their own sake). He contends that the key to finding happiness via work is to find work or to re-craft your current work so that it will engage your signature strengths on a daily basis for a greater good—this is what he means by "calling." Haircutters who engage emotionally with their clients (rather than mechanically cutting hair), nurses who attend to caring for patients and their families (rather than mechanically performing mundane tasks), and kitchen workers who see their work as art (rather than merely utilitarian) are all examples of how work can be a calling rather than simply a job or career (pp. 166–176).

LOVE

As the preceding chapter made the case that work is more than labor in exchange for money, chapter 11, titled "Love," makes the case that love is more than affection in exchange for some other gain. Seligman points out that there are different ways to love and different ways to be loved. There is the kind of love parents feel toward children, the kind that children feel toward their parents, and the kind that romantic partners feel toward each other. Moreover, there are different loving styles. Some have "secure" loving styles while others have "avoidant" and "anxious" loving styles. People also have optimistic and pessimistic orientations toward their partners. Various kinds of styles of loving and of being loved can work well together, but one particular combination is especially problematic: two pessimists married to one another. Marriage serves as a buffer against many of life's stresses, but when two pessimists are together, the stresses of life tend to exacerbate due to the relationship itself (pp. 185–195).

Noting that he is not a marital therapist and therefore could not rely on firsthand clinical experience relating to marriage, Seligman cites John Gottman's research (2000) on love and marriage, noting that Gottman has been able to predict divorce with over 90 percent accuracy. These behaviors are predictive of divorce: (1) harsh startups in disagreements, (2) criticisms of partner, (3) displays of contempt, (4) defensiveness, (5) lack of validation, and (6) negative body language (Gottman and Levenson 1992). In contrast, the following behaviors have a positive association with good marriages: (1) sharing one thing with each other about one's day in the morning, (2) having a low-stress conversation with one's partner at the end of a workday, (3) showing physical affection, (4) having one date a week, and (5) showing admiration and appreciation (Gottman 2000, ch. 4). Seligman suggests that putting in the actual quantity of time here into each of these expressions is crucial—in other words, actual time should not be replaced with "quality" time (pp. 196–202).

Because much of this advice is related to communicating with one's partner, Seligman also offers guidance in this chapter on attentive and responsive listening. When listening to our partners, we should have a good listening environment (e.g., the television should be off, the kids should be asleep), and when our partner is talking, we should focus on understanding rather than on rebutting or problem solving. Some of us are naturally good at loving and at being loved. But others of us need some guidance and practice—and he offers practical advice, some of which is outlined above in this chapter, which, he believes, will contribute to our authentic happiness (pp. 202–207).

RAISING CHILDREN

In chapter 12 on "Raising Children," Seligman proposes what he calls a positive psychological view of child rearing. Noting that there has been very little research in this regard, he writes about the way that he and his wife have raised their children (p. 208).

He divides his advice into two broad categories: child rearing through age seven and child rearing after age seven. Before age seven, parents should focus on cultivating positive emotions in their children. After age seven, they should focus on cultivating their children's strengths and virtues. He offers three principles of building positive emotion in children and eight specific techniques for doing so: (1) positive emotion broadens and builds the intellectual, social, and physical resources that your children build upon later in life; (2) augmenting positive emotions in your children can start an upward spiral of positive emotion; and (3) the positive traits that your child displays are just as real and authentic as his or her negative traits. Noting that children are naturally cute and positive, he suggests that these seem to be the gifts of evolution—something to counteract the crying and the whining. They also seem naturally oriented toward playing and exploring—traits that keep them growing (pp. 209–212).

He also offers eight techniques for cultivating positive emotion in children. They include: (1) sleeping with your baby, which cultivates secure attachment and does not reinforce the negative effects of crying for attention; (2) playing synchrony games, which entail demonstrating to children that they can affect their environment by means of stacking and moving blocks and other such activities; (3) selectively using the word "no" and finding other substitute words, such as "be gentle," because a "no" worldview can become internalized; (4) praising selectively and punishing for reasons that children understand, so they can learn what is expected of them; (5) attending to sibling rivalry by increasing attention and affection, and by "promoting" children with chores that can engage them; (6) engaging in "bedtime nuggets," such as asking children what the best parts of their day were, and, when they are older, what they are looking forward to tomorrow (when he and his wife asked their children the latter question at age three, they would get too excited and were unable to sleep); (7) selectively and strategically making deals with their children, such as buying them a deeply wished-for toy in exchange for a particular wished-for behavior (though this deal can, at most, be used twice—otherwise it could easily be abused by children as a way to get otherwise unattainable toys); and (8) making positive rather than negative New Year's resolutions, such as a resolution to learn the piano rather than to stop drinking soda (pp. 212–231).

Seligman does not offer as detailed advice about how to build strengths and virtues in children, but he includes the Children's Strength Survey (developed by Katherine Dahlsgaard) which has 24 statements with various subparts related to wisdom and knowledge, courage, humanity, justice, temperance, and transcendence. Acknowledging that he does not have evidence to back this claim, he nonetheless believes that newborns have the capacity for all 24 strengths, but that they develop the ones for which they are praised and that certain strengths rise to the fore. He offers two words of advice: (1) no matter what strengths emerge, encourage them; and (2) try to create opportunities for your children to display their strengths in daily activities, once you have identified them (pp. 231–246).

REPRISE AND SUMMARY

In chapter 13 titled "Reprise and Summary," Seligman suggests that readers might retake the Fordyce Emotions Survey and compare these scores with the scores they received when they first took the test (in chapter 2). He then points out that his "central theme" to this point in the book has been that there are several roads that lead to authentic happiness, each very different from the others. He reminds readers that the first part of the book focused on positive emotion, and that it suggested various ways to improve positive emotion in relation to the past, the present, and the future; and that it distinguished between pleasures (which are momentary and emotional) and gratifications (which are more abiding and characterized by states of absorption, engagement, and flow) (pp. 247–248).

Because gratifications come about through the exercise of our strengths and our virtues, the second part of the book described the 24 ubiquitous strengths and provided tests for readers to identify their own "signature strengths." The third part of the book discussed ways of deploying one's signature strengths in three great "arenas" of life, namely, work, love, and parenting. This, in turn, led to his formulation of the good life, which consists in using one's own signature strengths as often as possible in these three arenas in order to attain authentic happiness (pp. 248–249). In the concluding paragraph, he notes that he has identified the *pleasant* life (rooted in pleasures) and the *good* life (rooted in gratifications). There is also a third—the *meaningful* life—which has the added feature of using one's signature strengths in the service of "something larger." This is the topic he addresses in the final chapter (p. 249).

MEANING AND PURPOSE

The final chapter titled "Meaning and Purpose" has quite a different flavor from the rest of the book, as it delves into speculations about philosophy and theology. Seligman begins by recounting a gathering of 10 intellectuals (scientists, philosophers, and theologians) that was sponsored by the Templeton Foundation, which supports research on religion and science. At the gathering, Robert Wright, a distinguished journalist, gave a presentation on the secret of life: that life is driven by win-win games. Evolution, he argued, has brought us to where we are because, in the long run, win-win rather than win-loss games are the most beneficial. In effect, a cell that incorporates mitochondria symbiotically triumphs over cells that cannot do so. And this, Wright suggests, can also be seen over the course of human history: groups of people have evolved from savages to barbarians to civil societies. To be sure, there have been setbacks, but this progress can be observed on the whole and in the long run. There is, as it were, a design without a designer (pp. 250–255).

Wright's presentation led Seligman to speculate that negative emotions have evolved to help human beings navigate win-loss games, such as deadly competitions where our very lives are at stake, and that positive emotions have evolved to motivate human beings to pursue win-win games, such as mating, raising children, and working together. This also led him to speculate that in the long run human beings might be able to bring God into existence by means of working toward authentic happiness. This, of course, would not happen overnight, nor, perhaps, even in the lifetime of our species, but he thinks that if the universe is headed toward more complexity and more positive ways of being, we might just have, at the end, a God who is omniscient, omnipotent, and righteous. This would not be a Creator God because this God would come at the end of creation. He concludes that the good life consists of attaining happiness by using one's own signature strengths every day in the main realms of life and attaining a meaningful life using these same strengths to foster knowledge, power, or goodness. A life that does this, he suggests, is "pregnant" with meaning, and if God comes or is found at the end of this process, then one's life is not only authentically happy but also profoundly sacred (pp. 256–260).

CHAPTER 7

REALISTIC HAPPINESS

The seventh book that we have chosen to review is Richard Layard's *Happiness: Lessons from a New Science* (2005). As noted in the introduction, Layard is a British economist. An important influence on his perspective is the thought of Jeremy Bentham, a utilitarian philosopher on whom many writers in happiness studies draw.

The book is divided into two parts, with seven chapters in each part. The titles of chapters in part 1 are: "What's the Problem?," "What is Happiness?," "Are We Getting any Happier?," "If You're so Rich, why Aren't You Happy?," "So what does Make Us Happy?," "What's Going Wrong," and "Can We Pursue a Common Good?" The titles of chapters in part 2 are: "What can Be Done?," "The Greatest Happiness: Is That the Goal?," "Does Economics Have a Clue?," "How Can We Tame the Rat Race?," "Can We Afford to Be Secure?," "Can Mind Control Mood?," "Do Drugs Help?," and "Conclusions for Today's World." It is worth noting that all but one of the book's chapter titles asks a question. And this is precisely one of Layard's main points: if we want to know how to be happy, we first need to know what questions to ask.

In our presentation of the book, we will focus on the chapters in the first part of the book and on the concluding chapter. This is partly because we want to keep chapters in our book reasonably short, but also because the second part of Layard's book focuses on the things we can do to make our society more conducive to happiness, while our book is more focused on the individual. On the other hand, some chapters in part 1 consider the effects of society on individual happiness, so his consideration of the larger picture will not be entirely neglected.

THE PROBLEM

Layard begins chapter 1—"What's the Problem?"—by noting the paradox at the heart of our lives: Although most people want more income and often spend much of their time and energy striving for more of it, the fact is that as Western societies have gotten richer, people living in these societies have not become any happier than they were 50 years ago. It is true that our lives are more comfortable. We have more food, clothes, and cars; bigger houses; more central heating; more holidays; a shorter work week; better work; and, above all, better health. But we are not happier, despite all the efforts of governments, teachers, doctors, and the business sector of society (pp. 3–4).

Layard believes that this "devastating fact" should be the starting point for all political and social discussions. It should cause each government to revaluate its objectives and each person to rethink his or her goals. Perhaps the clearest lesson from the studies of happiness is that it is not easy to make people happier once subsistence income is guaranteed. If we want people to be happier, we need to know what conditions generate happiness. He acknowledges that we do not yet know all the answers as to how to make people happier, but we do have a lot of evidence, enough to rethink government policy and to reappraise our daily choices. The primary source of this evidence is the new psychology of happiness, but neuroscience, sociology, economics, and philosophy are also important. By bringing them together, we can produce a new vision of how we can live better, both as social beings and in terms of our inner spirit (p. 4).

For Layard, the Enlightenment philosophy of Jeremy Bentham's is an excellent starting point because it claims that the best society is one where the citizens are the happiest. It is egalitarian (because every person's happiness counts equally) and humane (because what matters most is what individuals feel). It also affirms that what counts as right, morally speaking, is that which produces the most happiness for the people it affects. Because it defines the common good as the greatest happiness of all, it requires us to care for others as well as for ourselves, and contends that care for others increases our own happiness (pp. 5–6).

What the new psychology adds to this is insights derived from empirical evidence on the nature of happiness. This means that we are now in the position to apply Bentham's philosophy using real evidence rather than mere speculation. More specifically, since happiness is a feeling, we can measure this feeling by (1) asking people or (2) monitoring their brains. Once that is done, it is possible to explain individuals' underlying level of happiness—that is, the quality of their lives as they experience it. Various factors contribute to a person's underlying level of happiness. Some of these come from outside of us (from society) while others come from inside of us (from our inner life) (p. 6).

Regarding the former, sociology and economics can play an important role in helping to identify the social factors that support and nurture happiness. The elementary economics that informs much government policy assumes that being able to acquire what we want is the key to personal happiness. As a result, income levels have, in effect, become a "proxy" for national happiness. But Layard thinks this way of thinking is too simplistic. Why? Because our wants are not, as it were, inborn but, rather, depend heavily on (1) what other people have, and (2) what we have gotten accustomed to (p. 7).

He also identifies two basic human desires that are dependent on external forces beyond one's own control—namely, security and trust. The question, then, becomes: how can the community promote a way of life that is more secure and trustworthy, especially when society has become increasingly mobile and anonymous? (pp. 7–8).

Concerning the internal factors that affect one's level of happiness, Layard notes that our thoughts (and behaviors based on our thoughts) affect our feelings, and he suggests, based on evidence to be presented later in the book, that people are happier if they are *compassionate* and if they are *grateful* for what they have. He notes that modern cognitive therapy has found ways to promote positive thinking leading to the development of traits of compassion and gratitude, and that Positive Psychology, which we focused on in the previous chapter, has more recently generalized these methods to offer a means by which all of us, depressed or otherwise, can find meaning and increase our enjoyment of life. In addition, we now have psychotropic drugs that provide relief to many who suffer from schizophrenia, depression, and anxiety. However, these developments prompt one to ask: how much additional progress is possible? And, of course, these developments raise the same question that increases in our material wealth and comfort also raise: why aren't we happier than we were 50 years ago? (pp. 8–9).

WHAT IS HAPPINESS?

Chapter 2 titled "What Is Happiness?" begins with evidence from neuroscience suggesting that our feelings of happiness can be objectively measured. Layard notes that what people say they feel is highly correlated with the different levels of brain activity in the relevant part of the cortex, and this means that there is no difference between what people think they feel and what they "really" feel (p. 20).

So, Layard asks, what is the feeling of happiness? And what are the best ways to measure happiness? In his view, happiness is feeling good—enjoying life and wanting the feeling to be maintained, and unhappiness is feeling bad and wishing things were different. He adds that most people find it easy to say how good they are feeling, and in social surveys such questions get very high response rates. Also, the scarcity of "don't knows" shows that people do know how they feel and recognize the validity of the question (pp. 12–13).

He suggests that when it comes to how we feel, most of us take the long view, and that we usually accept the short-term ups and downs of life and care mainly about our average happiness over time. This average is made up of a whole series of moments of relative happiness or unhappiness, and these can be compared with one another. But, most importantly, happiness begins where unhappiness ends (p. 13).

As for how happy people feel in general, the most obvious way to find out is to ask them. He compares the happiness levels of people in the United States and Britain and suggests that they are very similar. A recent study found that in the United States, 38 percent of the respondents said they are very happy, 53 percent quite happy, and 9 percent not very happy. The corresponding percentages for Britain were 36 percent, 57 percent, and 7 percent. But he also notes that people's feelings fluctuate from hour to hour and day to day, and these feelings tend to vary depending on what activity they are engaging in and with whom. One study of about 900 women in Texas showed the following average feelings of happiness (on a five-point scale): having sex scores highest (4.7); socializing, relaxing, praying/worshipping/meditating, eating, exercising, and watching TV come next (4.0–3.6); shopping, preparing food, talking on the phone, taking care of one's children, computer/e-mail/Internet, and housework come next (3.2–3.0); and working and commuting are last (2.7–2.6). In the case of personal interactions, feelings of happiness range from interactions with friends (3.7) and one's boss (2.4), with the other categories (relatives, spouse/partner, own children, clients/customers, coworkers, and being alone) falling in between. The average happiness at different times of the day are lowest at the beginning of the day and steadily climb upward, with a significant spike at noon and a sharp drop over the next couple of hours, and then a steady increase thereafter—in other words, happiness is the highest at lunch and when work is done for the day (pp. 13–17).

These findings suggest that happiness is a feeling and that feelings, and how they change, can be observed throughout our waking life. But Layard is especially interested in the long-term *average* happiness of each individual. In this regard, although our average happiness may be influenced by the pattern of our activities, it is mainly affected by our basic temperament and attitudes and by key features of our life situation—our relationships, our health, and our worries about money (p. 17).

He admits that skeptics may find his focus on the long-term *average* happiness of each individual a bit simplistic as it implies that happiness is a *single* dimension of experience ranging from extreme misery to extreme joy. Skeptics say: Isn't it possible to be both happy and unhappy at the same time? And are there not many *types* of happiness? He suggests that the general answer to these questions is no. It is not possible to be happy and unhappy at the same time because positive feelings damp down negative feelings and vice versa. He cites various studies in support of this point and concludes that we have just one dimension of experience, but that it runs from the extreme negative to the extreme positive. On the other hand, the fact that happiness-unhappiness is a single dimension does not mean that there are not different degrees of both. After all, happiness can be excited or tranquil, and misery can be agitated or gloomy and dispirited, and these differences correspond to different levels of "arousal." He provides a chart titled "Two dimensions of feeling," which has a vertical unhappiness/happiness line and a horizontal unaroused/aroused line, with descriptive words for each quadrant: (1) unhappy/unaroused: *depression*, (2) unhappy/aroused: *agitation*, (3) happy/unaroused: *contentment*, and (4) happy/aroused: *joy*. He adds that one of the most enjoyable forms of aroused experience is to be so engrossed in something that you lose yourself in it, and cites in this connection to Csikszentmihalyi's studies of "flow" (1990, pp. 21–22).

As for the argument that there are *types* of happiness, Layard cautions against this way of thinking because it tends to introduce moralistic distinctions reflective of one's culture and invites the argument that some types of happiness are *intrinsically* better than others, which, in his view, is untrue. On the other hand, it is obvious that some enjoyments, like those provided by cocaine, cannot last long, and also work against a person's long-term happiness, so they should be avoided. Other unhealthy enjoyments, such as the pleasures of a sadist or a serial killer, should be avoided because they decrease the happiness of others (pp. 22–23).

In concluding sections of the chapter on the relation of happiness to physical health and the function of happiness, Layard discusses the fact (supported by many research studies) that happiness improves your health. But he adds that because it does so does not make happiness "supremely important." What makes it supremely important is that it is our overall motivational device, for we seek to feel good and to avoid pain (not moment by moment but overall); and if we did not have this drive we would have perished as a species long ago. He disagrees with those who argue that we have separate drives (sex, food, etc.) that function independently of our general sense of happiness or well-being, noting that we often have to choose between satisfying different drives. He suggests that there must be some overall evaluation going on that compares how different drives contribute to our overall satisfaction, so when one source of satisfaction becomes more costly relative to another, we choose less of it. In other words, a pattern of "approach" and "avoidance" is central to our behavior, and it is governed by an "evaluative faculty" that tells us how happy we are with our situation, and then directs us to approach what makes us happy and to avoid what does not. Because we take a "longish" view of our happiness, we make choices that reflect our plans for the future, which sometimes involves delaying gratification. We want to be happy, and we act to promote our present and future happiness, given the opportunities open to us (pp. 24–26).

To be sure, we make mistakes from time to time, such as in the case of cigarette smoking and the self-starvation of anorexia nervosa. Also, we may be short sighted and rather poor at forecasting our future feelings. After all, natural selection has not produced perfect bodies, and neither has it produced perfect psyches. Still we are clearly selected to be healthy, although, of course, we sometimes get sick. And similarly we are selected to feel good, even if we make mistakes about forecasting our happiness. In any case, Layard suggests that it is simply impossible to explain human action and human survival without taking into account the desire to achieve good feelings, that is, the desire to be happy (p. 26).

But this raises the obvious question: Why aren't we happier than we are? Why are depression and anxiety so widespread? Anxiety clearly played a role in our survival as a species, and even today it is a good idea to be anxious while driving a car (or writing a book!) as such anxiety will save a person from making some bad mistakes. Even depression may have had its evolutionary function, for when dogs are confronted with an invincible opponent, they show signs of depression that turn off the opponent's will to attack, and this same effect may have been true of human beings (Nesse and Williams 1996). In Layard's view, however, these mechanisms of anxiety and depression are much less essential than they were several millennia ago. We have largely conquered nature, having defeated most vertebrates and many insects and bacteria, so much of our anxiety and depression is no longer necessary. The challenge we now face is how to use our mastery over nature to master ourselves and to give us more of the happiness that we all want (p. 27).

ARE WE GETTING HAPPIER?

Layard ends chapter 2 with the question, "So how are we doing?" Chapters 3–5 in part 1 explore the questions whether we are getting happier, whether there is a relationship between wealth and happiness, and what factors make us happy? The basic answer to the question—are we getting happier?—is no. He provides three pieces of evidence in chapter 3 in support of this conclusion: (1) when we look at the same people over their lifetimes, we find they do not become happier as they become richer; (2) when we compare the Western developed nations, the richer ones are no happier than the poorer ones; and (3) depression, alcoholism, and crime (three concrete expressions of unhappiness) have increased rapidly in the post-World War II period. In chapter 4 he provides two explanations for why people are no happier even though they are financially better off. The first is social comparison. For example: At work, I compare my income with what my colleagues get, and if I find out that they get a raise above inflation and I get inflation only, I get angry. This obvious piece of psychology—that is, common sense—is unknown to standard economics, which holds that if one person's income rises and nobody's falls, things have improved because no one has suffered (but, in fact, I *have* suffered, for income is much more than purchasing power). We also use our income, when we compare it to others, as a measure of how we are valued and, if we are not careful, as a measure of how we value ourselves (pp. 31–44).

Layard also notes that when people compare their wages, they tend to do so with people close to themselves rather than with, say, persons who make a whole lot more—or a whole lot less—money. What matters, in other words, is what happens in your own "reference group," because what they get might have been feasible for you. This is why in Olympic competitions the bronze medalists are happier about their result than the silver medalists are about theirs—the bronze medalists compare themselves with people who get no medal (and are, therefore, happy), while the silver medalists believe they might have gotten the gold (and are, therefore, less happy). Because comparisons are made at such close quarters, the most intense rivalries are often within organizations and within families, and if people change within their reference group in an upward direction, this can affect their happiness in a substantial way. For example, cases where people have become objectively better off but nevertheless feel subjectively worse include women whose pay and whose opportunities have improved considerably relative to men but whose happiness level has fallen relative to men. What was once unfeasible for them has become feasible, so although women have more, objectively speaking, they have less, subjectively speaking (pp. 44–46).

The second reason happiness has not risen with economic growth is habituation. When an improvement occurs in our standard of living, as when we buy a new car or television set, we are excited about it at first, but then we get used to it, and, finally, we eventually take it more or less for granted. So if we want to sustain the happiness we experienced with our initial improvement, we need to keep on having more of these experiences in order to sustain our happiness—we are on a kind of "hedonic treadmill." Thus, the secret to happiness is to seek out those good things in life to which you can never fully adapt. People get used to material possessions easily, such as cars and houses. Advertisers understand this and invite us to "feed our addiction," but other experiences do not pale in the same way, such as the time we spend with our family and friends, and the quality and security of our job. These are the things we should be giving our attention to, if we want to be happy (pp. 48–49).

In short, the central mechanisms that account for the fact that our happiness has risen less than expected are social comparison and habituation: we constantly distort our perception of reality by making unhelpful comparisons. One "secret of happiness," then, is to enjoy things as they are, without making comparisons, and another is to discover the things that truly make us happy (p. 53).

WHAT MAKES US HAPPY?

Layard takes up the question of what makes us happy in chapter 5. Genetic predisposition is one important factor. Researchers have found that identical twins are "remarkably close" to each other in happiness (or well-being) while nonidentical twins are not. Family upbringing is also an important related factor. For example, a study found that persons who have the inferior version of the gene that supplies serotonin to the brain are in danger of becoming depressed *if* they were *also* mistreated as children; conversely, adults who were mistreated as children are in danger of becoming depressed, but only if they have inferior versions of the gene. This finding demonstrates how genes and experience can interact to determine our makeup (pp. 59–62).

As for factors in our adult lives that affect happiness, Layard identifies five whose effect is negligible and seven whose effect is substantial. The negligible factors include age, gender, education, physical appearance, and IQ. The seven significant factors are family relationships, financial situation, work, community and friends, and health (in this rank order); and personal freedom and personal values (which cannot be ranked but are highly relevant to happiness). Regarding family relationships, Layard notes that habituation plays a role in either decreasing unhappiness (for example, the first year of a divorce is the worst) or moderating happiness (for example, the first year of marriage is the peak of happiness). He also notes that, in general, married persons are happier than single persons and unmarried persons who live together, and the primary reason for this is the stability of the relationship. On the other hand, he emphasizes that the quality of the relationship matters more than its form, and research is mounting that confirms the importance of love as a major contributor to happiness. Regarding work, research studies indicate that *unemployment* is much worse than *nonemployment*—that is, it is much worse to be forced out of work than choosing to leave work to raise children or to retire. Also, studies indicate that one does not get used to unemployment, but it hurts less if others are out of work as well. Furthermore, even when people return to work, its effects are still felt as a psychological scar. Layard also notes that there is an "indirect negative effect" of unemployment on the happiness of those who are at work, which is that the employed fear that soon they, too, could become unemployed. So, in this sense, happiness is not gained from making comparisons with the unemployed. If love is the necessary condition for happiness in a marital or committed relationship, a sense of fulfillment is critical to happiness in work, and the crucial factor here is the extent to which one has personal control over what one does (pp. 63–68).

Concerning community and friends, Layard notes the importance of the quality of our community in contributing to our safety and to our ability to make friends. The quality of community isn't easy to assess, but one good measure is this question: "Generally speaking, would you say that most people can be trusted, or that you can't be too careful in dealing with people?" In an international survey based on this question, the proportion who said "Yes, most people can be trusted" varied from 5 percent in Brazil to 64 percent in Norway. The study worked this way: Researchers dropped wallets that included the owner's name and address in various countries and then counted the number of wallets that were returned to the owner. They found that the proportions were closely related to the replies regarding trust. In short, what love is to committed relationships and fulfillment is to work, trust is to community and friendships (pp. 68–69).

Although health is an important factor in one's average level of happiness, it is never the highest determinant. This is probably because people tend to adapt to physical limitations, and, this being the case, healthy members of the public generally overestimate the loss of happiness that people actually experience from serious medical conditions. On the other hand, people do not adapt to chronic pain or to mental illness, so, in this regard, these two health issues are comparable to unemployment in work. Concerning personal freedom, Layard emphasizes the relationships among the three main dimensions of freedom: personal, political, and economic. He is especially concerned with the quality of government and its effects on the happiness of the citizenry. Key factors in the quality of government are the rule of law, stability and lack of violence, voice and accountability, the effectiveness of government services, the absence of corruption, and the efficiency of the system of regulation. A comparison of Swiss cantons showed that people were much happier in those cantons where they had more rights to demand referendums than was the case in other cantons—the difference in overall happiness was as great as if they had double the income (pp. 69–70).

Finally, concerning personal values, Layard notes that our happiness depends on our inner self and our philosophy of life, and that people find comfort from within, in all sorts of ways, but they usually include some system of relying for help on the deep positive part of oneself rather than on the efforts of the conscious ego. He specifically cites cognitive therapy, Buddhist mindfulness, the Twelve Steps of Alcoholics Anonymous, and the *Spiritual Exercises* of Saint Ignatius as systems that help one discipline one's mind and moods. These "systems" need not involve calling this source of comfort "divine," but one of the most robust findings of happiness research is that people who believe in God are happier than those who do not. At the individual level, we cannot be sure whether belief in God makes people happier or whether happier people are more disposed to believe in God, but because the relation also occurs at the national level Layard suggests that it is reasonable to assume that belief to some extent causes happiness (pp. 71–72).

Layard concludes his review of the seven factors that contribute to happiness with a brief discussion of the relationship between happiness and the realization of our life goals. Noting that earlier research on the quality of life emphasized that personal happiness is relative to one's expectations, he points out that if this were true, the simplest way to be happy would surely be to lower your expectations and your goals. He supports those who have reacted against this conclusion on grounds that it tends to work against the quest for greater justice and higher standards of excellence. He contends that we could not be happy without setting goals for ourselves, and that every happy person seeks new understandings and new achievements. On the other hand, our goals need to be calibrated to our own personal interests and abilities: If our goals are too low, we get bored, but if they are too high, we get frustrated, so the secret is to have goals that stretch us far enough but not too far. Unlike our predecessors, most of us in developed countries no longer have to struggle to keep alive, so we have more choice over our goals: Getting them right is the challenge (pp. 73–74).

WHAT'S GOING WRONG?

In the concluding paragraph of chapter 5, Layard notes that, in many ways, life is better than it was 50 years ago and yet we do not seem to be any happier. In chapter 6 titled "What's Going Wrong?" he focuses on the seven sources of happiness identified in chapter 5. He suggests that if these are the primary sources of happiness, we can take a close look at each of them and determine whether it has improved or deteriorated over the past 50 years. In this way, we may be able to put our finger on why we are no happier despite the social improvements that have taken place in that time (p. 75).

In his judgment, the primary sources of happiness that have deteriorated are family relationships, community and friendships, and personal values. In his discussion of the deterioration in family relationships, he focuses on the increasing divorce rate, out-of-wedlock births, and families headed by a single parent. In 1950, divorce was uncommon, but now only a half of all American 15-year-olds are living with their biological father. He observes that the main change in divorce occurred between 1960 and 1980 and peaked in 1980; that out-of-wedlock births increased from 5 percent of all births in 1960 to 33 percent in 2000; and that families headed by a single parent increased from 9 percent to 27 percent. In his consideration of community and friends, Layard focuses on the rising crime rate and decreased trust. In the United States, the major increase in the crime rate occurred between 1950 and 1980; the tide began to turn in the early 1980s, but crime is still many times higher than it was 50 years ago. The fact that the increase occurred during a period of unusually low unemployment and that the reversal occurred when unemployment was rising is evidence that unemployment is not a direct cause of crime. In his view, a major change in attitudes toward self and society and their relationship is behind these higher crime rates and family breakups. In 1952, 51 percent of Americans thought that people led "as good lives— moral and honest—as they used to." This percentage dropped to 43 percent in 1965, 32 percent in 1976, and 27 percent in 1998. Thus, three out of four persons in the United States now believe that people are less moral than they used to be. Also, fewer persons in the United States belong to associations of community members and friends, whether these associations are organized around sports, politics, service, religion, or ethnicity (pp. 78–81).

These trends in family life and community trust are major shifts and help to account for why happiness has not risen. But how are they to be explained? Economic growth as such does not provide the answer because this growth has been going on for the last 150 years. The explanations need to be specific to changes in the past 50 years, and Layard identifies three such changes: the change in gender roles, the cultural emphasis on self-realization, and the influence of television. He argues that the driving force behind these changes has been science and technology (p. 82).

Concerning gender role changes, a major factor has been labor-saving technology that has made housework less time consuming and made it possible for women to go out to work. In addition, the world of paid work became more desirable with higher wages, and, with new technologies that reduced the need for male muscle power, more jobs became accessible to women. Medical technology also contributed by means of birth control pills that separated sex from the likelihood of pregnancy. It was also becoming easier for families to split up (because women had their own income) and for married persons to have extramarital affairs (because of reduced risk of pregnancy). Laws prohibiting divorce except in cases of "matrimonial offense" were also relaxed. While we might have expected that the percentage of happily married Americans would increase with the rising divorce rate, this has not been the case. From 1973–75 to 1996–98, the percentage of persons who described their marriages as "very happy" declined from 70 percent to 64 percent for men and from 67 percent to 62 percent for women (we wonder if divorce functions somewhat similarly to unemployment, for if the unemployment of others has a negative effect on those who are still employed, it may be that divorces have a negative effect on those who remain married) (pp. 82–85).

Layard also attributes these adverse trends in family relationships and in community and friendships to the revolutionary effect of television. He points out that television has significantly reduced our social life and that its depictions of violence, aggression, sex, and chaotic relationships have made these behaviors more prevalent in real life. It is striking, and saddening, that suicides increase following actual suicides reported on TV or portrayed in a television drama. Furthermore, by presenting images of wealth and beauty, television raises our norms for judging our income and our spouses. Before TV, a weekly trip to the movies would similarly widen one's awareness of the wealth and beauty that existed beyond one's own social environment, but its impact was nothing like watching 25 hours of television each week. In 1982, nearly half of the characters in major shows were millionaires, and although two-thirds of real Americans work in blue collar or service jobs, only 10 percent of television characters do. The effects of this exposure to imaginary wealth are profound, for the more television people watch, the more they overestimate the affluence of other people, and the lower they rate their own relative income (pp. 87–89).

Also, TV viewing seems to reduce our happiness with our bodies and our spouses. When women were shown a series of pictures of female models, their mood level fell, and when men were presented the same pictures, they felt less good about their wives. In three hours of television viewing each day, one cannot fail to see a parade of beautiful women, and this means that television creates discontent by bombarding us with images of body shapes and riches we do not have (p. 90).

Concerning the deterioration in personal values, Layard focuses on moral values, noting that many people consider morals to be produced by human responses to the problems of living together and no longer consider moral principles to have divine sanction backed by the threat of eternal punishment. The change has been liberating—especially from false guilt—but it is also an invitation to license unless a strong social ethic replaces the old religious sanction. He discusses the various reasons for why such an ethic has been severely weakened in recent decades and considers some of its consequences. Especially worrisome is the death of deference. Today, we rightly refuse all deference to inherited position, but increasingly young people have withdrawn respect from those who should normally receive it, such as schoolteachers, police officers, and parents. Young people used to go directly from the care of their parents to an adult relationship with an employer, but they now enter an intermediate "youth culture" that is unrelated to the adult world and only partly influenced by adult values. This, oddly enough, is the result of progress: i.e., more wealth and more time to spend on education. It is also the result of earlier puberty. Layard notes that most children emerge relatively unharmed, but many young people today are uncertain of their role in society (pp. 90–92).

In his view, the goal of self-realization is not enough, for no society can work well unless its members feel responsibilities as well as rights. This raises a fundamental and totally reasonable question: "Why should I feel responsible for other people?" His answer is that we should feel responsible for other people, and they for us, because this contributes to the goal of general happiness (pp. 92–93).

ACHIEVING A HAPPIER WAY OF LIFE

In the concluding chapter, titled "Conclusions for a Better World," Layard presents four key points: (1) happiness is an objective dimension of all our experience, and (2) we are programmed to pursue happiness. Therefore (3) it is self-evident that the best society is that which produces the greatest happiness, and (4) our society is unlikely to become happier unless people work together to pursue happiness as a common goal. Regarding points 1 and 2, he notes that our happiness is a real and "objective" phenomenon and is, therefore, measurable; and the very fact we *are* programmed for happiness means that what makes us happy is generally good for us and has therefore helped us evolve. This applies not only to our love of food and sex, but also to our instinctive capacity for cooperation (p. 224). Regarding points 3 and 4, he acknowledges that various arguments have been advanced against the proposition that the best society is the happiest society, but none of them, in his view, stand up under careful scrutiny. Moreover, the greatest happiness ideal has two functions. It can help us think dispassionately about how to organize society, and it can inspire us with a passionate commitment to the common good as well. The value of a concept of the common good is that it helps to unite the efforts of its members, and, in his judgment, increasing the general happiness is the "right concept" of the common good. Even though none of us will ever completely reach that ideal, we are likely to live closer to it if we commit ourselves to it (p. 225).

Finally, Layard offers his "picture of a better society" based on the goal of achieving a happier way of life. It comprises the following commitments: (1) we should monitor the development of happiness in our own countries just as we monitor the development of income; (2) we should rethink our views and habits with regard to many standard issues (especially those relating to work); (3) we should spend more time helping others, especially those in poorer countries; (4) we should focus more attention on caring for the mentally ill (which is the greatest source of misery in the West); (5) we should find ways to improve family life (by, for example, introducing more family-friendly practices at work); (6) we should promote (and subsidize) activities that support community life; (7) we should do everything we can to eliminate high unemployment by ensuring that everyone has a chance to work and enforcing those who are unemployed to take advantage of the opportunities offered to them; (8) we should fight against the constant escalation of wants and desires portrayed on television (by, for example, prohibiting commercial advertising to children); and (9) we should improve moral education (pp. 232–234).

Suggesting that the ninth commitment is perhaps the most important, Layard describes the kind of moral education he has in mind: it would involve teaching the principles of morality not as interesting points for discussion but as established truths that are essential for a meaningful life, so as to inculcate empathy and altruism. A society cannot flourish without some sense of shared purpose, and neither can the individual flourish when the goal is the pursuit of self-realization. If one's sole duty is to achieve the best for oneself, then one's life becomes just too stressful and lonely, and, in the end, one will not succeed. Instead, one needs to feel that one exists "for something larger." This "something larger" should be a commitment to the common good, and this common good, in Layard's view, should be the pursuit of the greatest overall happiness (p. 234).

But this includes one's own happiness as well. If the pursuit of self-realization is doomed to failure, seeking your own happiness is not, and the idea that you should not think about your own happiness because you can only be happy as a by-product of something else is a dismal philosophy, a formula for keeping oneself busy at all costs. While one cannot be happy without a wider goal than beyond oneself, neither can one be happy without self-knowledge and self-acceptance—happiness comes from outside and from inside, and the secret is compassion toward oneself and others. The principle of the Greatest Happiness is "essentially the expression of that ideal" (p. 235).

CHAPTER 8

EVOLVING HAPPINESS

The eighth book that we have chosen to review is Daniel Nettle's *Happiness: The Science behind Your Smile* (2005). As noted in the introduction, Nettle is a psychology professor at the University of Newcastle. The book consists of an introduction and seven chapters. The introduction begins with this quotation from the Declaration of Independence: "all men are created equal, [and] they are endowed by their Creator with certain unalienable rights, that among these are Life, Liberty, and the pursuit of Happiness." He notes that happiness seems to provide the most hope for giving our lives purpose and direction. In effect, pursuing happiness provides a "guiding light" for what we should do with our lives and our liberty (p. 1). But the very fact that the pursuit of happiness may be this "guiding light" makes it all the more important for us to have a clear understanding of what happiness is. In this regard, one thing is clear: happiness has multiple senses which need to be identified and differentiated from one another (p. 3).

Nettle concludes the introduction with a brief overview of the book. Chapter 1 deals with concepts of happiness; chapter 2 asks whether people are, more or less, happy or unhappy; chapters 3 and 4 explore why some people seem to be happier than others; chapter 5 focuses on happiness and brain science; chapter 6 concerns how, practically speaking, persons can become happier; and chapter 7 offers an evolutionary explanation as to the paradoxical nature of happiness. Happiness, Nettle argues, is a handmaiden to evolution's purposes, giving us not actual rewards but, rather, a personal sense of purpose and direction (pp. 4–6).

COMFORT AND JOY

Nettle begins chapter 1, titled "Comfort and Joy," by making the case that happiness is a topic worth scholarly attention. Some great psychologists, such as William James, focused on topics such as happiness. But later psychologists thought that James and his contemporaries did so because they did not know any better, mainly because they lacked the enlightened methodology and the sophisticated tools for more scientific psychology (e.g., by studying eye blinking or by observing rats). Nettle points out that the 1985 *Penguin Dictionary of Psychology* does not have an entry on happiness, and that psychologists, until recent decades, would use terms such as "subjective well-being" or "positive emotionality" instead of the word "happiness." He endorses James's anthropological view of psychology, namely, that psychologists should study people's own ideas about what they think they are doing. If people think and talk about happiness, then this is reason enough to study it (pp. 7–10).

Nettle observes that in recent decades emotions have been deemed worthy of study, despite their subjective nature and their resistance to precise quantification. In the 1960s, Paul Ekman took photographs of American actors displaying six basic human emotions: anger, fear, surprise, joy, disgust, and sadness. That Americans were able to match the face with the emotion that was being represented should come as no surprise, for one would expect this congruence within the same culture. But, when he showed these photographs to New Guineans, they were also able to match the faces with the emotions being represented. This study therefore suggests that there is something universal about these emotions and how they are represented by means of facial expression (pp. 10–12).

Nettle argues that evolutionary psychology provides grounds for studying happiness. The point of evolutionary psychology is to study how the mind works in light of evolutionary problems our ancestors would have faced. This is not to suggest that a rigid determinism controls all of our particular thoughts, but, rather, it is to indicate that our shared human history influences patterns of thinking. The example of a large carnivore attempting to eat human beings is a case in point. The best (i.e., most advantageous in terms of survival) emotional response to the threat of being eaten is fear, and so, in time, human beings became "hardwired," as it were, to have such emotional responses in these types of situations. The problem is that this hardwiring can lead to irrational behavior today. Nettle points out, for example, that many people are more afraid of spiders than automobiles, but, statistically speaking, it is far more likely for us to die from a car accident than a spider bite. However, in our evolutionary history, spiders—not cars—were a real threat, and so fear of spiders has become a part of us. In other words, fear has become an effective—sometimes *too* effective—program our minds run (pp. 12–14).

Nettle thinks that happiness is also a program that our minds run and that it, too, is a product of evolution. He argues that we are not programmed for happiness, but, rather, that we are programmed to pursue happiness, and part of this program entails certain beliefs about what we think will make us happy. This theoretical perspective based on evolutionary psychology allows him to make sense of several findings about happiness in empirical research: (1) people consistently think that the future will yield more happiness, but it rarely does; (2) people have trouble thinking about what will make them happy in the future; and (3) wealth beyond subsistence usually does not increase happiness all that much (pp. 14–15).[1]

Nettle next defines happiness, noting three different senses of the term. In the first sense, happiness refers to an emotional state, such as *feelings of joy* or *pleasure*. One might be happy to see the Grand Canyon or happy to eat a piece of pecan pie with vanilla ice cream on top. These feelings are temporary, and they constitute, as it were, the lowest level of happiness. The second sense involves *judgments about emotions*, as in taking the balance of one's week or one's life. To be happy in this sense means feeling that one, on the whole, has more positive experiences than negative experiences. It could also entail the feeling that things are better than they might have been. Examples may include the feeling that one is satisfied with one's accomplishments after, say, attaining a college degree—but in order to distinguish it from joy, this feeling would have to continue well after the euphoria of graduation has passed. The third sense of happiness is what Nettle calls the good life or what Aristotle calls *eudaimonia*. By this Nettle means human flourishing, the sense that *one has fulfilled one's potential in life*. In this sense, happiness is not an emotion—it is more like a state of being than an emotion. He offers no description of this state, since each person's potential is different (pp. 17–21). How we define happiness is important not only for conceptual clarity but also for scientific research. The lowest level of happiness may be measured physiologically or with brain scans, the second level may be measured with surveys or questionnaires, but the third level of happiness is more difficult to measure: How, after all, can one know whether one has fulfilled one's potential? (pp. 22–23).

Nettle notes that Positive Psychology (which was discussed in chapter 6) has explored happiness a great deal. However, he suggests that many Positive Psychologists have been imprecise in their use of the term happiness. For example, they write about "flow," a state in which (1) one is absorbed in a given activity that one enjoys, (2) one has the skills for this activity, and (3) this activity stretches one's skills to their limits. While Nettle thinks that flow is a good thing to pursue, he also observes that many persons who have a lot of flow—artists, for example—are actually more often depressed and addicted than persons who do not have a lot of it. Nettle's identification of three levels of happiness is an attempt to sort out this conceptual confusion (pp. 24–27).

Another conceptual ambiguity in the writings of Positive Psychologists concerns the question whether their account of happiness is simply advice or is, rather, a moral position. Some Positive Psychologists make claims that certain ways of life are more worth living than others. Nettle finds this claim problematic. The problem is that Positive Psychology attempts to offer a prescription for the third level of happiness, that is, an account of what the good life is and how one should go about attaining it. While this may be a laudable intention, the fact that this level of happiness depends on the individual means that there can be no phenomenology of the good life without moralizing. Thus, the problem with Positive Psychologists is that they attempt to go beyond the first two levels of happiness when they write about happiness apart from emotion. In his view, Martin Seligman's *Authentic Happiness* should be titled *The Good Life* because it is primarily concerned with the third level of happiness. He indicates that the remaining chapters of his own book will be dedicated to levels one and two of happiness, with the bulk of the book focusing on level two, what he refers to as "subjective well-being" (pp. 27–30).

Nettle next continues his analogy of emotions as programs. Following Paul Ekman (1992), who, as noted, identified six basic human emotions (anger, fear, surprise, joy, disgust, and sadness), he suggests that there are four basic negative emotions, each having its own built-in response: fear (run); anger (fight); sadness (save energy to recover); and disgust (spit out or avoid). However, the response to joy (the only clearly positive emotion of the six) is to maintain things as they are so as to keep experiencing joy. This is why it is hard to go back to work after finding out a piece of really good news—we become preoccupied with continuing to keep experiencing joy. While one can live in a constant state of fear, one cannot live in a constant state of joy. Why? Because constant joy is not adaptive—we need to be able to return to work, to concern ourselves with other tasks. And so the joy program, for good reasons, shuts down after a short period of time (pp. 30–32).

Nettle next explores the relationship between experiences of joy (first-level happiness) and estimations of life satisfaction (second-level happiness). He cites several research studies that address this relationship. One study found that people would report higher life satisfaction—for all aspects of their lives—after they found a dime on a copying machine. Another found that people would report higher life satisfaction if they were questioned on sunny rather than rainy days *unless* the weather was explicitly mentioned (attention to the weather brought to the fore that mood was affecting their judgment). A third study (also noted in chapter 7) found that Olympic bronze medalists report higher satisfaction than silver medalists. Apparently, bronze medalists feel that it is better to get a medal than no medal, whereas silver medalists are dissatisfied with being so close to first place but not achieving it. Nettle concludes that the frame in which we view life, whether in comparison to others or in comparison to our own past, has a profound effect on our estimations of life satisfaction (pp. 32–38).

If, in terms of evolutionary psychology, the happiness program is like the fear program, one would expect that the goal of the happiness program is to lead us to beneficial things (e.g., a pleasant environment, an attractive partner) and that we would have the capacity to gauge what will make us happy with a good deal of accuracy. However, neither of these assumptions turns out to be true. There are several tendencies that affect our capacity to gauge what will make us happy. One is that people tend to overestimate the effects of certain wished-for events, such as winning the lottery, on their happiness, because they fail to appreciate the *adaptation effect*, which holds that people tend to get used to their living conditions. Another tendency is the *endowment effect*. People tend to think, wrongly, that they would be much less happy if they were not able to maintain their current lifestyles. However, the adaptation effect holds here too. In other words, people tend, in most circumstances, to adjust. Yet another tendency involves *how events end*. In one striking study, researchers found that people were more willing to hold their hand in very cold water that got warmer for a longer period of time than in very cold water that did not get warmer. Similar experiments have been conducted with colonoscopies. How experiences end affects our overall evaluation of them to such an extent that people will choose more pain when it makes no sense to do so (pp. 37–42).

Nettle concludes that human beings are not objective when estimating their life satisfaction. How people report their life satisfaction is affected by current mood, how one compares with others, how one's current experiences compare with past experience, the adaptation effect, the endowment effect, and the ending of the experience. A major implication of this research is that happiness can be affected to a great extent by attending to the frames in which we view our lives. Nettle closes the chapter by suggesting that when society bombards us with air-brushed models and tales of the rich and famous, it contributes a great deal to the general unhappiness of those of us who cannot compare to social elites (pp. 43–44).

BREAD AND CIRCUSES

The title of chapter 2, "Bread and Circuses," comes from a quotation by Juvenal, a Roman satirist, who said that "the public has long since cast off its cares . . . and longs eagerly for just two things: bread and circuses!" (p. 46). While Juvenal was a Stoic who believed that people subject themselves to misery on account of their own vain desires, Nettles wants to make the opposite point: most people, if their basic needs are met, would consider themselves happy if they have minimal entertainment. This is an optimistic point of view with regard to happiness. However, other thinkers—the happiness pessimists—have been skeptical of this point of view. For one reason or another, such thinkers believe that happiness is either elusive or simply impossible (pp. 45–48).

Nettle suggests that these contrasting points of view can be tested empirically. Are people basically happy? Or are they basically unhappy? In a series of studies completed in the early 1990s and spanning 42 countries, people were asked to rate their life satisfaction on a 10-point scale, with 1 being the lowest and 10 being the highest. Various countries had strikingly different averages, with Bulgarians scoring themselves at 5.03, the Swiss at 8.39, the Americans at 7.71, and the British at 7.48. Countries having acute political or economic difficulties scored themselves lower than countries that were not having such difficulties, but poorer countries that were stable scored themselves in 6 to 8 range. It seems, then, that in recent decades people across the world are generally happy (pp. 48–52).

Or, at least, they *report* being happy. One possible explanation for high happiness scores is that unhappiness is not simply unfortunate—it is also unattractive. An evolutionary perspective here would suggest that people try to manage their impressions on a routine basis to win friends, to attract partners, to advance in the workplace, and so forth. People also tend to rate themselves as above average as automobile drivers and as more likely than others to achieve their goals. Nettle speculates that this, too, could be related to impression management, but that there could be deeper motivations as well. Life is uncertain—we simply do not know if we will have a happy marriage or if our work will last. But if we take an optimistic view, this is not only attractive to partners and employers, but it is also more likely to lead to striving. Conversely, a pessimistic view is more likely to lead to passivity. Thus, reporting high levels of happiness might be related to impression management, but it may also be related to the desire to keep moving forward—a stimulus, in other words, to hope. In point of fact, Nettle cites studies that support the view that happiness is related to striving. When people are asked how happy they will be in 10 years, they usually report that they will either be happier, or, if they scored themselves as very happy in the present, they think that their happiness will continue. People do not tend to imagine themselves as less happy in the future, and this fits nicely with Nettle's evolutionary perspective (pp. 53–58).

Nettle closes chapter 2 by reflecting on the apparent contradiction that people are basically happy, and yet they spend lots of time and money on programs that promise to make them happier. Why? This, Nettle argues, is precisely as evolution would have it: We are programmed to be satisfied with a wide range of possibilities, whether living on the side of a volcano or living in a luxurious mansion. And yet we are programmed not to be completely satisfied, because then we would not have motivation for improvement. This could be disappointing to those who want to attain happiness, but it could be

comforting to those who are dissatisfied to know that others, in all likelihood, are not much happier than they are (pp. 58–64).[2]

LOVE AND WORK

In chapter 3—"Love and Work"—Nettle explores the relationship of love
and work to happiness. One major study that he draws on is the National
Child Development Study (NCDS) in Britain. This longitudinal study has
focused on persons born in the United Kingdom within the span of a single
week in 1958 and has followed these subjects to the present day. He draws on
other empirical work to support his claims, but the bulk of the chapter rests
on the NCDS (p. 68).

Here are some of its findings. The women in the study, on average, tend
to score higher than men on happiness. On the other hand, they report more
negative emotions, such as worrying and feelings of worthlessness. Some
interpreters of the data conclude from this that women experience or express more emotion, both positive and negative, than men do. Income level
does not seem to relate to happiness, but social class does appear to be a positive factor. On the other hand, the key factor as far as work is concerned
is personal autonomy—that is, how much control one has over one's job and
one's own life. People are happy, of course, when they are given a raise; but
once they adapt to their new income level, their happiness returns to its
previous level. How does marriage relate to happiness? Marriage accounts
for a wider range of variability than either income or social status. Married
people tend to rate their life satisfaction higher than people who are cohabi-
tating, single, separated, divorced, or widowed. The widest range of scores,
as well as the lowest point of scores, is in the category of widowhood, and
Nettle thinks this is related to the endowment effect—in terms of happiness,
it is better not to have had than to have had and lost. He does not conclude
from these scores that marriage leads to happiness; rather, it may well be the
reverse, namely, that happiness leads to marriage (pp. 68–83).

Other interesting findings with regard to happiness are that having a
severe disability or chronic health problems affects life satisfaction negatively, as does living conditions, such as noise pollution, because one does
not adapt to noise despite the fact that many people think that they *will* adapt
to it. On the other hand, cosmetic breast surgery seems to affect life satisfaction in a positive way and is associated with less mental health problems
(pp. 83–84).

Nettle concludes the chapter by returning to the issue of adaptation.
While it is true that people tend to return to a base level of happiness no
matter what their circumstances, there is more to the story than this. Some
life circumstances, such as getting a raise or purchasing a new car, will cause

peaks in happiness, but, in time, people tend to get used to their new income and to their new car. Other changes in life circumstances, such as accepting a decrease in pay in order to take increased time off so that one will have more control over one's time, do lead to substantial happiness increases. Nettle suggests that one way to think about these differences is to employ Robert Frank's distinction between positional and non-positional goods (1999). Positional goods are those that have value in comparison to what others around you have, such as the size of one's big screen television. Non-positional goods, such as living in the woods or by the ocean, have value in and of themselves. Evolutionary psychology suggests that although we are wired to keep going after positional goods, we would be better off not trying to "keep up with the Joneses" and instead making more evidenced-based decisions with regard to how we pursue happiness (pp. 85–90).

WORRIERS AND ENTHUSIASTS

Are some people, by virtue of their personalities, happier than others? In chapter 4, titled "Worriers and Enthusiasts," Nettle suggests that common experience seems to suggest so. We all know people who seem to be happy no matter what their circumstances may be, and we know others in the same or similar circumstances who always seem to be anxious and brooding. Research studies tend to support these impressions. There do seem to be real and stable differences between people with regard to personality characteristics, and these do seem to be related to happiness (pp. 91–92).

What is a personality characteristic? It is an attribute that marks one individual off from another that is (1) stable over time, (2) stable across situations, and (3) not universal to all persons. If, say, one is anxious if one happens to be in a pool of sharks, this does not make one an anxious person because most everyone would be anxious in this situation. A better measure of personality would be to ask individuals how they react when they are in a new city. Are they excited or are they anxious? These kinds of questions tend to be better indicators of personality characteristics (pp. 93–94). Noting that there are a variety of personality typologies, Nettle doesn't seek to evaluate these typologies, but simply points out that they all have two aspects in common: (1) all of them have some way of describing how people respond to negative events, such as threats or losses (this is often called neuroticism or negative emotionality); and (2) all of them have some way of describing how people respond to positive events or opportunities (this is often called extroversion or sensation seeking). He then relates these two basic personality characteristics—neuroticism and extroversion—to happiness research. As one might expect, neuroticism is a good predictor of low happiness scores; this, in fact, seems to be something of a tautology. However, some scales of happiness have been designed to be more discriminating, such as by asking persons how often they feel very unhappy and how often they feel very happy.

Strikingly, while persons with high neuroticism scores predictably have high scores of experiences of being very unhappy, they also have high scores of experiences of being very happy (pp. 94–101). In contrast to neurotics, extroverts tend to score higher on happiness, and Nettle attributes this to the fact that extroverts seek out pleasure to a greater extent than neurotics do (and when they are asked, it is likely that they had been to a party or had sex more recently). Being an extrovert has its costs, too, as extroverts are more likely to have unstable marriages and to experience serious accidents (e.g., rock climbing accidents) (pp. 102–104).

Other personality characteristics, such as agreeableness and conscientiousness, also seem to be related to happiness. Agreeable persons are more likely to perform favors for others (and vice versa), which may contribute to happiness. Conscientious people are more likely to achieve goals and to complete tasks, which would contribute to high levels of satisfaction (pp. 104–105).

What is the upshot of these findings? Nettle points out that various personality characteristics are better predictors of happiness than, say, whether one is married or one's income level. Also, these personality characteristics, such as neuroticism, can predict these other factors, such as the stability of one's marriage. Thus, what is striking about personality characteristics is that they are not only a better predictor of happiness than life events, but that they also seem to account for life events. In effect, the personality findings show that happiness stems less from the world as it presents itself to us and more from how we address the world (pp. 105–114).

WANTING AND LIKING

In chapter 5 titled "Wanting and Liking" Nettle focuses on the brain systems underlying emotions and moods. He begins by recounting the basic premise of Aldous Huxley's *Brave New World* (1946), where happiness is eliminated by means of genetic engineering, social programming, and a drug called soma. Soma has the power to eliminate unhappy thoughts in minutes. Nettle compares soma with Prozac, an antidepressant that affects the selective serotonin reuptake inhibitors (SSRIs). Specifically, Prozac increases serotonin activity in brain cells by disabling certain mechanisms in the brain, and this increase in serotonin activity is associated with higher levels of happiness. Even when people who are not depressed take Prozac they experience higher scores on extroversion and positive emotions. The effects of Prozac and similar drugs have entered public consciousness to such an extent that serotonin has been called the happiness chemical (pp. 115–119).

Nettle next discusses several other features of the brain, noting that the amygdala is the emotional hub of the brain, and, if damaged, it can cause animals and human beings to have difficulty recognizing emotions and experiencing them at proper times. The nucleus accumbens receives a track of neurons that communicate with each other by means of the chemical dopamine. If a stimulant is diffused into the nucleus accumbens, rats will want to feed, but if a suppressant is diffused into the nucleus accumbens, rats will ignore tasty food right in front of them. The dopamine system, then, seems to be controlling pleasure (p. 121), and it can be altered by means of stimulants and suppressants (pp. 119–121).

Nettle moves on to discuss brain stimulation reward. In experiments with rats and with monkeys, electrodes are implanted into the brains of the subjects, and researchers transmit an electron current through the lateral hypothalamus. The results are striking. Researchers have found that rats will press a lever that produces the electronic stimulation up to 3,000 times, and, while doing so, will ignore other attractive options, such as food and sex. This electronic stimulation is certainly related to desire, but, strikingly, it may not be related to pleasure. By studying behavioral responses, such as licking the paws and facial expressions, researchers have concluded that although the rats really want the electronic stimulation, their behavioral responses suggest that they do not find it pleasurable. Wanting and liking, Nettle points out, seem to be different mechanisms in the brain (pp. 122–126).

This distinction can be observed among various drug users. For example, nicotine is highly addictive (wanting) but does not yield much pleasure (liking) because it stimulates the dopamine system. Other drugs, such as heroine, do yield a great deal of pleasure, because they stimulate the opioid system, a system related to liking, and these drugs can be used as powerful painkillers because the pleasure they produce outweighs the pain of a given procedure. One can give someone a morphine injection, but not a cigarette, as a painkiller because they are operating on different brain systems (pp. 126–129).

Nettle also discusses research on right brain and left brain activity. Some research has demonstrated that the left brain is associated with positive emotions (e.g., humor), while the right brain is associated with negative emotions (e.g., disgust). Also, when one side of the brain is engaged, the other side reduces its activity, and we can measure whether one is "right brained" or "left brained" by measuring the level of activity when the brain is at rest. He predicts that a drug that increases serotonin levels would lead to increased left brain activity; that people with high neuroticism scores will demonstrate higher levels of right brain activity; and that other personality characteristics will be able to be correlated with the dopamine and serotonin systems (pp. 134–139).

Nettle concludes this chapter by returning to the question of personality. If it is the case that individuals are "hardwired" in certain ways in the brain, is it possible to change happiness? This is the question of the next chapter (p. 140).

PANACEAS AND PLACEBOS

Nettle begins chapter 6, titled "Panaceas and Placebos," with the observation that it might be tempting, especially in light of the evidence presented in chapter 5, to believe that happiness cannot be changed. Of course, brain functioning is directly related to our experiences of happiness. On the other hand, the brain is extremely flexible and changes its chemistry in order to adapt as needed. So finding out that something has a basis in the brain doesn't mean that it cannot be changed. In any case, people want to believe that happiness levels *can* change (as evidenced by the fact that 2,000 self-help books, what he calls "panaceas," are published annually). And these happiness "panaceas" offer a wide range of solutions: some are based on practical common sense, others seem to work on a kind of placebo effect, and still others are simply quackery (pp. 141–144).

How do these happiness solutions work? Nettle suggests three possibilities: (1) by reducing the impact of emotional negativity, (2) by increasing positive emotions, and (3) by changing the subject. Negative emotions tend to be pervasive. If, for example, we are rejected by our lover, we tend to think, for a brief period, that we are unlovable. But if someone praises us, we tend not to think we are the greatest or that everyone we encounter will praise us. Evolutionary psychology suggests that this is as it should be—threats and negativity should take precedence over positive emotions. Nettle supports this view by citing what he calls the life/dinner problem. We expect that a gazelle would have more motivation to keep running than the hungry cheetah that is chasing the gazelle. The cheetah is motivated by desire (dinner) while the gazelle is motivated by fear (loss of life). So the gazelle will run longer and tolerate more discomfort because its very life is at stake. Presumably, the cheetah can find something else to eat and shouldn't spend all of its energy on a single attempt. For human beings, the upshot is that we can spend a lot of time ruminating about some crass or stupid comment we made when it would be better to forget about it. This tendency to worry too much is a leftover from our evolutionary past where it was more important than it is today to stay socially connected (pp. 145–148).

Nettle discusses cognitive-behavioral therapy (CBT) in this connection. The point of CBT is to challenge the false assumptions behind our negative thoughts and emotions, and to expose them as irrational. Oftentimes our negative emotions cause us to exaggerate, even to "catastrophize," our problems. At one time, this may have been useful. But today such negativity is usually counterproductive. Many studies have shown that CBT is an effective way of reducing negative emotions even if we do not know exactly how CBT works. But CBT does not increase happiness. It simply decreases the impact of negative emotions (pp. 148–150).

On the other hand, pleasant activity training does attempt to increase happiness. How? It works simply by increasing the number of pleasant activities that we engage in, such as watching movies, spending time with family and friends, and boating. But why would anyone need to be told to do pleasurable things? How can this be a key to happiness? Nettle suggests that the distinction between wanting and liking is of use here, for many people tend to focus on their wants (e.g., a promotion, a nice house, an attractive mate) to which they adapt over time, whereas if they focused instead on their likes (e.g., eating chocolate ice cream, having sex, traveling to new places), they would be happier. The reason that many—perhaps most—persons focus on their wants instead of their likes is that, in evolutionary terms, it is better for the species to focus on wants than likes because this leads to advancement and progress, but not necessarily happiness. As it turns out, happiness is not, as it were, a priority of evolution (pp. 151–154).

A third way to affect happiness is by changing the subject. Nettle is referring here to the hedonistic paradox—namely, that those seeking happiness do not find it while those not looking for it seem to find it as a by-product. Things that one might seek or pursue that have yielded happiness for others include experiencing nature; reading, watching, or listening to stories; organizing and intervening in the activities of the world, such as volunteer work or collecting stamps; or participating in a religious tradition. All of these activities connect one to something larger than oneself, and these activities help to expand the complexity of one's self-image. Studies by Patricia Linville (1985, 1987) have shown that persons with more complex self-images tend to be happier than those with less complex ones. If, for example, one identifies oneself solely as a baseball player, one's self-image is dramatically affected when one has a bad game. But if one understands oneself to be a baseball player, a father, a husband, a deacon, a friend, a writer, and a builder, one can withstand setbacks in one of these areas because one's sense of self worth is not tied exclusively to that one identity. In short, happiness depends to a great extent on gaining a distance from one's desires (wants) and focusing instead on pleasures (likes) that are pursued not for the sake of happiness but that will, nonetheless, yield happiness along the way (pp. 154–160).

A DESIGN FOR LIVING

Nettle begins chapter 7, titled "A Design for Living," by referencing the robots in *Mostly Harmless* of Douglas Adams's series *The Hitchhiker's Guide to the Galaxy* (1992). In the story, there are robots that are programmed with the capacity to be happy. This programming entails details about the conditions that will bring happiness about, and the robots also have the ability to learn from experience. Nettle thinks that this is, more or less, how human beings are programmed by evolution. Some of the "rules" that human beings have been given include that it is better to have a mate than not, to have wealth than not, and to have high social status than not. Human beings have also been programmed to be competitive, so their wealth, for example, is always relative to their neighbor's wealth. Another key feature of our happiness program is adaptation—that is, we should never be completely happy, or, at least, not completely happy for too long. Otherwise, we would become complacent. These basic assumptions allow Nettle to make sense of a great deal of the empirical work on happiness, such as (1) most people say that they are happy; (2) hardly anyone says that they are perfectly or completely happy; (3) happiness with regard to positional goods is relative to those around you; (4) people get used to positive life changes—that is, they adapt; and (5) people become very unhappy after negative life events like injury or divorce, but, in general, they adapt to these situations as well (pp. 161–165).

Nettle notes, however, that there are other findings that need further explanation, such as the fact that human beings generally are not good at predicting what will make them happy and often choose to engage in activities that bring no pleasure. Returning to the distinction between desire (wanting) and pleasure (liking) introduced in chapter 5, and further explored in chapter 6, Nettle suggests that human beings operate with two systems—desire and pleasure—and that the former is related to dopamine and is long term while the latter is related to opioids and is short term. We are thus rewarded with pleasure in certain circumstances, and in others we are prodded forward with the promise of future happiness. In a sense, happiness works like a mirage—something that is always on the horizon, just at the end of the next rainbow. These assumptions explain why we are bad at predicting what will make us happy and why we work long hours for promotions that, in the end, will not make us happy—these are products of the desire system (pp. 166–167).

Nettle also discusses the topic of the future of happiness. Will we be happier in the future? He is somewhat skeptical of this point of view, since human beings are subject to adaptation, and, in fact, happiness levels have not risen in the past 50 years despite gains in material wealth. Then is it possible that we will we be *less* happy in the future? Nettle thinks that this is a real danger. Rates of major depression, for example, seem to be on the rise. It is hard to say why this is the case, but he identifies a number of culprits in this regard. By means of television and magazines, our global culture routinely exposes us to the rich, the famous, and the beautiful, highlighting the fact that there is always someone higher in social status than us. Also, work patterns have changed during the last 50 years—we are commuting further and working longer hours. Patterns of social and community engagement have also decreased. We are spending more time alone working and watching television than ever before. The price we pay for this is a reduction in our social capital, and our self-images are becoming less complex, meaning that we have less of a defense against unhappiness if something goes wrong in our work lives, because all of our eggs are, as it were, in one basket. To be sure, there are exceptions to these trends—such as voluntary simplicity—but these trends seem well-established, and there is reason to believe that, as far as pleasure is concerned, we are not as happy as we could be. Happiness, he concludes, is not the only good in life, and we should not expect to be completely happy. But if we can be above neutral—more happy than not—this is not to be disparaged or taken lightly. Also, if we put our minds to things other than pursuing happiness, then we might either find it along the way or realize that it was there all along (pp. 175–184).

CHAPTER 9

FORECASTING HAPPINESS

The ninth book that we have chosen to review is Daniel Gilbert's *Stumbling on Happiness* (2007). As noted in the introduction, Gilbert is a Harvard University psychology professor. The book has six parts. Part 1 has one chapter; the others have two each. In the foreword, Gilbert indicates that this book engages the scientific literature about how, and how well, the brain imagines what will make it happy in the future. Its primary contribution is that it offers an explanation for why our efforts to become happy so often fail (pp. xiii–xvii).

PROSPECTION

Part 1 titled "Prospection" is concerned with looking forward in time. In chapter 1—"Journey to Elsewhen"—Gilbert asserts that human beings are the only animals that think about the future. While other animals sometimes appear to do so—as when, for example, squirrels bury nuts for the winter—this is, in fact, a kind of programmed (or instinctual) behavior. The most these animals can really do is to think about the immediate future; they do not engage in predicting but only in what Gilbert calls "nexting" (pp. 3–8).

The capacity to think about the future, scientists speculate, emerged somewhere around three million years ago on account of the doubling of the human brain from about 1.25 lbs. to 3 lbs. Most of the growth occurred in the frontal lobe, thus changing the structure of the skulls of *Homo habilis* as they evolved into *Homo sapiens*. The frontal lobe is what gives human beings the capacity to think about the future. This was discovered, dramatically, by means of a freak accident in 1848. Phineas Gage was working on the railroad when a small explosion caused an iron rod to enter his face, below his cheek. The rod went through his frontal lobe and exited the top of his skull. Surprisingly, he felt fine, but he had undergone a major personality change: He was no longer able to think about the future. Another famous case in the history of brain science involves a patient referred to as N.N., who suffered a frontal lobe injury in a car accident in 1981. A psychologist asked him what he was going to be doing tomorrow, and he was unable to give a response. When he tried, he described it as a complete blank (pp. 9–17).

In the 20th century, surgeons experimented on human beings by destroying the frontal lobe. They discovered that frontal lobotomies were an effective treatment for anxiety. Why? Because anxiety involves thinking about the future. Frontal lobotomies removed the capacity to think about the future and, therefore, there was no reason to be anxious. This is also one reason why meditation works—one trains one's mind (and brain) to be focused on the present and not on the future (pp. 13–15).

Some studies suggest that we spend 12 percent of our time thinking about the future. Why do we spend so much time thinking about the future? Gilbert offers three reasons. One is that thinking about the future is pleasurable. We enjoy thinking about the nice meal we are going to have, what our date will be like, or what we would do with a million dollars if we won the lottery. A second is that thinking about the future helps us to prepare for unpleasant events; some studies indicate that they are less unpleasant if we are prepared for them. A third is that human beings like control and the illusion of it. This is why, for example, it is more fun to watch football games live than watching a recording (even if we do not know the outcome) because, on some level, we like to believe that our cheering can make a difference. This is also why people believe that if they pick their own lottery numbers they have a better chance of winning; and why toddlers like knocking over blocks— they like to see that they have done something, *controlled* something. Knowing something about the future and reacting accordingly is a pleasurable act of control. However, the problem is that we are not very good at foresight, and the rest of the book is dedicated to explaining why (pp. 17–27).

SUBJECTIVITY

Part 2 deals with subjectivity, and it is concerned with the fact that experience is not observable by those not having the experience. The first chapter in part 2, titled "The View from in Here," begins with the story of Lori and Reba Schappel, twins who are joined at the forehead. They have different personalities—Reba is shy and artistic, while Lori is outgoing and would like to marry and have children—but what they share in common is that neither wants to be surgically separated from the other. Furthermore, both report that they are happy. Strikingly, many conjoined twins say that they are happy and do not want to be separated. Assuming that most of us would be profoundly depressed about our lives if we were in their situation, Gilbert wonders how the Schappel twins can be happy. He uses their happiness as a jumping-off point to discuss definitions of happiness. He notes that there are three broad ways in which people talk about happiness: (1) emotional happiness, (2) moral happiness, and (3) judgmental happiness (pp. 31–33).

Emotional happiness is a subjective state, and philosophers often refer to such states as "irreducible." The color yellow is irreducible, and so is, some think, the emotional experience of happiness. Just as we explain yellow in terms of other things (school buses and lemons have yellow in common), emotional happiness is explained in terms of similar experiences (e.g., holding a kitten and getting a promotion). There are, of course, differences in these experiences, and Gilbert explains these differences in terms of degree or points on a scale (pp. 34–37).

Moral happiness is feeling happy for the "right" reasons. If one feels happy about overeating, stealing, and murdering, there is nothing admirable about the reasons one feels happy. Suspecting that such persons must be missing something, philosophers suggest that, in order to be happy, one must be virtuous. For Gilbert, the problem with this point of view is that it confuses causes (virtuous behavior) with consequences (feeling happy). Many times virtuous actions can lead to feelings of happiness, but one also can be extremely virtuous and completely unhappy (pp. 37–40).

Judgmental happiness is *being* happy about something while not necessarily *feeling* happy about it. For example, one may be happy about how one's life has turned out but not have any feelings about it. Or if a man's spouse just received a promotion and she gets to spend six months away training in an exotic place while he has to take care of the children, he might be happy for his wife but unhappy with the situation. These are judgments about happiness, and they are more cognitive than emotional (pp. 40–41).

Gilbert returns to the experience of Lori and Reba Schappel in light of these definitional matters. How can we compare the experiences of Lori and Reba and our own? If they say they are happy, do they mean the same thing that we mean when we say that we are happy? Gilbert proposes two possibilities. One is the "experience-squishing hypothesis." This position is based on the suspicion that persons like Lori and Reba do not have the full range of happy experiences that others of us have. So when they experience happiness as an 8 on a scale of 1 to 10, what they rate as 8, we, in our experience, would rate as 4. Another possibility is the "experiencing-stretching hypothesis." This position holds that there are different levels of happiness but that having more life experiences can lead to more unhappiness. Gilbert cites an example from his own life. He likes to smoke a cigar on vacation while watching the sunset. His wife doesn't understand why he needs to smoke the cigar because she is perfectly happy watching the sunset and not smoking the cigar while doing so. While watching the sunset without the cigar is an 8 for her, it would be a 7 for him. However, had he never smoked a cigar, he thinks that he, too, would have experienced an 8 watching the sunset without smoking a cigar. Which hypothesis is the correct one? In Gilbert's view, we really can't say. All that we *can* say is that all claims about happiness are contextual and depend on one's perspective (pp. 50–59).

In the second chapter in part 2, titled "Outside Looking In," Gilbert returns to the question whether people can be wrong about what they feel, but he raises this question in a different way. The point of this chapter is to deal with the question whether it is possible to study happiness scientifically. He thinks that such an endeavor is possible, but he begins with evolutionary psychology in order to raise more difficulties before he offers a way out of them (pp. 60–61). He points out that our brains were programmed to respond to certain kinds of situations before other kinds. For instance, when seeing a wolf, our brains know how to respond—run!—before we know to what, exactly, we are responding. This all happens in milliseconds, but it is striking that we know how to respond before identifying that to which we are responding. The fact that our brains work like this—that we know what to do and how to feel before we know the precise details of a given situation—affects our emotions (pp. 61–63).

Gilbert cites an interesting study in this regard to lend empirical support to this claim. In this study, the subjects (all male) were to cross a dangerous bridge. Some of the men were approached by an attractive woman while they were crossing the bridge. Others were approached after they had successfully crossed the bridge. The woman gave all of the men a survey as well as her phone number should they want the results from the survey. As it turned out, the men who were approached on the bridge were more likely to call her. Why? Because the men on the bridge were in a state of physiological arousal (fear), and when she approached them, they mistook fear for sexual attraction. People can, it seems, be wrong about what they are feeling (pp. 63–64).

Gilbert next discusses the distinction between experiencing and being aware of one's experience. These two activities are rooted in different areas in the brain, and we can have one without the other. For instance, some persons suffer from *alexithymia*, a condition in which one does not have awareness of one's experiences. Even though such persons know the meaning of words such as happy, sad, angry, afraid, and so forth, they are incapable of talking about how they feel. They just don't know if they are experiencing any of these states (pp. 64–69).

Perhaps, then, there is no point in studying happiness, because happiness is a subjective state, and we cannot know with certainty how another person feels, whether what he or she feels is the same as what we feel, or even what we ourselves are feeling. These are all real difficulties. Still, Gilbert believes that happiness and other subjective states can be studied, if only imperfectly. After all, there is some degree of error in all measurements. Furthermore, there are a variety of ways to take measurements when studying happiness, such as electromyography and physiography. In his judgment, however, the best way to measure happiness is by asking people to report on their own experience. All other measures of happiness must correlate with these reports. All of the problems with measuring happiness remain, but we can offset these problems by measuring often and by measuring large numbers of people so as to minimize degrees of error (pp. 69–79).

REALISM

Part 3 deals with realism, that is, the relationship between reality and perception. The first chapter, titled "In the Blind Spot of the Mind's Eye," begins with the professional lives of Adolf Fischer and George Eastman. Both men worked for the improvement of working conditions for industrial workers—for fair wages and decent working conditions. Fischer was executed for a crime he did not commit, and, as he was about to hang, he exclaimed that this was the happiest moment of his life. He was executed by the powerful industrialists in Chicago who were against unions. Eastman, on the other hand, was very well-respected and wealthy, though he committed suicide. Gilbert notes that most of us, if we were Eastman, would expect that we would be happy, and most of us, if we were Fischer, would expect that we would be unhappy. Why, then, do these men's experiences indicate the opposite? Gilbert suggests that we have trouble imagining what, in fact, will make us happy. The problem is not with these two men but with *us* and our imaginations. This chapter explores the mistakes our imaginations often make (pp. 83–86).

Gilbert attempts to demonstrate the flaws in our imagination by pointing out flaws in our memory and in our perception. He notes that our brains do not simply store information. Rather, they take snapshots of events, and, when we remember these events, our brains re-create the past rather than simply recall it. Moreover, there is an element of fabrication in how our brains remember. Dozens, perhaps hundreds, of studies have demonstrated this phenomenon with word lists and other kinds of experiments. Our brains work similarly with perception (both seeing and hearing) in the present as well. Depending on the context, our brains will fill in sights that it expects to see and sounds that it expects to hear even if they are not there (pp. 86–92).

Philosophers, most notably Immanuel Kant, came to recognize that our brains do not simply perceive reality—they construct it. This shift occurred in the 18th century, a move from realism to idealism, and this shift underscored the importance of perspective. Our perception of reality is an interpretation of the world, not the world as it actually is (pp. 93–95).

Children discover idealism when they are young. Jean Piaget showed that very young children assume that everyone knows what they know. When, for example, they know where a hidden piece of candy is because they watched someone hiding the candy, they expect their friends who did not see it being hidden to know where the candy is. This is because very young children do not distinguish between the world and their mind (pp. 95–98). Similarly, we adults fail to distinguish between things in the world and things in the mind (though not in such a simplistic way) precisely because our brains are good at imagining. Our brains do so effortlessly and quickly without our realizing that they are doing so. Gilbert offers a simple thought experiment to drive this point home: Imagine that you have been offered spaghetti for dinner tomorrow night and then rate how much you will enjoy it. People typically rate such offers very highly despite the fact that they were not told anything about the dinner. For all they know, it could be spaghetti out of a can or with grape jelly and hummus. The point is that our brains usually fill in the details with our imaginations, and this can lead us to make false assumptions. Our imaginations construct our perception of reality, and very often they skew it (pp. 98–102).

Gilbert returns at the end of the chapter to Eastman and Fischer. He provides the reader with more details this time, noting that Fischer may have seen himself as a Christ figure and believed that he would be remembered in history. This is why he could exclaim that his hanging was the happiest moment of his life (he was becoming famous). On the other hand, Eastman had lived a full life, but for medical reasons he was unable to do things that he very much loved to do. So he decided to end his life. In this light, his death does not seem like a failure. If our earlier assumption had been that Eastman died unhappy, our assumption was wrong. In effect, Gilbert played a trick on us to show, experientially, how our brains tend to work, and to make us aware of our blind spots (pp. 102–105).

The second chapter in part 3, titled "The Hound of Silence," focuses on how our imaginations fail to notice absences. Gilbert begins this chapter by recounting an episode in the adventures of Sherlock Holmes. Silver Blaze, a racehorse, was missing. The police accused a man (a stranger to the horse) of having stolen the horse, but Holmes identified the real thief by paying attention to a suspicious absence—the absence of the barking of the dog who was kept in the stables with the horse. He correctly ascertained that the thief must have been someone the dog knew well; otherwise the dog would have barked and awakened others, thereby preventing the thief from taking the horse. Gilbert notes that, unfortunately, Holmes (a fictional character) is an exceptional man, and most of us are not nearly as perceptive (pp. 106–107).

He goes on to cite a number of interesting studies in support of his point that we often fail to notice absences. One involved asking persons to identify patterns in letter sequences. Subjects were able to identify the presence of the letter "T" as the key variable, but they were unable to identify the absence of the letter "T" as the key variable. In general, most of us have a limited ability to identify absences in a variety of situations, and this, Gilbert suggests, causes us to draw some curious conclusions. In one study, persons were asked whether they would prefer to take a vacation that was average all around or a vacation that involved exceptional beaches but a poor nightlife. Most chose the latter. But, when asked which vacation they would be more likely to cancel, they chose the same vacation. Gilbert thinks this is because, when selecting a vacation, people tend to think of its positive features, but, when canceling, they tend to think of its negative aspects (pp. 107–111).

Our imaginations also fail to account for absences in thinking about the future. For example, we tend to overestimate the impact of blindness if we ourselves were to become blind, because we fail to see that persons with blindness live interesting and satisfying lives. The same is true of many other illnesses and disabilities. We also overestimate the satisfaction of experiences like babysitting for a relative. When we agree to babysit, we think about it in terms of affection and meaning (questions of "why"), but when the time comes to do the babysitting, we regret our offer to help out because we are reminded of the more mundane practical realities of babysitting, such as changing diapers and moving car seats (questions of "how"). Our perspective changes as we approach events in time. Even as our imaginations may sometimes give us too many details, they may also fail to give us enough. Both of these factors contribute to the difficulty we experience in predicting what will yield happiness in our own lives (pp. 111–119).

PRESENTISM

Part 4 deals with presentism, the fact that our current experience colors how we interpret both the past and the future. The first chapter in part 4, titled "The Future Is Now," deals with presentism with regard to both the future and the past. Gilbert begins by citing claims made in the first decade of the 20th century that no machine could be created to enable humans to fly long distances. Even Wilbur Wright thought, in 1901, that it would take 50 years before human beings would be able to fly. Gilbert also cites examples from popular culture from the 1950s that, on the one hand, depict futuristic flying cars and sidewalks that function as conveyer belts and, on the other hand, depict men working in the future while women stay home and bake. Whether scientific or popular, predictions about the future tend to have a heavy dose of presentism. This is why teenagers get tattoos when they are young but often regret them when they are older. We simply have trouble looking into the future and reliably estimating how we will feel (pp. 123–127).

We also tend to view the past in light of the present. Gilbert cites various studies that demonstrate this dynamic in regard to personal relationships, political views, pain, bereavement, and so forth. What people think they felt in the past is highly influenced by what they are feeling at the present—life satisfaction, one study showed, is affected by the current weather (pp. 125–126).

Gilbert also discusses how the brain works with regard to events (e.g., seeing certain sights or hearing certain sounds), memory (e.g., remembering certain sights or sounds), and emotions (e.g., the emotional experience of seeing or remembering certain sights). For example, when we see something, such as a pencil, the vision area in the brain is activated, and we have the experience of seeing a pencil. Or, when we remember seeing something, such as a penguin, the same area in the brain is activated, and we can have the experience of seeing a penguin. This exercise works better when we close our eyes because otherwise our actual perception is competing with our memory of what we perceived before. There is, as it were, a kind of "reality first" principle in the operating of our brains. This is as it should be, Gilbert suggests, for otherwise we could run a red light if we were thinking about a green light (pp. 129–133).

We can, then, both perceive and preview, and we can also feel and "pre-feel." Our pre-feelings can tell us what we'd likely be experiencing if we found our lover cheating on us. Sometimes our pre-feelings can also predict how much we will enjoy certain things, such as purchasing a painting for our living room, and they can do this better than if we try, rationally, to predict how we will feel. Other times, however, our pre-feelings can get in the way because they are skewed by our present feelings. For example, depressed persons cannot accurately judge how much they will enjoy a certain event in the future because they can't imagine any enjoyment in the future. Also, whether our stomachs are full or empty determines how hungry we think we will be and actually influences what we buy in the grocery store. Another reason, then, why we have trouble figuring out what will make us happy is that it is hard to imagine tomorrow in terms other than today (pp. 134–139).

In the second chapter in part 4, titled "Time Bombs," Gilbert focuses on time. He notes that when people think about time, they tend to do so in spatial terms. For instance, we think of the future as ahead of us, and the past as behind us; or, in the West, we think of the past on the left and the future on the right (other cultures depict time differently). It is hard to visualize time because time is an abstraction, something that does not exist as an object. The purpose of this chapter is to make the point that because we have difficulty thinking about time, we have difficulty thinking about what will make us happy in the future (pp. 140–141).

The first half of the chapter deals with variety. Gilbert notes that when we go out to a restaurant, we do not normally order the same thing as our friends. Instead, we order different things and then share our food with one another. This variety makes our meals more enjoyable. Another way to make experiences enjoyable is to use time as a variable. For instance, drinking champagne and kissing our loved one at midnight on New Year's Eve is pleasurable, largely because we do not do it every night at midnight. Similarly, one way to make sex in a committed relationship more enjoyable is to have it less often. Or, if a couple likes to have sex a lot, then introducing variety, such as different sexual positions, into the sexual relationship often proves to be pleasurable. But what is striking about this research is that it shows that one should not change *both* time *and* type of variety because this leads to *less* satisfaction. So if we go to a favorite restaurant once a month, we should order our favorite dish; but if we go to a favorite restaurant every day, we should order different dishes (pp. 141–147).

Gilbert also points out that we predict future satisfaction in terms of present experience. For example, if we are really hungry now, this affects how satisfied we think we will be with a spaghetti dinner tomorrow. We are occasionally able to take account of the effect of time, though even our attempts to account for time are affected by our current starting point (pp. 147–151).

The second half of the chapter deals with comparison. Gilbert notes that we tend to think of money in relative rather than absolute terms. For instance, if a cup of coffee costs $1.50 today, but $2.50 tomorrow, it is likely that we would be reluctant to buy the coffee. However, in his view, this is the wrong comparison to make. We should not think about what coffee used to cost but, rather, what else we could get for $2.50, and on this basis we should judge whether the cup of coffee is worth $2.50. There are all sorts of marketing tricks that play into this psychology, such as by placing a few really expensive items next to the items that retailers are hoping to sell; by asking for a modest donation after asking for an extraordinary one; or by showing potential home buyers modest homes after showing them shabby ones. These comparisons tend to influence our decisions, causing us to see "good deals" where there really are none. Predicting how happy we will feel in the future needs to take account of presentism in its variety of forms. This, however, is harder than it sounds, and Gilbert goes on to show why in the next part of the book (pp. 151–162).

RATIONALIZATION

Part 5 deals with rationalization, the process of the ways in which we make things seem reasonable to ourselves. In the first chapter in part 5, titled "Paradise Glossed," Gilbert considers the conventional wisdom that such calamities as the death of one's spouse or child, sudden and chronic illnesses, experiencing a natural disaster, or going to jail have a devastating effect on people. However, recent research suggests that people are much more resilient than has been assumed in conventional wisdom and in professional psychology. Also, individuals tend to overestimate the effect that a negative life event—such as losing a game or doing poorly in a job interview—will have on them. Why is this so? Gilbert suggests that the human mind tends to exploit ambiguity, and experiences are naturally ambiguous. This helps to explain why, for example, most people think they are better than average drivers. Unlike pigeons and rats, we human beings respond to the world not only as it is presented to us but also as our minds represent it to us, and our minds tend to look for facts that will confirm the positive image that we have of ourselves (pp. 165–176).

There are, however, limits to this tendency to look for facts that will enable us to have a positive image of our experiences. As Gilbert points out, people are generally not overjoyed about hemorrhoids and in-laws. Our interpretation of the facts must have some correspondence to reality—that is, the view we have of ourselves must be credible to us. In other words, our "psychological immune system" needs to defend us without making us too defensive. Indeed, if the facts are too disturbing to our wants and our needs, we tend to scrutinize the facts in a much more rigorous way than when the facts concur with our wants and our needs. This is especially true when it comes to political positions where we seek out facts and studies that support our own views while downplaying the significance of inconvenient facts. This, of course, is bad science, but we tend to be bad scientists when it comes to evaluating ourselves (pp. 176–188).

The second chapter in part 5, titled "Immune to Reality," continues with the theme of rationalization. Gilbert notes that although we may in fact "cook the facts" when we take positive views of ourselves, we tend to do this unconsciously—otherwise this "cooking the facts" would not be credible to us. He focuses in this chapter on the effect of painful experiences, and one striking point he makes in this regard is that people tend to feel happier after *very bad* experiences than after *bad* experiences. Why is this? He suggests that our psychological immune system comes to our defense after very bad experiences in order to help us rationalize them, whereas with normal bad experiences no rationalization is needed. As a result, we often feel worse after bad experiences than after very bad experiences. One study in this regard involved people receiving electric shocks in order to join a club. People who received the higher-voltage shocks rated the experience more positively than those who received the lower-voltage shocks. Afterward, the higher-voltage group rationalized the pain by stating that the club was a very elite group. An upshot here is that our psychological immune system will rationalize very bad events—such as divorces ("he was not right for me") and lost jobs ("I never liked that job anyway")—but, with regard to everyday unhappiness—such as spilling coffee on our shirt or stubbing our toes on the sidewalk—our psychological immune systems do not help us all that much (pp. 189–201).

A variation on this theme is that people tend to rate situations they are simply stuck with more positively than situations they can eliminate from their lives. We tend, for example, to forgive family members for their rudeness or social ineptness, but, if friends were to act the same way, we'd likely part ways. We also tend to highlight the positive features of our purchases, such as cars, once we own them; but, while we are considering buying, we focus on their flaws. This is also why it is worse to receive inconclusive results from a test for genetic defects than either a positive *or* a negative result (pp. 201–204).

Another striking point that Gilbert makes is that we think we will especially regret acts of commission while, in fact, we tend to regret acts of omission. This is because it is easier to rationalize acts of commission than to rationalize acts of omission. This is true of persons of all ages. One reason for this, Gilbert suggests, is that we can "learn things" from foolish actions (a rationalization), but it is harder to "learn things" from what we did not do. Whether these rationalizations will help us to proceed with greater caution in the future is difficult to say. But, in any event, we don't learn much from acts of omission (pp. 196–197).

Another finding that Gilbert focuses on in this chapter involves the effects of explanations on happiness. Explaining negative events, such as traumas, can be beneficial. He cites studies that demonstrate that writing about one's traumas can lead to improvements in one's physical and psychological health by such measures as fewer visits to the doctor, higher levels of viral antibodies, and higher self-reporting of subjective well-being. On the other hand, explaining positive events tends to mitigate the effects of pleasant experiences. This, he suggests, is why it is more exciting to receive a note from a secret admirer than from someone whom we know, and also why people enjoy mystery movies with an ambiguous ending more than mystery movies in which everything is explained. Unexplained events are rare, and, therefore, we are more likely to keep thinking about them, prolonging the emotional impact. Thus, explanations tend to mitigate our emotions, both positive and negative, and therefore make it hard to predict what will make us happy. Our minds have various techniques for keeping us immune to various unpleasantries of life, but these same techniques can also prevent or mitigate our happiness (pp. 204–211).

CORRIGIBILITY

Part 6 deals with corrigibility. Corrigibility means that something is capable of being corrected, improved, or reformed. Gilbert wonders whether, with a little practice and a little coaching, we can learn to be happier. The first chapter in part 6 titled "Once Bitten" focuses on practice, while the second chapter titled "Reporting Live from Tomorrow" focuses on coaching (pp. 215–216).

Gilbert points out in the first chapter that many of us repeat experiences that we say we will never do again. For example, people tend to marry someone who is a lot like the person whom they've divorced or to take long camping trips that they swore they'd never take again. The problem here is that we often fail to remember our experiences correctly, because we tend to remember unusual events but not ordinary ones. We recall, for example, where we were on the morning of September 11, 2001, but not on the morning of September 10, 2001 (pp. 216–222).

We also tend to remember endings more than beginnings and middles. Gilbert remembered disliking the movie *Schindler's List* while his wife insisted that he did like the movie. To settle the debate, they rented the movie again and discovered that they were both right. He enjoyed the whole movie until, at the very end, the real life people on whom the movie was based were honored in the closing minutes of the film. He thought the final two minutes were "stupid," and this colored his memory of the film. He cites more scientific studies to support this point, such as ice water experiments, how women remember childbirth, and how couples remember relationships that have ended badly (pp. 222–226).

Gilbert also points out that the theories we have about ourselves affect how we remember feeling. For example, in our culture, women are believed to be more emotional than men. Yet various studies demonstrate that this is not true. On the other hand, when men and women remember their experiences, women remember being more emotional than they were while men remember being less emotional than they were. Similar dynamics occur between cultures. Asian Americans tend to think of themselves as less happy than European Americans. In one study, Asian Americans actually scored higher than European Americans on self-reporting measures of happiness, but, when asked later how they felt, Asian Americans remember being less happy than they reported. So the reason why practicing is not a very effective method for making ourselves happier is that we tend not to remember our previous experiences correctly (pp. 226–232).

In the second chapter in part 6 on whether we can become happier with a little bit of coaching, Gilbert begins by pointing out that most of everything that we know—for example, that the earth revolves around the sun and that there are more people in China than in Nebraska—is secondhand knowledge. Knowledge is social, and we rely on this knowledge to live our lives. Yet, when it comes to happiness, we tend to be reluctant to listen to the experiences of others. Instead, we rely on our own imagination, the distortions of which Gilbert has been challenging throughout the book (more on this point below). In other words, we refuse to be coached by others about our own lives when it comes to happiness. Also, he notes that we tend to rely on widely shared ideas about what will make us happy. Cultural beliefs about what will make us happy are social, just as scientific knowledge about the earth is social. But these ideas do not have evidence to back them up—they are, as it were, false beliefs. One false belief is that money will bring us happiness. Gilbert points out that research has consistently demonstrated that wealth has decreasing marginal utility—the more we have, the less value, in terms of pleasure, it yields. Money is important to provide for our basic needs, but, in terms of happiness, there is not much difference between earning $100,000 a year or $1,000,000 a year. Another false belief is that having children will make us happy. Many studies have shown that children are a lot of work and that mothers (who, generally, are still the primary caretakers of children) are happier taking naps and shopping than caring for their children. Where do these "false beliefs" originate? Unlike scientific knowledge, there is no authority advocating for them. Gilbert thinks that they are the product of evolution, as he points out that it is good for society to believe that money will make you happy and that having children will make you happy—these ideas serve the ends of creating a stable society (pp. 233–245).

There is, then, a kind of social knowledge that undermines our happiness—social knowledge based on false beliefs. There is another kind of social knowledge—the actual experiences of happiness that others have had—that would give us our best chances of finding happiness, but it is a kind of knowledge that many persons are likely to reject. What, then, affords our best chances of discovering happiness for ourselves? Gilbert thinks it is by asking other people in situations that we are considering for ourselves how they feel, right now, and basing our decisions on this kind of surrogate knowledge rather than on what we imagine to be the case (pp. 245–251).

Gilbert anticipates the objection that many of us would prefer to use our own imagination (rather than relying on someone else's experience) on the grounds that we know ourselves best; that we are all unique; and that, therefore, we are in the best position to know what would make us happy. But this leaves us depending on our own imaginations, and there are three problems with our imagination: (1) our imaginations tend to fill in information that is not there (realism), (2) our imaginations tend to project the present into the future (presentism), and (3) our imaginations tend to re-create the past to make it more palatable (rationalization). In reviewing these three problems with the imagination, Gilbert cites several studies showing that surrogates were able to predict another person's future happiness with much greater accuracy than those who tried to imagine how they themselves would feel. Gilbert concedes that most people will not take this simple advice to heart (i.e., to accept the coaching of others), because people tend to see themselves as unique—not necessarily superior, but unique. People also tend to overestimate the uniqueness of others, and so we often will not look to others for advice about our own lives. He doesn't think that he has offered any real solution as to how to find happiness, but he thinks he has provided some good reasons for why, when we do find happiness, we stumble onto it (pp. 251–257).

CHAPTER 10

Becoming Happier

The 10th book we have chosen to review is Tal Ben-Shahar's *Happier: Learn the Secrets to Daily Joy and Lasting Fulfillment* (2007). As noted in the introduction, Ben-Shahar is an Israeli psychologist who teaches at Harvard University. In *Happier*, he articulates his vision for living a happier life. The book is divided into three parts. Part 1—"What Is Happiness?"—consists of chapters on the question of happiness, reconciling present and future, happiness explained, the ultimate currency, and setting goals; part 2—"Happiness Applied"—consists of chapters on applying happiness to education, work, and relationships; and part 3—"Meditations on Happiness"—consists of seven mediations on the following topics and themes: self-interest and benevolence, happiness boosters, beyond the temporary high, letting our light shine, imagine, take your time, and the happiness revolution. There is also a preface and a conclusion. Each chapter includes exercises intended to promote self-reflection as well as to serve as practical guides to help the reader live a happier life. In addition to the exercises at the end of each chapter, there are also "Time-In" exercises. These are shorter exercises also designed to help the reader implement reflection and action into his or her life. He has subsequently published a sequel that is entirely composed of these "time-in" exercises (Ben-Shahar 2010). We will focus primarily on chapters in parts 1 and 2, the parts of the book that present his basic understanding of happiness. We will confine our discussion to the sections of chapters that focus on the nature of happiness and not discuss the exercises designed to help readers become happier.

THE QUESTION OF HAPPINESS

In the first chapters in part 1 titled "The Question of Happiness," Ben-Shahar begins with an experience that raised the question of happiness for him in a personal way. At age 16, he won the Israeli national squash championship. He had trained for five years for the championship, believing that the fulfillment of his goal was essential to his realization of happiness, because this, he thought, was the only way he could rid himself of the nagging sense of emptiness that he felt inside of him. When he won, he was in fact happier than he had ever been, happier even than he had imagined that he would be. But this elation did not last. After celebrating with family and friends, he had an experience that he would never forget: the waning of the bliss and the return of the emptiness. He was afraid that happiness simply might not be possible because he knew, intuitively, that simply substituting a new goal would not lead to happiness (pp. 3–4).

As a result of this experience, Ben-Shahar became obsessed with the question of happiness. He began reading Plato, Confucius, and modern psychology. He talked with friends and read self-help books. In college, he decided to study philosophy and psychology, as these disciplines seemed to be the best guides on the question of happiness. He wondered, is happiness an emotion, an experience of pleasure or bliss, or the absence of pain? He concluded that although emotions are enjoyable and inherently significant, they are also fleeting and therefore cannot be the basis or foundation of happiness (pp. 4–6).

Now, years later, he accepts the fact that he cannot answer the question "What is happiness?" with complete precision and clarity. The answer eludes him. Nor has he found five easy steps to happiness. But he *has* discovered general principles that can lead to a happier life for people in certain circumstances—people who are not struggling with major mental health issues, such as depression, or who are living in social conditions in which it is unlikely that one could ever be happy, such as when one finds oneself living in a war zone. Also, for some people in certain acute circumstances, such as the death of a loved one, these general principles may not be of much use (pp. 7–8).

One such discovery is that the question "Am I happy?" is the wrong question to ask. Why? Because it assumes (1) that one can know what happiness is, (2) that there is a universal standard of happiness, and (3) that one can judge one's own level of happiness in relation to someone else's level of happiness. He is skeptical of attempts to quantify happiness in these ways. The question "Am I happy?" assumes that happiness is an endpoint, a goal that one can reach, and this belief, as he knows from his own experience, will only lead to a dead-end. The right question to ask is: "How can I become happier?" (pp. 7–8).

RECONCILING PRESENT AND FUTURE

In chapter 2, titled "Reconciling the Present and the Future," Ben-Shahar begins with a story about his training for a squash tournament. He ate nothing but health food for about a month leading up to the tournament, with the understanding that he could go on a two-day junk food binge when it was over. But when the time for the binge came, he no longer wanted the junk food because he knew that eating it would be unpleasant for his body. This experience led him to certain insights about happiness. He knew that if he ate the hamburgers he would feel pleasant now but would feel ill later—*present benefit but future detriment*. He calls this the hedonistic archetype as it focuses on present pleasures. But then it occurred to him that he could eat a vegetarian hamburger, which he did not like much, and that this experience would *bring future benefit but present detriment*. He calls this the rat race archetype where pleasure is delayed in the name of future gratification. A third model is one in which *one experiences neither present nor future pleasure*, the equivalent of eating a tasteless hamburger that is also bad for you. He refers to this as the nihilistic archetype. A fourth model is one that *constitutes pleasure now and in the future.* This, the happiness archetype, involves eating a hamburger that is both good and good for you (pp. 13–15).

Most of us will act at times as hedonists, rat racers, nihilists, and happy persons, but an effective strategy toward becoming happier is to increase the time we spend on activities that are both pleasurable now and will continue to bring pleasure in the future. So when, for example, one of Ben-Shahar's students came to ask him when she should stop focusing on the future and begin focusing on the present, he responded by reformulating the question, suggesting that she should instead think about what would make her happy now and in the future (pp. 16–25).

This outlook can be applied to many aspects of life. For example, in school, one should find ways to enjoy what one is studying and not simply focus on grades; in work, one should pursue, to the extent possible, vocations that one is committed to rather than simply working for a paycheck; in relationships, one should enjoy the time spent together in the present as well as cultivate ways to grow closer in the future. To be sure, this outlook has certain limitations. After all, one should not expect all of life to be pleasant. Sometimes, in fact, sacrifices in the present are necessary (as when studying for an exam); conversely, there are times when indulgence in hedonistic pleasures is conducive to happiness so long as it does not have long-term negative consequences (as with drug use). He concludes that if the rat racer's illusion is that reaching some future destination will bring lasting happiness, the hedonist's illusion is that only the journey is important. The nihilist's illusion is that neither the journey nor the destination matter. The attainment of happiness—or becoming happier—entails enjoying the journey toward a chosen and worthy destination (pp. 16–27).

HAPPINESS EXPLAINED

In chapter 3, titled "Happiness Explained," Ben-Shahar notes that when we are questioned about why we want certain things we may not be able to produce a good or convincing explanation. But when the question is "Why do you want to be happy?" we can give a simple and definitive answer: "We pursue happiness because it is our nature to do so." As Aristotle claimed, happiness is the meaning and the purpose of life and the final or ultimate end toward which all other ends are directed (pp. 31–32).

What, then, is happiness? Ben-Shahar defines happiness as "the overall experience of pleasure and meaning," and notes that happiness is not a state; rather, it is "a generalized aggregate of one's experiences." By "pleasure" he means emotion, which is related to motion and also to motivation. So happiness entails (1) experiencing positive emotion and (2) having a sense that, on the whole, life is pleasurable. Although pleasure is necessary for happiness, it alone is insufficient; one must also have meaning. Conversely, meaning alone is insufficient for happiness; one must also have pleasure—and there is a synergistic relationship between the two (pp. 33–44).

What, though, does he mean by "meaning"? He defines meaning as a sense of purpose that is connected to one's values and one's passions. Meaning, in other words, is living life with a sense of calling or vocation. He does not specify the kinds or types of activities that constitute meaningful ones, because we should choose these activities based on our own values and passions. He notes that an investment banker who does his or her work from a sense of personal passion could be living a more meaningful and authentic life than a monk who is trying to conform to the expectations of others (pp. 37–39).

Ben-Shahar offers some specific suggestions with regard to cultivating meaning in one's life: one should live with a calling, and one's calling should also be rooted in daily activities. For example, one might find meaning in one's family life, but, for this calling to be rooted, it should manifest itself in daily activities, such as playing a board game or taking a walk with one's family. Another key to happiness is living up to one's potential. One needs to be stimulated and challenged in order to thrive. However, this does not mean that someone who has the potential to be President of the United States needs to become the President of the United States; what is needed is engaging and stimulating work, not success per se. On the other hand, this does not mean that one needs to give up on success in order to find meaning. Rather, the goal is to find challenging and meaningful activities that may also lead to successes (pp. 39–42).

He concludes this chapter with a discussion of quantity and quality, and what he calls the "lasagna principle." Lasagna is his favorite food, and when he visits his mother, she makes him a tray of it. But this does not mean that he would like eating lasagna every day. Similarly, he likes watching movies and feels that two movies a week contribute to his happiness, but two movies a day would be physically and emotionally draining. The same principle holds for involvement with his family, the most important thing in his life. He would not want to spend every minute of every day with them. He needs time to work and time to be alone. Finding happiness—or becoming happier—involves identifying the activities that give us meaning and pleasure, and finding the right balance with regard to the time we spend on these activities (pp. 42–46).

THE ULTIMATE CURRENCY

Ben-Shahar begins chapter 4, titled "The Ultimate Currency," with the story of Marva Collins, who taught during the 1970s in the inner-city school district in Chicago, where there was little hope and optimism. Many of the children in these schools were considered to be "unteachable." It was assumed that their lives were destined for the streets. But she disagreed. And in 1975 she founded a school of her own, initially located in her own home. The kids began reading, including Plato and Shakespeare, and many went to college. When she was in the company of persons who had made a great deal of money running multibillion dollar corporations, Collins asked herself why she wanted to remain a teacher. The answer came when Tiffany, an autistic child who had been told by the experts that she was "unteachable," spoke her first words to Collins: "I love you, Mrs. Ollins." Seeing Tiffany writing her numerals, beginning to read single words, and even speaking was worth more to Collins than anything that money could buy. She later turned down offers by the Reagan and Bush administrations in the 1980s to become the nation's secretary of education (pp. 51–53).

The basic point of this chapter is that happiness, and not money or fame, is, to use Ben-Shahar's phrase, "the ultimate currency." Wealth and fame are secondary to happiness and are, in fact, important only if they can enable or lead to happiness. They are not, in Ben-Shahar's view, valuable in and of themselves. Material wealth can liberate us from work that we would rather not do. Yet as various studies have demonstrated, money does not buy happiness. Furthermore, these studies suggest that attainment of wealth sometimes yields *decreases* in happiness, as people have less to strive for once they have "made it" (pp. 53–58).

If money can't buy happiness, why is so much time and energy directed toward gathering wealth? Like many other contemporary writers on happiness, Ben-Shahar suggests that an evolutionary perspective may shed light on this question. Long ago, when we were hunters and gatherers, it was necessary to hoard in order to survive the winter months. Over time, these hoarding practices cultivated a hoarding mentality that is no longer necessary today. But focusing on material wealth can leave us emotionally bankrupt. Strikingly in making this point, Ben-Shahar compares individuals to businesses: Just as businesses can go bankrupt, so, too, can persons. Businesses need to take in material profits, but persons, in order to be happy, need to take in emotional profits. The net balance between positive and negative experiences needs to come out on the positive if a person is to avoid emotional bankruptcy. Ben-Shahar suggests that societies, too, can become emotionally bankrupt—and that this is precisely what we have been witnessing in Western societies during the 20th and 21st centuries. Income levels may be higher, but so, too, are rates of major depression (pp. 57–60).

SETTING GOALS

In chapter 5, titled "Setting Goals," Ben-Shahar notes that goal setting (the goal of winning the squash championship) first put him on the path to seek the nature of happiness. At first, his experience of unhappiness after achieving his goal of winning the squash championship caused him to think that goal setting was the problem (that, in other words, one needs to let go of goals to achieve happiness). But, in time, his views changed, and he now sees setting goals, the right kind of goals, as essential to happiness (p. 65).

He begins his discussion of setting goals by observing a relationship between goals and success. He notes that having clear objectives and time lines instigates active movement toward the goal and ultimately the achievement of it, and that declaring that one will achieve a certain goal can have remarkable power in this regard. When, for example, Thomas Edison declared that he would showcase the light bulb on December 31, 1879, none of his attempts to create a light bulb had been successful. Yet, at the end of the year, he presented the light bulb as promised and on schedule. Words, Ben-Shahar notes, have power because they inspire commitment (pp. 66–67).

While the relationship between goals and success seems reasonably clear and convincing, the relationship between goals and happiness is less so. As noted in other chapters in this book, empirical research indicates that individuals tend to maintain a certain level of happiness. Despite certain emotional peaks and valleys (after winning the lottery or becoming paraplegic), people tend to return to their previous states of happiness. This means that we need not be all that concerned about the failures and misfortunes that befall us, but it also means that our successes and fortunes won't last forever either. However, there is another way to think about goals. The point of goals should not be achieving them, but, rather, *pursuing* them—and the goals that we set for ourselves should be consistent with our values and with what gives us pleasure and meaning (pp. 68–72).

Ben-Shahar also suggests that our goals should be self-concordant. Goals like making a lot of money and gaining prestige are usually based on extrinsic rather than intrinsic factors, such as social pressure. In contrast, self-concordant goals are based on intrinsic factors and are therefore idiosyncratic. Identifying self-concordant goals for oneself is difficult because it involves introspection and honesty about what one really desires and finds pleasurable in contrast to what others tell us we should desire and experience as pleasurable. To be sure, money and prestige can be related to self-concordant goals. If an author loves writing and also becomes a best-selling author, there would not seem to be any incongruence here. The problem is when we sacrifice our self-concordant goals for the sake of money or prestige. When this happens, we sacrifice meaning and pleasure in our daily lives for extrinsic goals that, ironically, will not benefit us much in terms of our happiness even if we attain them. In the final analysis, achievement is important but not primary; the primary factor is commitment to self-concordant goals (pp. 72–75).

HAPPINESS IN EDUCATION

In chapter 6 titled "Happiness in Education"—the first of three chapters in part 2 on "Happiness Applied"—Ben-Shahar cites Mark Van Doren's claim that "Our best chance for happiness is education" (quoted in Ben-Shahar 2007, p. 83). But then he points out that education is often a cause for *unhappiness*! He cites his brother's experience as a case in point. His brother loved psychology and would read about it on his own. But this changed when he decided to study psychology in college—then he began to dislike it. Why? Ben-Shahar thinks that it was because his brother had to do certain assignments in his psychology classes. They were often time consuming and difficult, so, when he was finished with them, he experienced relief, the kind of relief one experiences when coming up for a breath of fresh air after being underwater for a considerable amount of time. He calls this the drowning model of education: the relief we feel after a completing a trying task. This relief is sometimes equated with happiness, and education—the stressor—is sometimes equated with unhappiness (p. 83).

Another model of education is the love-making model. Here the relief after completing a task is not so much a breath of fresh air—"I'm glad that's over!"—but, rather, a climax, something like an orgasm. In this model, education is like foreplay, and when one comes to an important insight or solves a problem, this is like an orgasm. But education itself, like foreplay, is also pleasurable, not just the solution or climax. The key for finding happiness in education is to seek meaning and pleasure in the work itself, not simply in the completion of the work. Love of learning should be emphasized, not achievements or grades (pp. 83–86).

What kinds of learning activities are likely to yield pleasure and meaning? Like many other contemporary writers on happiness, Ben-Shahar draws on Mihaly Csikszentmihalyi's concept of "flow" to spell out what these activities might look like. According to Csikszentmihalyi, flow is a state in which one is immersed in an experience that is rewarding and we feel that action and awareness converge. States of flow are when we are at our best, when peak experience and peak performance merge. If we are underworked, we are bored; if we are overworked, we are anxious—flow finds the right balance between the poles of task difficulty and our skill level. Therefore, in order for education to be pleasurable and meaningful, educators need to be able to provide the conditions for the state of flow (pp. 86–89). Ben-Shahar notes that Csikszentmihalyi's research shows that 12-year-old children make a clear distinction between work and play, and that children view their education as work. Perceiving education as work largely prevents students from enjoying their education because there seems to be a bias or prejudice against work in Western cultures. He thinks that this prejudice is a part of our Western psyche, our cultural constitution, as it were, and he cites the story of Adam and Eve as an example of this bias against work. When Adam and Eve were in the Garden of Eden, they lived a life of luxury and of leisure—all their desires were fulfilled, and no work was necessary. But when they were banished from the Garden, their punishment was work. Work, sin, duty, punishment—these concepts all came to be mingled together in the Western psyche. Ben-Shahar finds evidence of this constellation of concepts today. In one research study, for example, respondents reported that they are happier during times of leisure than during times of work, but they also reported that they had more flow experiences at work. If flow is related to happiness, it is work—not leisure—that leads to happiness, though we often think (and report) otherwise. He takes this to mean that work, including schoolwork, should therefore be reframed as a privilege rather than as a duty, because work holds some of the greatest potential for happiness that we have available (pp. 91–93).

Ben-Shahar believes that education should not be about inculcating basic skills but about cultivating curiosity. Children are naturally curious—they want to learn—but education often takes the excitement out of what should play into their natural questioning and growing (p. 94).

HAPPINESS IN THE WORKPLACE

Ben-Shahar begins chapter 7, titled "Happiness in the Workplace," with an account of his conversation with a young lawyer who had been working hard and was about to be made partner in his law firm. The young man seemed to have it all: a beautiful apartment overlooking Central Park, a new BMW paid for in cash, and he seemed to want for nothing as far as his financial situation was concerned. Yet he was unhappy. His work seemed to be one chore after another for 60 or more hours a week. When Ben-Shahar asked him what kind of work he would enjoy, he replied that he would like to work in an art gallery but had decided not to pursue this line of work because he wanted a more lucrative profession (p. 97).

Ben-Shahar suggests that we should ask ourselves (1) whether we are happy at work, and (2) what would make us happier. He also suggests that to the extent possible bosses and supervisors should help their supervisees achieve a sense of flow at work. He gives three practical tips in this regard: (1) assignments should allow employees to express their talents and skills; (2) whole tasks, rather than partial tasks, should be given to workers when possible, so that they can see the fruits of their labor; and (3) employees should be able to recognize why their work matters—that is, how it helps others (pp. 98–99).

But he also points out that, for many workers, their bosses make no effort to help make their work meaningful. So, in the end, this task falls on workers themselves. He also notes that some work, to some people, cannot be reframed so as to be made meaningful in any way. In such cases, he recommends finding a new line of work. He realizes that sometimes people have to compromise happiness for the sake of material needs, but he thinks we often and needlessly sacrifice pleasure and meaning in our work life (p. 100).

In his judgment, individuals should, if possible, follow what they are passionate about in their work. As Abraham Maslow once noted, one of the most fortunate things that can happen to a person is "to be paid for doing that which he passionately loves to do" (quoted in Ben-Shahar 2007, p. 101). Also, as psychologist Amy Wrzesniewski and her colleagues have noted, persons can experience their work as a job, which is mainly perceived as a chore (the focus being financial rewards rather than personal fulfillment); a career, which is pursued for motivations such as money, prestige, and power; or a calling, which is pursued not for prestige or any other extrinsic factor but, rather, because one is passionate about the nature of the work itself. Many individuals, following the advice of career counselors, pursue what they do well rather than what they really want to do. Ideally, work should be related to what gives us meaning and pleasure as well as being something we can do well (pp. 101–105).

There are, of course, times when, due to financial constraints, persons do not have the luxury of pursuing work that would give them meaning and pleasure as well as draw on their strengths. But, even in these cases, it is often possible to view (or reframe) one's work as meaningful. One can imagine, for example, that being a medical doctor would afford a sense of meaning while being a hospital custodian would not. Yet many physicians see their work as a chore, and a study of hospital custodians found that while some custodians viewed their work as a chore, others found it engaging. This study found that the latter sometimes learn to craft their work in ways that make it meaningful to them. The upshot is that even if we do not have complete autonomy in pursuing the kind of work that we would like to, we do have autonomy in crafting the work that we currently have, and this may make all the difference in terms of experiencing one's work as meaningful and pleasurable (pp. 105–107).

HAPPINESS IN RELATIONSHIPS

Chapter 8 titled "Happiness in Relationships" begins with a discussion of the research findings of Ed Diener and Martin Seligman (2002) indicating that the difference between "happy people" and "very happy people" had to do with the quality of their relationships. "Quality," however, is a rather vague term, so Ben-Shahar seeks to identify its essential characteristics. One is *unconditional love*. Returning to the squash national championship, he notes that in a conversation with his mother, he mentioned that he wanted to meet a girl who would love him for "who he is" and not simply because he had won the national championship. But his mother replied: "Your being the national champion *is* a reflection of who you are." It revealed, for example, his passion and dedication. Later he came to see that she was right, that external factors can highlight, or make manifest, internal characteristics (pp. 111–113).

What, then, does unconditional love mean? Does it mean that we love someone for no reason? He is skeptical of this point of view. While emotions are a strong part of love, lasting love must also have a rational basis. We love others for many reasons, reasons that may or may not be conscious. Of course, we may also love others for superficial reasons, such as money or fame. But he thinks that we should love other persons for reasons related to the "core self" that he defines as involving our "deepest" and "most stable" characteristics. Being loved for our wealth, power, or fame is to be loved conditionally, but to be loved for our passion, our drive, and our warmth is to be loved unconditionally. Thus, to love someone unconditionally is to love their core self, regardless of external factors, which are subject to change and to circumstances beyond one's control (p. 114).

But unconditional love is not the only condition necessary for happiness in relationships. *Pleasure* and *meaning* are also necessary. As with work and education, the key to cultivating happiness in our relationships is seeking pleasure and meaning both now and in the future. This means that we should not sacrifice too much present pleasure in the relationship for the sake of the future; nor, on the other hand, should our relationships be based purely on pleasure now, for lasting relationships also need to be meaningful. Furthermore, it is absolutely essential that we do not sacrifice our core self in our relationships, as when, for example, a woman sacrifices her core self by permanently giving up work for the sake of the family. In these situations, when sacrifice is mistakenly taken for love, both partners in a relationship will become resentful. This does not, however, mean than one should not stand with one's partner during a time of need; the point, rather, is that persons need to hold onto and to express their core selves in relationships. In a very real sense, it is more important to be known than it is to be validated, because intimacy depends on sharing and knowing, not on sacrificing and accepting—and because there is always more to share, there is always more potential for deeper intimacy and more passionate relationships (pp. 115–120; Schnarch 1998).

MEDITATIONS ON HAPPINESS

Part 3 consists of seven meditations on happiness and a brief conclusion. We will not discuss these meditations in detail but simply identify the themes, topics, or issues that they address. The first meditation is on self-interest and benevolence, and it challenges the dichotomy between self-interest and benevolence. Here, Ben-Shahar notes that teaching is his calling. He does not teach out of a sense of duty; he teaches because it makes him happy. He does not agree with those who believe that if we follow our own self-interests, this will necessarily be hurtful to others. After all, self-interest and benevolence are not mutually exclusive. In fact, when we help others we often *increase* our own happiness (pp. 125–128).

The second meditation deals with what he calls "happiness boosters." He notes that there are times in one's life when one experiences "happiness droughts." What we need are temporary happiness boosters to get us by. A happiness booster is a brief activity that yields pleasure and/or meaning in the present. For example, reading for pleasure or playing golf twice a week might make a job that one dislikes, such as working in a steel mill, more tolerable. Sometimes, too, one might want to consider changing one's work, if possible. If a career change is, in fact, possible, it is usually wise to explore this change as fully as possible before making the change. If, for example, one is a teacher but wants to become a stockbroker, one can (and should) learn about the stock market and actually manage stocks in one's free time before making the change. If one enjoys free time with this activity, it is more likely that one will enjoy this work in the future (pp. 129–133).

The third meditation challenges the view that happiness is more or less stable and that there is little one can do to affect it. Although some contemporary empirical research shows that lottery winners, not so long after they win, return to their original states of happiness, there is also evidence that people can and do become happier, such as when one works through a difficult problem with a psychotherapist or when one discovers a new idea that

changes one's life forever. Also, the fact that there may be a genetic or devel-
opmental component to happiness that determines ranges of happiness does
not mean that it also determines set points with regard to happiness. So,
although one might not be able to change one's genetics and circumstances,
one can change one's practices, and, therefore, affect one's happiness level
(pp. 135–140).

The fourth meditation makes the point that the greatest threats to happiness are not external forces but, rather, internal forces. More specifically, the
idea that one is unworthy of happiness is the greatest threat to happiness.
The belief that we are not worthy of happiness has deep cultural roots in the
West. Ben-Shahar cites Sigmund Freud's ideas on aggression and the death
instinct and Thomas Hobbes's view that life is "nasty, brutish, and short" as
cultural expressions of a deep pessimism about human nature. (We could add
Augustine's doctrine of original sin and John Calvin's doctrine of total de-
pravity.) If these thinkers were right, how could human beings ever possibly
be happy? In face of these great thinkers, Ben-Shahar thinks we need to focus
on the inherent worthiness of human beings. If we don't, we are likely to ignore the good things in our midst, including life itself (pp. 141–145).

The fifth meditation involves a thought experiment. He invites his readers to imagine that they are 110 years old and that they have the chance to
travel back in time to give advice to their younger selves. He asks, "What do
you say when you meet? What advice do you give yourself?" In effect, this
exercise invites us to consider the lessons that we have *already* learned in life.
Regrettably, he notes, we have a tendency to underestimate or ignore what
we have learned in life. To support this claim, he cites the many examples of
terminally ill persons who live a richer life *after* their diagnosis because they
become aware of the many gifts of life—for example, that time is a very pre-
cious thing. In effect, their lives have changed by means of the capacities that
they always had but that, for one reason or another, had previously seemed
inadequate in making them happy (pp. 147–149).

In the sixth meditation, Ben-Shahar focuses on the importance of time, a
limited resource, to happiness. He cites his own recent experience: Writing
this book was deeply meaningful and very pleasurable for him, but when the
due date for the manuscript approached, he was traveling around the country conducting workshops and giving lectures. He was doing things that he
loves doing, but he had overcommitted himself. Citing research (Kasser and
Ahuvia 2002) suggesting that in contrast to material affluence, time affluence
(that is, having enough time to do our work and to pursue activities that are
pleasurable and meaningful to us) is a predictor of our well-being, he concludes that our happiness depends to a significant degree on knowing when
to set limits and how to protect our time (pp. 151–156).

Ben-Shahar begins the seventh meditation by praising the wonders of
the Scientific Revolution, especially as reflected in our ability to control the

material world. As a result, Western society has become less spiritual as it has emphasized the material. This focus on the material world has also led to a focus on material possessions—what we can see is what we can know, and what we can see is what has value. He wants to recapture nonmaterial goods, such as happiness, which means, practically speaking, that the questions we ask should not be which job will make us a lot of money but, rather, which job will give us the most meaning and the most pleasure. He calls this "happiness perception." From the topic of happiness perception, he moves to the topic of the happiness revolution, which he contrasts with the Marxist revolution, which was materialistic, and suggests that the Marxist revolution failed because it limited freedom. The happiness revolution is internal and it maximizes freedom. It will not be brought about by means of a bloody revolution. Instead, it will be peaceful and gradual because it will entail a cultural change of perception, creating an abundance of happiness and goodness (pp. 157–163).

In the conclusion, Ben-Shahar notes that happiness is usually not an event—it is a process. Happiness is something that we experience moment by moment by engaging in activities that give us meaning and pleasure, and the more we can do this in the various aspects of our lives, the happier we will become (pp. 165–169).

PART III

Some Questions about Happiness

CHAPTER 11

THE ARTIFICE OF HAPPINESS

The 11th book that we have chosen to review is Ronald W. Dworkin's *Artificial Happiness: The Dark Side of the New Happy Class* (2006). As noted in the introduction, Dworkin is a practicing anesthesiologist. This is the first of two books reviewed here that offer trenchant critiques of the happiness movement in the America. The book consists of 10 chapters. We will offer brief overviews of each chapter.

TOO MUCH HAPPINESS

In chapter 1, titled "Too Much Happiness," Dworkin argues that millions of Americans have become artificially happy. He suggests that many of them are being made to feel happy while the causes of their unhappiness remain unaddressed. As an example, he recalls the time when a woman asked him to prescribe Prozac for her son because he wanted to join the navy. She contended no one who was "happy" would want to join the navy. When he refused her request on the grounds that the prescription was not medically indicated, she criticized him by saying that he was not treating her son's "disease." His book is about a change in the culture of medicine—what he calls "medical ideology"—where everyday unhappiness, as opposed to clinical depression, became a disease. He charts three "treatments" that came to the fore over the past 40 years or so: obsessive exercise, alternative medicine, and psychotropic medication. All three of these treatments, he argues, contribute to the artifice of happiness (pp. 1–3).

He offers several examples of what artificial happiness looks like. John, a 35-year-old lawyer, takes Prozac to stay in a loveless marriage, a marriage that he maintains because he doesn't want to face the financial implications of divorce. John says that his wife is still a "bitch" and that he can't stand her, but, because of his medication, he doesn't care so much anymore—he is happy. Dworkin thinks that people with artificial happiness don't move forward in their lives because they do not have the motivation to do so—unhappiness provides this motivation, but it is being medicated away (pp. 3–8).

Linda, who is 42 years old, had been in a troubled marriage for many years but lacked the motivation to sue for a divorce. Then things changed when she began taking Paxil. Prior to taking Paxil, there ensued a cycle of attack, guilt, and reunion when she would fight with her husband. This cycle led to the only emotional bonding that they had. However, once she began taking Paxil, she felt no need to fight, so the minimal emotional bonding that occurred in her marriage dissolved. Also, prior to taking Paxil, she was hesitant to pursue divorce because she felt ambivalent about single parenthood and was anxious about what her financial situation would be. But once on Paxil, these cautionary behaviors dissipated, and she sought a divorce and began dating men. Because the drug affected her ability to achieve orgasm, she wanted to stop taking it, but her doctor instructed her to keep taking the drug until the divorce was settled. As Dworkin sees it, this situation is troubling because her doctor seems to be making strategic life choices for her while she herself is in, as it were, an altered state of mind (pp. 8–12).

In his view, the shift in medical practice that turned unhappiness into a disease was not the result of a grand conspiracy on the part of doctors, pharmaceutical companies, and insurance companies. Rather, it stemmed from the "realm of ideology." He suggests that this ideology has deep populist roots, and that it is based on the assumption that medicine can—and should—address every life problem. Americans, he argues, are too happy, and they are happy for the wrong reasons. If this trend continues to spread across the whole life span—medicating not only adults but also children and elders—the result could be an American nightmare (pp. 13–19).

UNHAPPINESS BECOMES AN ENGINEERING PROBLEM

In chapter 2 titled "Unhappiness Becomes an Engineering Problem" Dworkin points out that in the early part of the 20th century generalist physicians were "wise confessor types." They were weak on science but strong on doctoring. That is, they were good at listening and in dealing with the practical problems of their patients. But as the century progressed, social troubles were given over to social workers, emotional troubles to psychologists and psychiatrists, moral problems to bioethicists, and spiritual troubles to self-help groups and organizations. As a result, doctors were reduced to "engineers of the body" (pp. 21–25).

In the 1960s, various individuals and groups began to lament this change. The golden age of medicine was over, these persons and groups decried, and doctors had become plumbers of the body who were more interested in earning high salaries than in spending time with their patients. But there was no easy way to go back. It was clear that doctors couldn't just begin talking to their patients again, and, moreover, their education and their life experiences were much more narrow and specialized than the education and the life experiences of doctors from the earlier part of the century. So they simply lacked the skills to become wise confessor types even if they had wanted to. How they found a way to connect with their patients again was by treating unhappiness (pp. 25–27).

When primary care doctors began to reconnect with their patients by means of treating unhappiness, they did so by treating it as "an engineering problem," that is, as a physical problem in the brain. They did this on the basis of groundbreaking research in the 1950s that suggested an association between neurotransmitters and depression. Primary care doctors extended this association beyond depression to everyday unhappiness, though, as Dworkin notes, no empirical evidence supported this practice at the time. Where the science was weak, ideology was strong, and "neurotransmitters" became the slogan of unhappiness, signaling a new ideology in medicine where unhappiness was constituted as a disease (pp. 27–29).

Dworkin discusses the resulting war between primary care and psychiatry over the unhappiness issue. As various domains of medicine specialized during the 20th century, the turf of primary care physicians was becoming reduced to taking the blood pressure of the elderly and treating the runny noses of children. Psychotropic drugs became a tool that primary physicians could use, and unhappiness was an area that they could claim. Because of the stigma of mental illness, many patients preferred to be treated by primary care physicians rather than by psychiatrists. From 1988 to 1998, the prescription of psychotropic drugs such as Prozac tripled, from 40 million prescriptions in 1988 to 120 million in 1998, and out of these 80 million new prescriptions, nonpsychiatrists wrote 60 million of them. When these numbers came to light, psychiatrists were obviously concerned (pp. 30–38).

Initially, these numbers were often interpreted as reflecting a shortage of psychiatrists, problems with health insurance coverage, and problems with reimbursement rates. But, in time, it became clear that primary care physicians were practicing a different kind of mental health, one that did not rely on talking with the patient but solely on medication. Psychiatrists published numerous articles demonstrating how primary care physicians were ill-equipped to practice psychiatry, but, since a major point of these articles was that primary care physicians were *underdiagnosing* clinical depression, this led to *more*, not fewer, prescriptions from primary care physicians. This was especially so after the launching of Prozac, which was shown to be more effective and to have fewer side effects than the other psychotropic drugs to date. While primary care physicians were driven by idealistic motivations—they truly did want to help their patients, not simply take turf from psychiatry—in time, Dworkin contends, their idealistic motivations faded (pp. 38–47).

FROM IDEOLOGY TO INTERESTS TO SCANDAL

In chapter 3 titled "From Ideology to Interests to Scandal" Dworkin discusses the shift from idealism to ideology among primary care physicians. With the medical institutionalization of the ideology of life problems—particularly unhappiness—on the grounds that these problems involve diseases with a physical basis in the brain, primary care doctors enjoyed an expansion of their power, especially under the introduction of managed care, as they could now treat patients who would otherwise have gone to specialists (and they were encouraged to do so). Dworkin argues that while this ideology began with good intentions, the ideology, in time, transformed into something more selfish: a means of gaining power and control, most notably through the treatment of patients for unhappiness, attention deficit/hyperactivity disorder (ADHD), and pain (pp. 49–52).

Dworkin cites several studies from the MacArthur Foundation Initiative on Depression and Primary Care to support his assertions. In one study, it was found that a primary care physician would prescribe antidepressants to "convince" his patients that they were in fact depressed. In another study, trained actors would visit primary care physicians, all presenting with the same concerns: 10-pound weight gain, sadness, and a recent divorce. Over half of these actors were prescribed antidepressants after a 16-minute interview. Since standard checklists for depression take 8 minutes, he suspects that primary care physicians were attempting to treat unhappiness simply by prescribing medications and without addressing the psychosocial concerns of their patients (pp. 52–54).

Another turf battle involved ADHD. This disease was first observed in 1902 by George Still, and, over the course of the century, it has been called various names: a defect in moral control, minimal brain damage, minimal brain dysfunction, and ADHD. Psychiatrists and neurologists fought over this turf, but when neurologists were unable to produce any physical basis for the disease in the brain by means of their brain scanners, psychiatrists won the day. That is, it was thought, by default, to be a behavioral, not a neurological, problem. But then primary care physicians, based on inference, suggested that ADHD had to be a brain problem, just as unhappiness is a brain problem, and they began prescribing Ritalin, the drug of choice for ADHD. Like unhappiness, attention deficit was now an engineering problem (pp. 56–57).

To be sure, Dworkin is not suggesting that ADHD is not a disease; nor is he suggesting that depression is not a disease. Rather, he is claiming that ADHD is overtreated and that primary care physicians had (and have) political reasons for overtreating it. The numbers, he suggests, simply bear this out. In the late 1980s, about 800,000 American children were being treated for ADHD. In 1995, this number rose to 1.5 million, and by 1999, it rose to 5 million. In light of the fact that Ritalin has existed for decades, he associates the rise in prescribing it with the implementation of managed care. Primary care physicians had the most to gain from this scenario, and, in point of fact, they fill 75 percent of the prescriptions for Ritalin (pp. 58–59).

He points out similar dynamics with the treatment of pain—his own turf as an anesthesiologist. Here, primary care physicians won yet another victory. But, in time, groups of physicians would become dissatisfied with the psychotropic approach to treating unhappiness, and thus a new phase of combating unhappiness was born: alternative medicine (pp. 59–63).

THE REVOLT OF THE ENGINEERS

In chapter 4, titled "The Revolt of the Engineers," Dworkin discusses the second force contributing to artificial unhappiness: alternative medicine. He begins his discussion by recounting the history of placebos. He notes that, for centuries, placebos were viewed in a pejorative light, as they were seen to be deceptive. However, during World War II, an anesthesiologist named Henry Beecher discovered that soldiers who had severe injuries could be effectively treated with placebos. One day, when he ran short of pain medication to treat the wounded, he decided to try an experiment. He gave his patients a placebo injection (saltwater) and told them that they had received pain medication. To his surprise, the patients were able to tolerate their needed operations as though they had received morphine. He attributed this to the psychology of the situation: the soldiers were relieved that they were out of harm's way, and this, combined with the placebo, reduced their pain (pp. 65–67).

Dworkin notes that a small group of primary care physicians applied Beecher's discovery to general medicine during the 1980s. These physicians proposed that happiness can be used to help fight disease in the same way that it helps wounded soldiers fight pain. In this view, unhappiness was not so much a disease as a risk factor. Nevertheless, unhappiness was something to be treated, and, shortly after this, primary care physicians began to embrace alternative medicine for similar reasons. Dworkin suggests that doctors turned to alternative medicine in the 1980s because their work as primary care physicians became boring. They longed for the days when they could connect with their patients, a desire or need that treating unhappiness with psychotropic drugs was unable to fulfill. By embracing alternative medicine, they were able to practice the kind of medicine that they dreamed about when they first decided to go to medical school. It took time, of course, for alternative medicine to be incorporated within mainstream medicine, and there was disagreement over whether alternative medicine functioned as a placebo or in some more spiritual way. But, in time, hospital administrators brought alternative medicine into the fold after they had discovered how much the public was willing to spend on it (pp. 66–69).

A couple of name changes reflected this incorporation: "alternative medicine" became "complementary medicine," which then became "integrative medicine." Journals were created, textbooks were written, a major office was established at the National Institutes of Health, and a scientific theory gained some traction to support this movement: psychoneuroimmunology. This theory basically held that psychological factors (psycho) could influence the brain (neuro) in such a way that the immune system could be affected (immunology). With the rise of psychoneuroimmunology (or PNI), doctors came to believe that happiness, even if a placebo, could be good for health. Dworkin points out that although psychoneuroimmunology remained a theory, it seemed intuitively right to doctors (pp. 69–88).

Dworkin suggests that the first wave of physicians who turned to alternative medicine did so for noble reasons; specifically, they did so out of a desire to recover more personal ways of doctoring. But subsequent waves of physicians did so for instrumental reasons; that is, they used alternative medicine as a technique to treat unhappiness. As it was first practiced, alternative medicine lost money because doctors spent too much time on their patients. But as it became institutionalized, it fit within the standard 20-minute patient consultation for traditional medicine. Prescribing meditation became a way to treat unhappiness in an analogous way to prescribing Prozac—a noble intention was transformed into an ideology, and money and politics continued to infect medical practice (pp. 77–95).

Dworkin thinks that the problem with alternative medicine and with the theory of psychoneuroimmunology is that the idea that everyday unhappiness is bad for your health inculcates fear in patients and drives them into medical care. Moreover, as with the practice of medicating unhappiness with psychotropic drugs, so with alternative medicine: people are not dealing with their psychosocial and moral problems. Rather, they are looking for (and finding) ways to detach from life and from the ways in which they might achieve "real," not "artificial," happiness (pp. 95–102).

ENGINEERING FOR THE MASSES

In chapter 5 titled "Engineering for the Masses" Dworkin discusses physical exercise as the third component of artificial happiness. In the 1960s, physical exercise was shown to have beneficial effects with regard to heart trouble—this, Dworkin notes, was science. But when in the 1980s physicians began to speak about endorphins and how exercise could treat unhappiness, this, in his view, was ideology. But, in any case, the tide was shifting, and the American public wanted to be able to take their health into their own hands, and exercise was one way to do it. Increasingly dissatisfied with passively taking pills and more frequently hearing testimony about "runner's high," they wanted to believe in exercise in an almost religious fashion, and exercise became, as it were, an expression of free will. Working out was a form of salvation by works. Embracing endorphin theory, primary care physicians began to endorse exercise, despite the fact that this theory is highly questionable. However, it was attractive to them because it offered biochemical explanations for the pleasurable effects of vigorous exercises such as running marathons, and this made their advice appear more scientific than the lessons from a high school gym teacher (pp. 104–112).

In 1979, the Surgeon General's office recommended exercise as preventive medicine. In 1984, however, only 15 percent of American physicians recommended that their patients exercise. This was because in the late 1970s and in the 1980s, a rigid division existed between preventive medicine and curative medicine. Preventive medicine was the domain of public health professionals, while curative medicine was the domain of medical doctors. It was considered rude and a form of moralizing for doctors to make recommendations about the private lives of their patients and their personal habits. But the false dichotomy between preventing and curing began to crumble when unhappiness became a disease and when exercise became recommended as a treatment for depression. Exercise was considered not only preventive but also curative, and doctors began to view health in moralizing terms (pp. 112–122).

Dworkin's critique is primarily of fitness culture, where people overexercise not for the sake of health but for the sake of happiness. In his view, this is "artificial" happiness. He cites the case of Jim Scott, a 40-year-old hospital orderly. Scott dislikes his job and finds very little meaning in it. There is no change and no hope of advancement; he has no goals with regard to work. But he does find happiness in the gym, for here he has goals, and, moreover, he can chart his progress. He is also proud of how he looks, as his bodily appearance is a direct result of his exercise. In Dworkin's view, however, success in the gym does not correlate with "real" success in "real life." Success in real life, Dworkin notes, is measured by income, fame, and power. He notes that fitness culture gained a newfound respect when doctors blessed it with moral authority. In this moral culture, when fat people die, Dworkin observes, they are also "damned," but, in contrast, when thin people die, their death is experienced as though it were, to use a theological term, a theodicy (pp. 122–130).

HAPPINESS HITS THE ASSEMBLY LINE

In chapter 6, titled "Happiness Hits the Assembly Line," Dworkin contextualizes his consideration of artificial happiness with a discussion of the rise of managed care. He argues that the rise of managed care was not only a cultural event but also a business event. As the costs of health care in the second half of the 20th century skyrocketed, small businesses could no longer afford to offer benefits to their employees. Managed care executives entered into this situation with their own interests in mind, but they also appealed to the desires of the American people. They did so by appearing sincere and democratic (in contrast to doctors who were perceived as being greedy and elitist). Americans wanted to live longer and to live healthier lives, and managed care executives adeptly responded to Americans' fears of missing out on health, longevity, and happiness by offering these hopes at an affordable cost (pp. 131–135).

The project of managed care was to make health care more affordable. And this, of course, meant cutting costs where possible. One way of doing so involved reducing the number of patient referrals to specialists. This, in effect, meant that primary care doctors gained a great deal of power with the implementation of managed care, especially at the expense of psychiatrists, because psychiatrists had no specialized procedure. In other words, primary care physicians could offer pills just as easily as psychiatrists. The result is that less than a third of all mentally ill persons in America are treated by psychiatrists. *The Quick Reference Guide for Clinicians* encouraged primary care physicians to treat their patients having symptoms of depression with two rounds of antidepressants before making a referral to a psychiatrist. As Dworkin points out, a significant number of misdiagnoses and false positives of depression are likely to occur when primary care physicians practice psychiatry, as it were, without a license (pp. 135–143).

Cutting costs also meant standardizing health care. Time with patients had to become quantified and more routine, and doctors had to see more patients to keep their practice profitable. And this inevitably led to unhappiness being treated as a biochemical problem that could be addressed with the right pills, whatever the patient's life circumstances might happen to be. Unhappiness was treated the way Henry Ford built cars: on the assembly line with formalized procedures and tight schedules (pp. 140–143).

MEDICINE AND RELIGION

In chapters 7–9, Dworkin focuses on the battles between medicine and religion. In all three chapters, he notes that he is talking about two heterogeneous groups: "doctors" and "religious people." He realizes that he may be misrepresenting any given person in either group, but that by talking about groups of people rather than individuals, his discussion is grounded in the type of work that sociologists do. In any case, while primary care doctors won the day with regard to unhappiness in competition with specialists such as psychiatrists, they still had to compete with organized religion, which had its own approach to dealing with unhappiness. The first step in winning this battle was to define life in medical terms, which enabled doctors to take control of the body (pp. 153–160).

Chapter 7, titled "More Revolution," focuses on the question of when life begins and ends. The chapter itself begins with abortion and concludes with physician-assisted suicide. Abortion was legalized in the United States in 1973, but none of the major scientific journals at the time commented on the moral significance of this decision. But this changed dramatically over the next 20 years. When the debates about cloning and embryonic stem cell research emerged, physicians and scientists had a lot to say—*against* religion. They argued that life does not begin at conception but when one has the ability of consciousness, for it is then that one can experience happiness and unhappiness, as well as pleasure and pain. And, with regard to abortion, because women can experience unhappiness and pain while a fetus in the first trimester cannot, their interests outweigh the interests of the fetus, which, in this view, is non-life. The same logic applies to a person who has experienced brain death (pp. 155–183).

What is striking about Dworkin's analysis is that he connects the question of when life begins—a question central to abortion, cloning, and embryonic stem cell research—to the question of happiness. In his view, doctors won the battle for life in part because religious people dug their own grave by embracing happiness as a goal of life. He cites a 19th-century preacher who proclaimed that the goal of life is not in gaining happiness but in passing God's test. However, in time, religious leaders changed their tune and embraced happiness as a life goal. During the 1950s and 1960s, religion joined forces with medicine in embracing happiness. Dworkin cites Norman Vincent Peale's *The Power of Positive Thinking* (1952), Billy Graham's *The Secret of Happiness* (1954), and Bishop Fulton Sheen's *Way to Happiness* (1954) as key texts in this regard.[1] But, in time, medicine would prove, or at least offer observable evidence, that it does a better job than religion. Religion had become, as it were, instrumental. By the time the competition between religion and psychology was apparent, it was too late, because by then, the war between religion and "real" medicine was already underway. Because neither religion nor psychotherapy could fix unhappiness, primary care doctors, with their psychotropic drugs, won the day (pp. 160–185).

In chapter 8, titled "The Plight of Sir John Eccles," Dworkin tells the story of how physicians and scientists won control over the mind by focusing on Sir John Eccles, winner of the Nobel Prize in Medicine for his work in the 1940s and 1950s on the motor neurons of cats. During the second half of the 20th century, Eccles championed a cause called "dualism." As Dworkin uses the term, dualism refers to the mind–body (or mind–brain) problem. The question is: Where does mind come from? Is mind only a product of the brain, meaning that the brain is primary? Or is it that the mind is primary, and that it controls the brain and the body? (pp. 187–188).

How is this debate related to happiness? The question of dualism intersects with the history of artificial happiness by asking whether happiness is related to the mind (and, therefore, to moral and spiritual concerns) or related to the brain (and, therefore, to neurological and psychiatric concerns). Dworkin notes that the medical profession itself was divided over the relevance of the mind. While neurology dealt with the brain, and psychiatry dealt with the mind, both were monistic in practice, assuming that brain has priority over mind. In contrast, religious people contended that unhappiness was a religious problem, not something to be fixed by attending to neurotransmitters but, rather, by attending to one's relationship to God. Thus, the question of the mind–brain problem involves happiness because, if only the brain matters, then only brain solutions to problems such as unhappiness matter (pp. 187–190).

Dualists and monists debated for decades. The problem with the dualist position is that it simply seemed irrational and antiscientific, and there was no satisfying way of squaring dualism with evolution and physics. But the problem with monism is that it was an uncomfortable existential reduction of human beings to molecules: If the mind has no influence, how can human beings have free will? And is the self only an illusion? (pp. 191–205).

This stalemate concluded in the 1980s when the idea of "emergent materialism" arose. This position holds that the mind-brain is a "biosystem" in which consciousness emerges from "special cellular systems," and the brain enjoys physical properties that no one cell has alone—the whole, in other words, is greater than the sum of its parts. On this view, it is possible to say that people have free will; that the self exists; that human beings really are different from other animals because we have minds; and that evolutionary theory, rather than viewing life from a reductionist perspective, suggests that human life is becoming *more* complex. This view was both scientifically plausible and emotionally satisfying, and, with this development in the mind–body debate, the medical profession now had control of not only the body but also the mind. The final battle would be for the spirit (pp. 198–210).

In chapter 9, titled "The Last Battle," Dworkin focuses on the life of the spirit, or what is commonly called "spirituality." Here, he argues that medicine won this battle by redefining spirituality, thereby taking control of it. He observes a split occurring between religion and spirituality in America emerging in the 1990s, when people began to describe themselves as "spiritual but not religious" (cf. Fuller 2001). This new sentiment reflected a distrust of organized religion and a disavowal of religious ideas or beliefs in favor of religious experience. He asserts that medicine had a great deal of influence in fostering this split, because in order for medicine to take control of spirituality, spirituality had to be defined in terms of feelings that, unlike ideas or beliefs, can be measured by means of brain scans (pp. 211–212).

How did medicine assert its influence over the definition of spirituality? This was not some kind of shrewd conspiracy among doctors, but, rather, merely a pressing of their monist or materialist worldview to its logical conclusions. Two factors weighed heavily here: (1) neuroscientists came to recognize the importance of culture and experience on neural activity, thereby reintroducing the possibility of the significance of religious experience; and (2) from the 1980s onward, the data became overwhelming in pointing to a positive association between religion and health. Doctors didn't know how religion made people healthier, but they observed that it did somehow, so, instead of fighting religion, they embraced it (pp. 212–220).

Religious people now found themselves among friends when interacting with scientists, but, in Dworkin's view, they gave up too much ground in letting spirituality become defined as a feeling and in allowing religion to be explained in terms of evolutionary biology. If religion is allowed to be explained in terms of evolutionary biology, then religion is no different from keen eyesight or superior strength in a given animal. There was a shift from belief in the existence of God to belief in the experience of God as something evolutionarily beneficial, and the latter degraded religion by making it instrumental and by bracketing its truth claims. In his view, religious persons who wanted to be respected by scientists had made a grave error (pp. 220–225).

He also thinks it is simply a mistake to disconnect spirituality from religion, and that this error is directly related to artificial happiness. For him, spirituality is an idea that connects human beings to God and to the infinite, and this connection also explains and details one's moral obligations. He contends that if one believes that one should love one's neighbors as one loves oneself and conducts oneself that way, then that person is spiritual. Thus, for him, spirituality is about believing certain things and behaving in a certain way—not in feeling certain things. By redefining spirituality as a feeling, clergy lose their relevance. People can meditate at home or on the golf course, or they can take drugs to experience spirituality. With their victory over spirituality (i.e., by separating it from religion), doctors gained control over the body, the mind, and the spirit—all in the name of happiness (pp. 225–235).

THE HAPPY AMERICAN

Dworkin's book is mostly concerned with describing what he means by artificial happiness and exploring the role that doctors have played in advocating it. But in chapter 10 titled "The Happy American" he describes the lives of people who are "artificially happy." Here, he focuses on interviews and conversations with various people, some personal friends among them. Most of these stories involve a description of a person's problems and what he thinks they should do in order to take steps to fix their lives.

For example, he opens the chapter by discussing the case of his childhood friend Kevin Grimm. When Kevin was a teenager, he worked as a manager at a local McDonald's and had the "luxury" of supervising a lot of young women. He tried college for a little while but dropped out because he missed the life of working in a restaurant. However, in his mid-20s he began to regret this decision because he saw that all of his friends were moving on with their lives, so he changed jobs to work at a department store. By his mid-30s, when most of his friends had established themselves in successful careers, he began to regret the course he had taken, and he would express this regret openly. He viewed himself as "a failure" and "a nobody." And he was unhappy and afraid. When he went to Dworkin for help, Dworkin tried to joke him out of his misery, but, in so doing, Dworkin also tried to respect the gravity of Kevin's situation. So he told Kevin that a man can't call himself a failure until he's at least 50 and that he still could succeed in life. He encouraged Kevin to go back to college and to consider going to nursing school. Instead of taking Dworkin's advice, he went to his primary care physician because he was unhappy. The doctor gave him a diagnosis of depression and prescribed a psychotropic medication. And while the drug improved Kevin's spirits, Dworkin recalls that it also turned off "the alarms" inside his mind, so rather than plan seriously for his future, he submitted to circumstances. In the end, he never sent in his college applications. In Dworkin's view, medication had robbed Kevin of his unhappiness at the moment he needed it most, because it would have acted as an incentive for Kevin to make a life change. Dworkin concludes this vignette by noting that Kevin died "young, angry, and afraid," though he does not indicate the cause of death. In any case, Dworkin seems to be intimating that psychotropic drugs were somehow responsible for his death, and the reader is left to wonder if Kevin committed suicide (pp. 237–239).

He presents a number of cases in this chapter, most of which deal with artificial happiness and psychotropic drugs. Also, in a more limited way, he considers artificial happiness in overexercising. In all of these cases, his critique is consistently that artificial happiness, no matter what form it takes, diverts people from addressing their life problems in a clear and direct way, and that medicine has sanctioned this diversion with its separation of happiness and life with the authority of science (pp. 251–253).

He also presents a substantial amount of commentary on how he thinks artificial happiness is affecting Americans across the whole span of life. The basic structure of his argument is the same here as well: people become locked into the life stage in which they became consumers of artificial happiness. Viewing the population as a whole, he sketches out what the Happy

Child, the Happy Adult, and the Happy Senior will look like if artificial happiness continues to spread. The very fact that more teenagers and more seniors are taking psychotropic drugs than in previous decades gives his cautionary tale considerable plausibility (pp. 254–277).

Where is all of this leading? Dworkin thinks that life, inevitably, breaks through artificial happiness, and when life is found to have been inauthentically lived, the end result will be despair, and people will yet again turn to their doctors—this time not for artificial happiness but for physician-assisted suicide. This, he believes, is the end result of believing that the purpose of life is happiness—a dark prophecy from a doctor who specializes in numbing people and putting them to sleep (p. 277).

CONCLUSION

In the final chapter of *Artificial Happiness*, titled "Conclusion," Dworkin ends on a personal note. He notes that he decided to become an anesthesiologist when he was 24 years old. At the time, this specialty seemed "macho" to him. It also seemed like the most scientific, or "the most engineering," of all the specialties, which, he believed, would allow him to keep his intellectual life alive. He discovered along the way that one could keep the world of ideas alive within a life devoted to medicine, and this book is the result of this discovery. What better question to tackle than the question of happiness—the central question, according to many, of life—in order to keep the life of ideas alive? (pp. 279–281).

What are the central lessons of this book? Dworkin hopes his readers are convinced that artificial happiness is a genuine problem. But he also notes that the solution to this problem should not be to combat *overmedication* with *undermedication*. This would do great harm to the persons who really do need medication to reduce their suffering. He simply wants doctors to think twice before they prescribe a psychotropic drug or a technique in integrative medicine. Thus, doctors are the primary audience for this book (pp. 281–282).

But the book has lessons for others as well. One group is medical educators. He envisions a transformation of medical education, much like the one that took place a century ago on account of the Flexner Report. The Flexner Report raised the bar for the standards of medical education, as it instituted the basic model of two years of basic science and two years of clinical education for medical students. The end result was the creation of "physician-engineers," doctors who became heavy on the sciences but light on the arts. Dworkin thinks that this needs to be corrected. Specialists should still be educated heavily in the sciences, but primary care physicians, he thinks, should be educated to become "wise generalists," with a third of their education being devoted to non-biomedical topics. Why? When unhappy people go to their doctors, these wise generalists could talk to them about their problems rather than simply medicating them (pp. 282–286).

Another group is religious leaders. They should resist the temptation of offering happiness to their flocks because this leads to the instrumental use of religion. They should help their flocks to become intrinsically, rather than extrinsically, religious, and they should not sugarcoat the fact that "Lasting happiness is a pipe dream" (p. 287). In his view, the question of life is: "How should one live?" The problem of artificial happiness is that it offers ways of being happy that are disconnected from how one should live (pp. 286–293).

He does not offer a vision of how one should live, but he suggests that the place to turn is not to doctors and to neurotransmitters but, rather, to the local bookstore. For a small amount of money, one can buy all of the world's wisdom, and read it in about a month. One can then apply this knowledge to one's life, modify one's behavior, and live according to the requirements of one's conscience—without drugs, without yoga, without running marathons, and without neurotransmitters. That one can do this without any of these devices points to the fact that artificial happiness is not only unnecessary but that it stands in the way of the realization of real happiness (pp. 292–293).

CHAPTER 12

AGAINST HAPPINESS

The 12th book we have chosen to review is Eric G. Wilson's *Against Happiness: In Praise of Melancholy* (2008). As noted in the introduction, Wilson is an English professor at Wake Forest University. The book consists of an introduction, a conclusion, and four chapters. The introduction presents the basic argument of the book, which is that the current emphasis on happiness at the expense of sadness poses a very serious danger for Americans, not only individually but also collectively (p. 6).

Wilson begins the introduction with a reflection on the "ominous times" in which we live—major oceanic flooding, destruction of the natural environment, a new cold war, and the renewed threat of nuclear warheads—and then adds another threat that is potentially the most dangerous of all: that we are on the verge of eliminating melancholia, which has been a major cultural inspiration for invention and innovation in the arts and the sciences (p. 4).

He wonders why we are driven to eliminate sadness from our lives, and what we should make of the American obsession with happiness. Could the elimination of unhappiness be a disaster on the scale of global warming and nuclear war? He admits that these questions cut across the grain of what most Americans report about themselves, noting that a recent poll by the Pew Research Center shows that about 85 percent of Americans say that they are either "very happy" or "happy." He also suggests that psychologists seem to be obsessed with Positive Psychology these days, and that the happiness industry has hit it big in popular culture as well, selling thousands of books. How can this be? How can people be happy when the world faces so many threats and perils: political, environmental, and economic disasters, personal and family problems, and so forth? Given these realities, can people really be as happy as they say they are? Wilson is especially critical of what he considers the overemphasis on happiness at the expense of sadness. Why? Because he believes that in order to live a full life, one must experience both happiness and sadness (pp. 4–6).

He wants to make clear that he is writing about this specific form of American happiness, and that he is not discounting joy per se. Nor does he wish to romanticize clinical depression. He knows that depression takes millions of lives every year. But, like Dworkin, he is concerned that persons experiencing melancholia (i.e., unhappiness) are taking medications intended for the clinically depressed. He acknowledges that there is a fine line between what he is calling melancholia and what society calls depression, but there is an important difference between the two. Both forms involve chronic sadness and ongoing unease, but depression leads to apathy whereas melancholia leads to activity and often creativity. The problem is that our culture confuses the two (pp. 7–9).[1]

THE AMERICAN DREAM

In chapter 1, titled "The American Dream," Wilson focuses on the relation between the American dream and the importance that Americans continue to attach to happiness as a life goal and as an expectation for the country as a whole. The first half of the chapter presents the "happy visions" of William Bradford (a leader of the first pilgrims to reach American shores) and Benjamin Franklin. The second half presents the melancholy countertradition of Herman Melville and Bruce Springsteen.

Wilson argues that our susceptibility to the appeal of happiness can be traced back to the first pilgrims and, more specifically, to the fact that even though happiness was not waiting to greet William Bradford and his fellow passengers when they reached Cape Cod, they nonetheless persisted in their optimistic hopes, hopes that they could find happiness by creating a religious utopia in the New World that was unavailable in the Old World (pp. 10–12). Later, Benjamin Franklin articulated the 18th century ideal of achieving financial security. In Wilson's view, his influence pervades the language of the Declaration of Independence, a document that declares our inalienable right to "life, liberty, and the pursuit of happiness," a phrase that, in effect, takes liberties with John Locke's declaration in his *Second Treatise of Civil Government* (1986, first published in 1690), which claims that everyone has the right to "life, liberty, and property." Wilson suggests that this connection between property (and, therefore, wealth) and the pursuit of happiness confirms what Franklin exemplified throughout his life, namely, that happiness is realized through material acquisition (pp. 10–15).

Wilson contends that the capitalist Franklin is not much different from the Puritan Bradford, for both overlooked the insecurity of the wilderness for the security of possession. This vision, he suggests, leads one to view the world through a narcissistic lens: the world becomes something to possess as a means to achieve security. The Puritans possessed land to create a land of religious freedom, whereas the capitalists possessed a savings plan to create a land of plenty. But the world, in fact, is much more insecure than either of these strategies assume (pp. 14–15).

Turning to contemporary influences, Wilson notes that our current technologies make it easy to escape from the world. Our digital age enables us to live in "virtual reality," and our medical technologies ensure that we receive "artificial health." Furthermore, our sacred institutions—our universities, churches, and political systems—are becoming "happiness schools." In universities, for example, the liberal arts education, which once emphasized the intrinsic value of education, is now, more or less, a precursor to trade. The serious writings of Herman Melville and Friedrich Nietzsche become the butt of quips and jokes; the science of economics is reduced to superficial notions of supply and demand ("I need a BMW to be happy and I will, therefore, work to get one"); and psychology has become shallow and superficial, reduced to the study of character types. As for the other sacred institutions, churches are in the business of helping people feel good, and politics has become entertainment (pp. 15–21).

In his view, the American quest for happiness is much more than a pastime—it has, in fact, become an obsession. But he also believes that, deep down, we really do not want happiness without sadness. We do not want a lopsided existence; we want to live full and authentic lives. The problem is that many Americans are blinded about what, in fact, leads to an authentic existence. He identifies those who are thus blinded as the "happy types." These "happy types" respond to different events in the same way: Every day is "great," every mountain view is "nice," and everyone they meet is "a character." Wilson notes that when we are around these "happy types," we long for difference and for some kind of indication that someone—some individual—is really there. No doubt these happy types simply want control over their lives, and there's nothing unique or strange about this, for we all desire control over our destiny. It's just that those who want complete happiness also want complete autonomy. He concludes that if they live their own lives at all, they do so through repression, because it is only by repression—by whatever means—that we can eradicate sadness from our lives (pp. 21–30).

The chapter concludes with a discussion of the American countertradition that exposes the superficiality of this fixation on happiness. The exemplars of this tradition, few but powerful, include Herman Melville, who teaches us that sadness reconciles us to realities, throwing us into the flow of life and locating us on the edge of experience, causing the heart to beat, throbbing between faith and doubt. It also assures the pining mind that it's fine to languish in incompleteness, and to embrace the darkness, for it is there, in this shuttered existence, that the brightest light will break through and shine forth. Sadness does not counsel quick escape but remaining in the bleakness, for out of its blankness something will come, a new insight, a fresh way of seeing and of being. Wilson also notes that Melville is not alone, for this "sullen American genius" shows up in the tormented canvases of Jackson Pollock, the nervous ebullience of Marilyn Monroe, the fevered confessions of Robert Lowell, the manic humor of Jim Carrey, the melancholy music of Bruce Springsteen, the haunted verse of Sylvia Plath, Tom Wait's guttural laments, the ruined faces of Edward Hopper, and Mark Rothko's blank squares (pp. 33–35).[2]

A MAN OF SORROWS

In chapter 2, titled "A Man of Sorrows," Wilson offers an account of his own failed effort to become a happy type, discusses conflicting images of Jesus as a happy savior and a man of sorrows, praises C. G. Jung for perceiving that Jesus's life was ultimately a parable for embracing melancholy and grasping the essential self, critiques the "optimistic Christianity" of Norman Vincent Peale and Billy Graham, laments the transformation of American cities into suburban malls and the resultant "mall mentality," and presents another exemplar of the melancholy spirit—the English writer William Blake.

In his account of his own failed effort to become a happy type, he confesses that he has purchased books on how to be happy, has tried to turn his chronic scowl into a bright smile, has attempted to become more active and less sedentary, and has pursued success in his career. But each time that he has embarked down the happy road, he has turned back because the road he was on was not the road to heaven—rather, it was the road to hell (p. 39).

He learned that his most "basic instinct" is toward melancholia, and that, if he is to be authentic, he must embrace—not repress—this truth about himself. He guesses that some of his readers have felt the same way that he does, and he remembers feeling this way from a very young age. As he grew older, he reluctantly adjusted to the demands of the daytime, but he recognizes that the darkness seems much closer to his essential nature. He forced himself to become a person of the daytime so that he could make friends and "succeed," but he knew, in some sense, that this was all a pretense. He thinks that some of his readers will be able to relate to his experience, that regardless of how happy we pretend to be, we have all undergone this struggle, this tension between our own dark feelings and "the grating call" of the bright, shiny, happy world. In time, we grow weary of the guilt we feel over our melancholy souls, and want to be left alone so that we can brood for as long as needed. To be sure, we can fly from sadness, but sadness has much to give. In fact, it is no exaggeration to say that it affords the chance to become who we are. Moreover, melancholy has the effect of depriving us from the enjoyment of a comfortable relationship to the objects or people around us. It defamiliarizes them, and when we become defamiliarized from the world around us, we are forced to look within ourselves, into the mystery of our own being (pp. 39–43).

He goes on to relate one of several experiences he has had that remind him that there is no life without death. He notes that although this motif might seem foreign to many contemporary Americans, it really shouldn't be, because it is a Christian notion (and America is believed to be a Christian nation). His reference to America as a "Christian nation" prompts a brief discussion of the popular association of Jesus with happiness. He notes that in the Christian tradition, there is a depiction and understanding of Jesus that has nothing to do with happiness but, rather, the reverse: a man of sorrows. He wonders how it happened that the "happy" Jesus became so popular, because there is little, if any, evidence for such a portrait in the Gospels. He discusses in this connection C. G. Jung's own experiences of melancholia that led to his insight that Jesus, during his crucifixion, was beset by a dark confusion and a bewildering and painful disintegration of the old self that set the stage for his transformation into a new being (pp. 47–53).

This discussion leads to a trenchant if unsurprising critique of Norman Vincent Peale, whom he describes as the promoter of a "saccharine version" of Christianity in which Jesus is more or less a successful man of this world, and of Billy Graham, who, he suggests, thinks that sorrow is a punishment for sin. He much prefers more European portraits of Jesus, such as Matthias Grünewald's *The Crucifixion* (circa 1515) and Salvador Dali's mid-20th-century *Christ of the St. John of the Cross* (pp. 50–55).

Identifying Graham and Peale as "ministers for the suburbs," he contends that suburban existence is essentially a mode of living that "puts people out of the fray," and that sequesters them from the "gorgeous turmoil" of the natural world. Viewing suburbia as a virus that originally spread to take over almost all available marshlands and forests, he notes that it has more recently invaded the cities, transforming them into suburban malls, with their smooth, blank, bland, and blinding exteriors. He suggests that it is no mere coincidence that the rise of the happy type has occurred simultaneously with the development of the "mall mentality." After all, happy types tend to put the world into "glittering boxes." Going to a mall in Erie, Pennsylvania is much the same as going to a mall in Fresno, California. He contrasts these "glittering boxes" with old, rundown buildings in the cities and towns of America that are, in his view, much more beautiful, largely because they exemplify the particular over the abstract, a preference that William Blake, a melancholy soul, challenged in his 1798 marginalia to the works of the painter Sir Joshua Reynolds (pp. 57–60).

Comparing his own living space—a 1920s house that he describes as an "old wreck of a building"—with the warm and efficient prefabricated houses in the suburbs, Wilson concludes this chapter with the observation that the happy types want glittering boxes, malls, houses in the subdivisions that all look the same, and the rough edges of life smoothed out, so that everything shines. In contrast, melancholy souls want old houses on rundown streets with large oaks. Moreover, happy types have perfect faces, perfect hair, and their clothes are all the same, while melancholy types have faces with wrinkles and gray hair, and their clothes, like their houses, are worn. When you look at happy people, you will see they are all the same—like the malls all across the country. And if you look too long, you will see that they are hollow and shallow, airbrushed like magazines (pp. 65–68).

GENERATIVE MELANCHOLIA

In chapter 3, titled "Generative Melancholia," Wilson continues his explorations into the lives of notable melancholiacs, including Marsilio Ficino, Emily Dickinson, Samuel Taylor Coleridge, and Joni Mitchell. Ficino, the 15-century philosopher, is especially relevant for our purposes here—to provide a balanced view on the subject of happiness—because he not only struggled throughout his life with fits of melancholia, but he also wondered if he could find a way to reframe his chronic melancholia in a positive way.

In the past, Ficino had attempted to get some relief from his melancholy by throwing himself into his work. But now, as he reached his 60th year, escapism was no longer working for him. He wanted to counter Western history's prevailingly negative view of melancholy, to find a positive way to interpret it. Through the good offices of his patron Cosimo de'Medici, he came upon a Greek text featuring an ancient work titled *Problems*, possibly written by Aristotle himself. Embedded in this book was the following passage: "Why is it that all those who have become eminent in philosophy or politics or poetry or the arts are clearly melancholi[a]cs?" Brooding over this passage, he saw, as it were, the light within the darkness: melancholia is a sign of grace, for melancholia is necessary for the intellectual life (pp. 69–73).

So he set about writing one of his last books, *The Book of Life*. In it, he made a case for melancholia on the grounds that it can lead to creativity. Exploring connections between inside and outside, the melancholy intellectual has special insights, because he broods over the inner and the outer worlds, and he finds his way on the borders of life, between life's many oppositions (pp. 74–75).

Wilson suggests that we find here the deep heart of melancholia, the very roots of its perseverance and its power. By pushing thinkers into a middle between two extremes and forcing a journey into a "fertile limbo," melancholia invites a vision of a third term, "a golden mean," as it were, "a synthetic element" that somehow reconciles, even if tenuously, the antagonisms that threaten to rip the universe apart. Ficino's hope was that melancholy philosophers like himself could discover this "healing idea," that they could recognize and tap into this concord between oppositions and opposing forces, knowing that body and soul, sensation and feeling, brain and consciousness are not mutually exclusive oppositions destined to be forever at odds with one another (p. 76).

How does this "healing idea" relate to those of us who are not philosophers? Wilson invites the reader to imagine being a witness to the birth of a child, a marriage, and a funeral. When the baby appears, you lament the fact that the baby will face many pains in the future, but you also cry tears of joy to celebrate its new life. So, too, at the marriage ceremony when you hear the proclamation that the two are made one, you are both happy and sad, aware that the couple has many hard days ahead, but that they will face them together. The funeral evokes similar opposing emotions. You experience sadness about the fact of death itself, and you know that you will one day die, but you also have the sensation that you are not dead but alive. Joy and sorrow are two sides of the same coin of life (pp. 77–79).

The problem, however, is that American culture pressures us to move to one side or the other, that is, to label ourselves as one thing or another, such as "introverts" or "extraverts," or "brooders" or "boasters." We know, too, what side or label it prefers: happy extroverts. This, Wilson notes, is one of the great "bifurcations" in our culture: those who are social and happy and those who prefer to be alone and to brood. Wilson calls both sides to the middle: to live in the limbo of these two antinomies. He realizes, though, that living in this limbo of in-between-ness has little appeal for either type.[3] He notes that "those committed to happiness at any cost and those bent on sadness no matter what are not very different from each other. Both are afraid of the wispy middle, that fertile and often febrile ambiguity between the poles of the cosmos." In effect, neither one is able to endure the limbo of in-between. It almost goes without saying that the "happy types, bent only on bliss, always take flight from this complicated limbo." But those who have committed their lives to dejection, Wilson suggests, are no different, because the sad types identify only with the darkness and, like their brighter opponents, cut half of life away, living only partial existences. Our task, then, is to somehow "stay strong" in the middle (pp. 82–84).

TERRIBLE BEAUTY

In chapter 4, titled "Terrible Beauty," Wilson discusses John Keats's poem "Ode to Melancholy" in the context of his tragically brief life, an essay by the novelist Walker Percy, and the music that Ludwig van Beethoven and John Lennon produced during deeply melancholic periods of their lives. He concludes with briefer comments on Georg Frederick Handel, Virginia Woolf, and Georgia O'Keefe. Through these illustrations, Wilson presents and explores what he calls "melancholy irony," contrasting it with the shallow and a selfish irony (which he calls "instrumental irony") that he discerns among jaded younger adults who use mockery as a means to distance themselves from real and moving experiences of the world. Melancholy irony has its basis in the relationships between melancholy, death, and beauty.

In relating melancholy and irony, Wilson identifies features of the melancholic temperament that might otherwise be overlooked. One is that melancholy resists dogmatisms of every kind, because it is the very nature of irony to remain "open-minded in the face of indeterminacy" and to "remain in an interpretive limbo." The other is that the melancholic temperament has a playful side that derives from the acceptance of the fact that one lives much of the time in a gloomy limbo, but, at the same time, remains open to the interplay between life's oppositions. This open stance borders on innocence; but this innocence, Wilson suggests, is not mere simplicity or gullibility. Rather, it is an openness to the world and to its multiplicity of forms, both to their emergence and to their passing (pp. 107–146).

CONCLUSION

In chapter 4, Wilson noted that John Lennon, in the throes of a deeply melancholic period in his life, underwent a form of psychotherapeutic treatment that involved returning to his deepest repressed pains and purging them through extreme screaming. This therapy proved effective: Lennon was able to channel his pain into his music.[4] In effect, his therapist, Arthur Janov, helped him to give voice to the repressed emotions underlying his melancholia. Wilson notes that the purpose of this therapy was not to cure Lennon of his melancholy. Rather, it enabled him to turn his deep wailing into his music. Wilson wonders, therefore, why so many people are trying to "cure" melancholy. He agrees that persons who are suffering from severe depression, suicidal ideation, and psychotic tendencies require medication, but he believes that the vast majority of Americans do not fall into these categories. If the numbers are correct, he notes that only 15 percent of Americans report that they are not happy, and that medication might be able to eradicate this 15 percent. For reasons that he has presented in the foregoing chapters, this would be terribly unfortunate for them and for the nation itself. In effect, those who say that they are unhappy are a saving grace to the others who say that they are happy. Many Americans, because they are afraid of the world's complexity, medicate away the sleepless nights. Is this where America should be heading? For Wilson, the answer, of course, is no. Why? Because to be against happiness as popularly understood is to know what it means to experience the joy that comes to those who embrace their sadness (pp. 147–151).

CHAPTER 13

EXPLORING HAPPINESS

The 13th book that we have chosen to review is Sissela Bok's *Exploring Happiness: From Aristotle to Brain Science* (2010). As noted in the introduction, Bok is a senior visiting fellow at the Harvard Center for Population and Development Studies and a moral philosopher. As the subtitle implies, this is a book that reviews understandings of happiness from the early Greeks to contemporary neuroscience. Intentionally multidisciplinary, it draws on writings of philosophers, psychologists, economists, geneticists, and neuroscientists. The book has nine chapters.

LUCK

In her opening chapter, titled "Luck," Bok recounts a lucky event, namely, the fact that she, or any one of us, was born at all. But her luck, she believes, was particularly noteworthy, because her young mother, who was advised by her doctor not to have any more children for medical reasons, decided to go ahead and try for another child on the grounds that it would be very difficult for her and her husband to be happy if they remained the parents of an only child. Many years later she came across a letter written by her father to her mother. In it he said that they were putting the outcome of the pregnancy and delivery in the hands of fate, and were doing so because they have always been lucky. For Bok, life itself is as much about luck as it is about anything else. Yet she has also learned that happiness is not something that just happens—to have luck, you need to give yourself a chance; happiness must be pursued (pp. 1–2). On the other hand, the purpose of her book is not to tell people how to be happy (and she is skeptical of any single vision of the path to happiness). Her purpose is simply to explore happiness, and she does this with two aims: (1) to bring together the recent empirical and scientific research on happiness with the historical, philosophical, and artistic inquiry into the nature of happiness; and (2) to reflect on these findings in light of moral considerations.

She notes that some of her colleagues in philosophy and in public health expressed objections to her project because a better place to begin, they felt, was with the question of suffering. Given the suffering that exists in the world today due to poverty and war, studying happiness, to these colleagues, seemed like a luxury. However, she points out that some of the great philosophical and political thinkers of all time wrote about happiness in times of great suffering. The study of happiness was never—and can never—be postponed until peace has arrived and suffering ameliorated, because that time will never come. Moreover, there is a particular need to study it now, as some of the ancient notions concerning happiness—that one should submissively accept misery and discrimination—are no longer credible in light of the progress made in terms of, say, the opportunities that women and minorities have gained in many countries of the world. Happiness is not what it used to be and, for this reason alone, it deserves study (pp. 5–7).

EXPERIENCES OF HAPPINESS

In chapter 2, titled "Experience," Bok notes that people tend to describe happiness in ways that are more vivid than definitions of happiness, so the purpose of this chapter is to identify the varieties of happiness and the variety of sources on which one can draw in seeking to describe such kinds of experiences. As she points out, when one begins reading about the varieties of happiness, one is struck by the many different kinds of experiences the word "happiness" is used to connote: experiences ranging from being liberated from slavery to feeling contentment while aimlessly walking on a sunny day. If people who live in the Arctic regions have many words for snow and ice, perhaps, she suggests, the same should be true for happiness. If we had or employed such a vocabulary, we could begin to make certain kinds of distinctions with regard to happiness, for example, temporal distinctions— "bliss" lasts for a moment, while "contentment" lasts for a considerably longer period of time—and we could begin to articulate different types of experiences related to happiness (pp. 11–12).

Bok discusses several methods by which we may come to perceive happiness more vividly. The first is introspection. Here she draws on William James, who, she notes, argued that we first have to rely on introspection when seeking to learn about an experience and that empirical observations should be coordinated with introspective observations. Another method is self-narratives. These self-narratives include the great classics of self-portraiture, as well as the numerous memoirs and journals that are proliferating today. The idea here is that one can go beyond one's own experience of reflecting on happiness to reflecting on the experiences of others. For example, one can read about the mystical experiences of Teresa of Avila or the pantheistic ecstasy of Henry David Thoreau, or any other writer in various genres from autobiographies to letters. Still another method that Bok discusses is thought experiments. She notes here Robert Nozick's Experience Machine, a thought experiment that is cited in many of the recent books on happiness. This thought experiment involves asking readers whether they would voluntarily hook themselves up to a machine in which they would feel total happiness. In reality, however, they would be living unconsciously and floating in a tank. Though complete in terms of feeling, their happiness would be based on utter illusion. Nozick wants his readers to conclude that the correct answer is "no," that happiness is more than feeling, and that they should not opt to be hooked up to the machine. Yet another method for thinking about experiences of happiness involves considering perspective. Here Bok notes Montaigne's practice of reading Aristotle and Seneca not only for the content of their works but also with an eye to their perspective and also Montaigne's own perspective on their perspective. The value of these methods, Bok suggests, is that they prevent one-dimensional conclusions about the extent to which marriage, for example, or religious belief or health correlates with happiness (pp. 15–34).

DISCORDANT DEFINITIONS

In chapter 3, titled "Discordant Definitions," Bok notes that there are an abundance of definitions of happiness. While people have no trouble identifying expressions of happiness when they see it in photographs—indeed, she notes, there is widespread cross-cultural agreement in identifying facial expressions associated with happiness—there is no agreement on definitions of happiness. She notes, for example, that happiness has been defined as increasing the right kind of satisfied desires (Aristotle); striving to have the fewest possible needs (Stoics); having many passions and many means of satisfying them (Charles Fourier); the rational soul's activity of virtue in a complete life (Sarah Broadie); finding out what is the "one thing necessary" in our lives and gladly relinquishing all the rest (Thomas Merton); the state of consciousness which proceeds from the achievement of one's values (Ayn Rand); having a rational life plan and in making progress on this plan (John Rawls); the feeling that power *increases*, that a resistance is overcome (Nietzsche); and having probed what is knowable and quietly revering what is unknowable (Goethe) (pp. 37–55).

As Bok observes, it should not be surprising that definitions of happiness abound. Like other abstract terms, such as beauty or love, there are no agreed-upon rules for defining it, and there are no canonical criteria to dictate when the term does or does not apply in a particular case. The fact that there are so many definitions of happiness might tempt us to dismiss the most compelling ones because they appear to be unscientific or vague, but she thinks there is much to be learned from comparing and contrasting particular definitions. There is no one definition of happiness, she suggests, but by juxtaposing conflicting definitions, we can gain a better sense of perspective—both the perspective of others and our own (pp. 56–58).

She also notes some perennial debates that are inherent in definitions of happiness. For example, there is the debate about whether people are the best judges of their own happiness or whether outsiders are better judges. Some think that happiness is purely a matter of subjectivity, while others maintain that there must be some kind of objective criteria against which claims about happiness must be judged. Another debate involves happiness and time. To what extent should one talk about happy moments, happy periods, and happy lives? Can one be judged to be happy only at the end of one's life, as Aristotle argued? Yet another debate involves the relationship between virtue and happiness. For instance, can serial killers who take great pleasure in harming others be considered happy? Also, should one strive to be happy or to be virtuous, and does striving to live a virtuous life lead to happiness as a consequence or does striving to happiness lead to virtuousness as a consequence? (pp. 39–54).

Bok does not settle these debates; nor does she defend a particular definition of happiness, though she does weigh in from time to time on a particular definition of or debate about happiness. Instead, what she does in this chapter is demonstrate the richness and the complexity of the term "happiness" itself.

ON THE HAPPY LIFE

In chapter 4, titled "On the Happy Life," Bok moves to discussions of happiness and notes in particular a few dialogues. She begins with Seneca's "On the Happy Life." Following the Stoics, Seneca argued that happiness involves living a simple life in pursuit of wisdom and virtue. He envisioned the happy life as one in which one is not too attached to wealth but lives a life in communion with nature; a life of sound mindedness and one that prepares for emergency; a life of kindness toward others; and a life of courage and of energy. Bok notes that many of these claims can be studied empirically today, and that these claims could provide a common area for fruitful dialogue between the humanities and the sciences (pp. 59–66).

She also discusses Augustine's little-known essay on the happy life written shortly after his conversion to Christianity. He relates that on his birthday he assembled a group of family and friends to discuss the matter of happiness, and that he proposed to the group that happiness is something that everyone desires. They all agreed. Then he proposed that no person can be happy without possessing what he or she desires; that everyone who is not happy is wretched; and that anyone who does not possess what he or she desires is therefore miserable. Again, they all agreed. Bok notes that Augustine and the group he had assembled considered happiness to be a state that is invulnerable to illness, death, or any misfortune. This means that, for them, happiness cannot be achieved in this life and can only be found in God. Thus, the key to happiness is possessing God. Augustine concludes the essay by defining happiness as the full recognition of "the One through whom you are led into the truth, the nature of the truth you enjoy, and the bond that connects you with the supreme measure" (pp. 66–69).

Moving on to other Christian and pagan thinkers and their writings about happiness, including Boethius, Aquinas, Pascal, Voltaire, Diderot, and others, Bok notes that these writings center on the relationship between God and happiness, morality and happiness, and reason and happiness. Pagan and secular thinkers, such as Seneca and Voltaire, have stressed the role of reason in happiness, whereas religious thinkers, such as Augustine and Pascal, have argued that happiness can only be found in God. Bok does not come down on the side of any single thinker or point of view, but she does intimate that part of exploring happiness involves seeking the wisdom of those who have gone before us (pp. 69–82).

MEASUREMENT

In chapter 5, titled "Measurement," Bok takes up the question as to whether happiness can be measured. At a minimum, anyone claiming to measure happiness is "in for" a number of questions, including: "What measurements could possibly encompass the depth and scope of conceptions of happiness? By what quantitative standards can one person's happiness be compared to another's? What numbers make sense in comparing even one person's different experiences [of happiness] from day to day or year to year? And by what indices can such personal experiences be established by outsiders?" (p. 83). Those, like Augustine, who think happiness is only achievable after death would discount all such measures. But some recent psychologists have boldly claimed that new sophisticated research methodologies have enabled happiness, for the first time, to be measurable (pp. 83–84).

Bok notes, however, that this claim has been uttered before. For example, two centuries ago, Jeremy Bentham proposed a "felicific calculus" that was based on "the greatest good for the greatest number." Similarly, Francis Edgeworth proposed a "hedonic calculus" based on the claim that different kinds of people and different societies had different capabilities for happiness. He also envisioned a "hedonimeter," a "psychophysical machine," that would one day be able to measure happiness with great precision. More recently, psychologists have been refining their empirical methods of studying subjective well-being in three areas: (1) reports of high affect; (2) reports of low affect; and (3) reports about life satisfaction. The two most influential names in these types of studies are Ed Diener (cf. Diener and Biswas-Diener 2008), who developed the Satisfaction with Life Scale; and Ruut Veenhoven (2004), who developed a similar construct. These scales involve different ways of asking people to what extent they feel happy and satisfied with their life (pp. 96–104).

However, Bok notes some of the problems with these attempts to measure happiness. She points out that sophisticated techniques that measure brain responses are not measuring happiness per se. Instead, these are measurements of responses in the brain that we *think* are associated with happiness in one way or another. She also points out that cross-cultural attempts to study happiness are fraught with interpretive difficulties, as "happiness" has different meanings in different cultures. She also notes that claims about certain variables, such as religion, as related to happiness are inconclusive because these associations vary by culture. For example, for Americans there is a positive association between religiousness and happiness, but Scandinavians are less religious but happier than Americans. The issues seem endlessly complex. And, moreover, the directionality of causation of many associations is difficult to establish: Are people happy because they are healthy, or are they healthy because they are happy? Are people happy because they are married, or do happy people tend to get married more often? Does religion contribute to people's happiness, or do happy people seek out religion? (pp. 96–104).

Bok closes her discussion of measurement by noting the proliferation of books with titles such as *The Science of Happiness*. She points out, however, that each offers its own way of measuring and its own take on happiness. Thus, they offer "a" science of happiness rather than "the" science of happiness. She also suggests that scientists and humanists should work together to further the study of happiness. The study of happiness is, and must be, an interdisciplinary endeavor (pp. 104–106).

BEYOND TEMPERAMENT

Bok next turns in chapter 6—titled "Beyond Temperament"—to the question to what extent temperament is related to happiness. She begins by noting William James's (1987) distinction between the "sanguine and healthy-minded" and the "depressed and melancholy," and contrasts this distinction with today's distinctions between "extroverts" and "neurotics." With regard to the distinction between extroverts and neurotics, she notes that (1) these categories seem more related to happiness than categories such as age, sex, and class; and that (2) these categories seem somewhat stable over the course of one's life. On the other hand, we do not know how or why the traits of extroverts and neurotics develop and how they interact with other personality traits, such as resilience or risk taking (p. 107).

She also discusses the traditional distinction between melancholic and sanguine temperaments, and considers various claims related to a variety of sanguine dispositions. She notes in this regard Sir Leslie Stephen's (1904) claim that, with regard to happiness and temperament, the following traits make all the difference: curiosity, imagination, capacious memory, and humor. She also notes Teilhard de Chardin's (1973) claims that the happy life is to be found in discovery and in ascent; that a zest toward living can be cultivated; and that happiness consists of adding "one stitch, no matter how small . . . to the magnificent tapestry of life." Another trait that she identifies as related to sanguine temperaments is resilience—the ability to bounce back from hardships in life. Persons suffering from post-traumatic stress disorder often lack this very trait. On the other hand, she suggests that resilience must be counterbalanced by empathy—someone who is too defensive and too well-guarded can do a lot of damage. So Bok grounds the discussion of happiness in the realm of moral considerations: considerations that, in her view, most authors on happiness leave out (pp. 114–124).

Bok discusses a number of other traits and characteristics related to temperament and happiness. She notes, for example, that how one experiences time is related to how one defines and experiences happiness. Some, for example, are organized and ritualistic with their time, while others are more spontaneous. Some focus on the present, while others focus on the past and the future. In other words, time is intimately related to one's temperament and also to one's happiness. Another such factor concerns cleanliness and orderliness. People have vastly different attitudes toward orderliness and cleanliness, and these factors, too, affect one's subjective well-being. Still other factors include attitudes toward risk taking, or how one feels about solitude, or the appreciation of beauty.[1]

In other words, there are a variety of preferences, whether fulfilled or unfulfilled, that can affect one's happiness. This being the case, Bok wants to challenge any easy generalizations about happiness—prescriptions, for example, that tell people they need to live an orderly life or that they need to live a life full of civic engagement. She is skeptical of all such prescriptions and proscriptions. She suggests that we turn to humanists and to the world of literature to challenge any easy generalizations, as well as to scientists who can falsify simplistic claims (pp. 130–131).

IS LASTING HAPPINESS ACHIEVABLE?

In chapter 7, Bok turns to the views of Bertrand Russell and Sigmund Freud on the question of whether happiness is possible. As noted in chapter 4, Russell's *The Conquest of Happiness* (1968) was originally published in 1930. This was also the year that Freud's *Civilization and Its Discontents* (1961) was published. Both authors, she notes, discounted the importance of their respective works, both were atheists, and both believed that the majority of people are unhappy. Both, too, used the category of "illusion" to discount those who disagree with their positions. And yet both men offered radically different views as to our hopes of achieving happiness in this life (pp. 132–137).

Bok interprets Freud as arguing for a "narrowly hedonic view" in which happiness is derived, in spurts, from the attainment of various pleasures or relieving of various tensions. In contrast, she sees Russell as contending that happiness is available to all who seek it, and that the main factors in this regard include preserving good health, having wide interests, maintaining physical vigor, cultivating loving relationships, having meaningful work, and fulfilling goals. Freud, however, viewed happiness as incompatible with modern life, which requires human beings, for good reasons, to sacrifice what would make them happy—in particular, sacrificing their sexual and aggressive drives—for the sake of civilization (pp. 132–137).

Bok notes that both men struggled with depression and unhappiness in their own lives. Freud frequently used opium to overcome his depressive spells, and Russell wrote his book on happiness when his marriage was in shambles. She also notes that their views may have been influenced not only by their personal dispositions and life circumstances but also by their historical context—that is, the context of modern warfare and of shifting political and economic structures and forces—and that it is quite possible that Europeans and Americans were more unhappy in the 1920s than they have been in recent decades (pp. 137–142).

Bok next shifts the discussion to what Philip Brickman and Donald Campbell have called the hedonic treadmill, which has been previously discussed in our book. To recapitulate, the basic idea is that people's happiness levels adapt to their situation. Lottery winners are happy after winning the lottery, but then they return to a lower level of happiness. The same goes for moving to a sunny climate, buying a new car, or many other such changes—people adapt. And they also adapt to tragic events in life, such as severe accidents or losing one's job. Bok notes, however, that some life events and circumstances, such as chronic pain and noise pollution, do not lend themselves to adaptation. She also notes that some of the early studies involving the hedonic treadmill are not holding up today, or, at least, other studies are contradicting previous data. Studies of paraplegia, which were widely cited in support of the hedonic treadmill, are now suggesting that some do not "return completely to the state of happiness they had enjoyed before their accident" (pp. 142–147).

She also discusses the scientific literature on the question whether there are set points of ranges of happiness. She notes the research by David Lykken and Auke Tellegen (1996) involving twins that suggests a genetic component to happiness. On the other hand, the role of genetics with regard to happiness should not be overstated. As neurophysiologist Felicia Huppert (2007) suggests: "The assumption that our basal level of happiness is primarily under genetic control is inaccurate . . . since genes need to be expressed—turned off or turned on. Interventions therefore make it possible to change set points, by modifying external circumstances, attitudes, and behavior. At times, our genes may play the predominant role, but only if we have certain experiences; alternatively our environment may have the greatest influence, but only if we have a particular genotype" (p. 149). In other words, genes do not have to be seen as challenging human independence (pp. 149–150).

Bok also indicates that numerous psychologists, especially Positive Psychologists, offer a resounding "yes" to the question of whether achieving happiness is possible. They rely on various research studies that use averages and correlations, but she cautions readers to keep in mind that there are limits to such methods—especially because happiness is such a personal and individual matter. She also reiterates her point that the advice that derives from the empirical literature needs to be grounded in moral considerations. One piece of advice from the empirical literature that satisfies her moral sensibilities is the cultivation of gratitude. But even here moral considerations still need to be weighed: gratitude to whom, she asks, and for what, and at whose expense? (pp. 150–154).

ILLUSION

Bok begins chapter 8 titled "Illusion" with the observation that few writers on happiness fail to address the relationship between happiness and illusion. Those who have a path to happiness—whether secular or religious—often claim that critics of their point of view are deluded. Augustine claims that happiness is only found in God—all else is illusion. Marx claims that religion is the opiate of the people, and that true happiness in society is to be found by following his prescriptions. Skeptics also appeal to illusion; that is, while they do not offer a path to happiness, they regard all such paths as deluded (pp. 155–158).

Some, however, make a case for illusion. Bok cites Horace's story of the Greek merchant Lycas of Argos (1959, p. 266) who delighted in imagined performances in an empty arena on his estate. His family was eventually able to drive out his disease (i.e., cure his delusions), but when they did he cried: "You call it rescue, my friends, but what you have done is to murder me! You have destroyed my delight and forcibly swept away from my mind the most gloriously sweet of illusions!" Bok points out that this story raises practical ethical questions about psychiatric treatment, such as when and on what grounds individuals might refuse treatment, but it also raises questions about moral development. After all, many traditions and thinkers, from Confucius to Kant, have stressed the importance of self-knowledge as essential to maturity (pp. 158–161).

Bok also cites the case of Madame du Châtelet as a defender of illusion. She and Voltaire become romantically involved in the 1740s, and she left her husband and children to be with him. However, when Voltaire began to treat her coolly, she nevertheless persisted in believing in their love. She wrote in her *Reflections on Happiness* (1997) that this belief gave her much happiness, and when it no longer was tenable, she turned to the illusions offered by gambling and study. Bok notes that Madame du Châtelet "insisted that such illusions don't deceive us, any more than do optical ones of the fictions we enter into so wholeheartedly at the opera" (pp. 162–164).

Bok also notes that psychologists, too, have weighed in on the relationship between illusion and happiness, and that some of them have viewed illusion positively in this regard—much more so than philosophers. She points out, for example, that Martin Seligman has suggested that we should hold onto our illusions in romantic relationships—though it seems unlikely that Seligman would support the kind and degree of illusion that Madame du Châtelet experienced with her relationship to Voltaire. In any case, Bok cites some empirical evidence that positive illusions as a form of optimism can be beneficial in terms of patient health outcomes and can also help persons be more resilient in the face of loss. One distinction that psychologists employ here, she notes, is between positive illusions and defense mechanisms, with the former viewed as interpreting or reframing reality in a positive light (adaptive) and the latter as altering reality by means of denial and repression (maladaptive) (pp. 164–166).

In conclusion, Bok brings the discussion of illusion back to ethics. With regard to the relationship of illusion to happiness, she comes down on the side of self-knowledge as a path to moral maturity, though she does not discount "the pleasures of daydreaming or imagination," nor does she ignore the fact that resilience sometimes requires temporary denial. But, in the long run, denial and rationalization can do great harm to one's moral compass because they enable complacency. She cites Barbara Herman's notion of "moral salience" (1993), which calls for the development of the balance of empathy and resilience "so as to be alert . . . to signals that might otherwise go unheeded" (pp. 167–172).

Finally, she invokes Kant's view that "uninhibited truthfulness toward oneself as well as in the behavior toward everyone else is the only proof of a person's consciousness of having character" (1978). She notes his distinction between truth and truthfulness, as well as his emphasis on truthfulness rather than on some unachievable full truth. What is critical here is the *striving* for truthfulness. Bok suspects that this striving for truthfulness, in connection with a desire to treat others as one desires to be treated might be one path toward happiness (p. 172).

THE SCOPE OF HAPPINESS

Bok concludes with a brief chapter on the scope of happiness. She uses the word scope in two senses: (1) the extent, range, reach, sweep of perceptions, thoughts, or actions; and (2) freedom, latitude, and leeway. She writes: "I see both meanings as relating to each of my two aims in this book: that of bringing together writing and thinking about happiness by philosophers, poets, religious thinkers, and others with research by natural and social scientists; and that of examining, against this background, the limit imposed by perennial moral issues about how we should lead our lives and how we should treat one another" (p. 173). She adds that some students of happiness have illuminated its scope by ranging freely across cultures and centuries and disciplines to draw on literature from earliest times, history, philosophy, religion, the arts, and the sciences, while others have examined particular problems, such as problems relating to work or love, as they relate to happiness in great depth. Both approaches are needed.

In her view, we need to look not only to personal accounts of the experience of happiness but also to works of literature, because otherwise, we will miss the various nuances of happiness. She also notes that philosophical analyses deepen our understanding of happiness, and social scientific research challenges our intuitive assumptions about happiness. She stresses the danger of coming to "premature closure" on the subject of happiness, and one way that we avoid doing so is to take into account these various perspectives on the subject of happiness. The depictions of happiness that she has explored in her book yield a "gorgeous many-hued tapestry," and, in her view, it is those who can see both the dark and the light in this tapestry who can help us all understand the human condition a little better (pp. 173–178).

CHAPTER 14

AFTERTHOUGHTS

In the foregoing chapters, our goal has been to present the books about happiness as accurately as we possibly could. We know, of course, that with any attempt to provide a relatively brief digest of a book, important features of the book will be left out. In some of the chapters, we alerted the reader to this very fact when we noted that we were being rather selective. However, we tried to represent the author's perspective on happiness accurately, and as we were writing our chapters we would often think of the author reading the chapter and hopefully saying, "Yes, this is what I say," or "Yes, this is what I claim," or "At least they have not misrepresented me."

In viewing this as our primary goal, we did not engage in any evaluation or critique of the various books. We felt that to do so would endanger the objectivity of our presentation of the book itself. We also wanted readers to have the opportunity to make their own evaluations of what the authors had to say without the interference of a third party. Knowing that readers of books come from very different perspectives, we felt that this was also a way to be fair to them. Our role, we felt, was not to try to persuade readers to endorse our own point of view, for our goal was simply to put together, as it were, a symposium of authors who had been prompted or inspired to write a book on happiness.

If we had a personal agenda, it was that we wanted to bring to readers' attention the fact that happiness is a topic that has been of interest to men and women throughout human history, and by including books that were written more than 100 years ago, we wanted to bring attention to the fact that the study of happiness is not a mere fad. No doubt, there have been times when more books about happiness have been written than during other times, but the study of happiness is an ongoing project, and there is every reason to believe that more books will be written about happiness as time goes on.

Having said all this, we felt it would not be too self-indulgent if were we to offer a few comments and observations of our own in these last remaining pages. This would not be a systematic evaluation and assessment of the books on happiness covered here, either collectively or individually, but it would indicate how two individuals who have immersed themselves in the happiness literature have found the experience personally rewarding. We do not expect that readers will agree with what we have to say, but we hope that our engaging in this "exercise" will inspire them to do something similar, for we believe that the authors of books on happiness hope that their own readers will not take a purely objective view of what they have written but will also give thought to how what they have read may affect them on a more personal level.

In order to create the appropriate atmosphere for this exercise, we imagined that we were privileged to attend a symposium to which the authors of the books reviewed here were invited to present and to discuss their views on happiness, and that we went to a coffee shop afterwards and talked about what we had heard. While we know that this scenario is rather contrived, it nonetheless enabled us to avoid attempting to provide the systematic evaluation and assessment mentioned earlier, a task that would undoubtedly be a book in itself.

So we ask our readers to imagine two auditors at a symposium on happiness going to their favorite coffee shop afterward. They order coffee and dessert and sit down at their favorite table to talk about what they have seen and heard. As this would be an informal setting, we will use our given names rather than our surnames in the following reflections.

REFLECTIONS ON THE PRESENTATIONS

Donald began the conversation by asking Nathan, "So what did you think of the symposium?" Nathan replied, "It was really interesting. I thought that Karl Hilty's discussion on time and happiness was especially valuable, and I appreciated Tal Ben-Shahar's practical advice about being intentional about increasing activities that give us meaning and pleasure in our daily lives. I also thought Daniel Nettle was really creative in interpreting a massive amount of scientific and empirical data in light of evolutionary psychology. How about you? What did you think of it?"

Donald answered, "I found it interesting too. I was especially impressed with the wide range of empirical data that various presenters reported. I also appreciated Daniel Gilbert's point about how difficult it is to know what will make us happy, and that the best way to predict our own happiness is by looking at others in situations that we are considering, such as deciding on a career, living in a certain part of the country, and so forth. I feel a little ambivalent about Positive Psychology, but maybe this is because I have been educated to think in the very ways that Martin Seligman wants to challenge, but I am not inclined to want to join forces with the critics of happiness, either. I think my favorite was probably Jean Finot because he really wants to make a case for happiness, but not at the expense of sadness or sorrow (which was a major concern of Eric Wilson), and I am impressed that he saw the need for a 'science' of happiness. At the same time, I couldn't help thinking that Bertrand Russell was right when he said that we should look at happiness from a commonsense point of view, even though I know that more recent empirical research has shown that what we take to be 'common sense' is not always supported by the evidence. I also appreciated Finot's point about journalism—that we hear so much about the misery of life that stories or experiences about happiness sound rather trivial. His own background in journalism, and the fact that he interviewed people and simply reported what they said to him makes this observation credible and timely too."

Nathan commented, "His point about happiness seeming almost trivial reminds of a line in one of Kurt Cobain's songs, where he says something like 'I think I'm dumb, but I might be just happy.'" "I think Finot was making that point," Donald replied. "We are led to believe that the dark portraits of life are superior to the bright portraits of life. Darkness, or unhappiness, is supposed to be profound. Happiness is dumb, or can be confused with being dumb, as Cobain seems to be saying. I also like Finot's analogy of portraits, because this suggests that frames, especially the way we frame ourselves, give our lives structure."

"A number of the presenters would support that way of thinking," Nathan noted. "Seligman talked about changing our views about the past, the present, and the future, and how we can work to change, or reframe, these aspects of our lives. Gilbert, it seems to me, talks about how we sort of do this automatically and unknowingly, and Nettle talked a bit about this, too. I think a few of the presenters used the term "psychological immune system" in this context. But your point seems to be how we can intentionally reframe our experience and how we can intentionally help others to reframe their experience, so that seems to be a little different from Gilbert's discussion and closer to Finot." Donald agreed.

Nathan then asked, "Were there statements by any of the presenters that you disagreed with or that you would have wanted to question the presenter about?" Donald replied, "Among some of the more empirical presenters, there seemed at times to be a lack of understanding and appreciation of humanities-oriented scholarship. When Martin Seligman claimed that his team read all of the world's philosophical and religious literature and boiled them down to six virtues, this seemed both unlikely and somewhat dismissive. And

Ronald Dworkin made a similar claim—that you could go to local book store and read what all of philosophy and theology has to say about happiness in a month—this seems anti-intellectual, in a way." Nathan agreed and added, "I think that is why I really appreciated Sisela Bok's presentation. Her book seemed to be in the spirit of William James's *The Varieties of Religious Experience*, though her theme would be the *varieties* of happiness. There is simply a wide range of human experience, and there is no way that statistical methods—averages and correlations—can tell us the whole story. There's no question that we learned a lot from what the psychologists and economists told us about the factors that are conducive to happiness and the social and political trends that have, in a sense, made the dream of universal happiness seem all the more utopian, like the evidence that David Myers presented on marriage and Richard Layard presented on the effects of local governments on citizens' level of happiness. But idiographic methods are essential, and I wonder if some of the most profound truths about happiness can be found in poetry?"

Donald agreed, "Even though Bok and others drew heavily on the humanities—and this, of course, was also true of Eric Wilson—no one talked in any real detail about what poets have written about happiness. In fact, I think that some of the most profound insights into happiness have been expressed by contemporary American poets. Stephen Dunn's 'How to be Happy: Another Memo to Myself' (Dunn 1994, p. 48) is a nice example. There's a poem by Lawrence Raab (1993, pp. 46–47) titled 'Happiness' that really resonated with me when I read it a number of years ago. He tells about the only time he felt perfectly happy. He was a freshman in college, and school had just gotten underway. He was sitting on the lawn, leaning against a tree, and reading a book. He tells about how he certainly had enough to worry about, that he hadn't made any friends, was not in love, and didn't like his classes, yet just at that moment he felt completely happy. Since he was surrounded by nature, I think his poem supports what Horace Fletcher was talking about—how the organic world testifies to happiness and how our fears and worries get in the way of our happiness."

He continued, "At the same time, Fletcher says that a person has just as much of a right to carry a frown as to wear a smile. Ronald Dworkin and Eric Wilson would back him up on this point. And in that light there's a poem by Linda Pasten (1998, p. 12) titled 'On the Obligation to Be Happy' in which she objects to the expectation that others have that she wear a happy smile when she doesn't feel that way, as if her sadness were some sort of hidden vice. It's the issue we talked about earlier—that sadness and sorrow are not inimical to happiness. And yet some of the presenters came dangerously close to suggesting that the two are incompatible."

Then Donald asked Nathan the same question: "Were there statements by any of the presenters that you disagreed with or would have wanted to question the presenter about?" Nathan responded, "I guess I felt myself wondering if Eric Wilson's presentation was really *against* happiness, as his titled indicated. He made a convincing case for the value of sadness and sorrow, but it seemed to me as I listened to him that, in doing so, he was really offering his own vision of, to use Seligman's term, *authentic* happiness! Also, although Bok's presentation really didn't cover from Aristotle to brain science—no single presentation, it seems to me, could do that—it was a very thoughtful and selective presentation that contextualizes happiness in ways that social scientists simply are not trained to do. She did a bit of moralizing, as did others, but it did not come across as heavy handed or even as advice but, rather, as caution. It also occurs to me that her presentation would seem to fit with other recent works on happiness that I have heard about, such as Sara Ahmed's *The Promise of Happiness* (2010), which is a critique of the obligation to be happy from a feminist perspective. That's what Linda Pasten also seems to be saying."

Nathan asked Donald, "Do you have any other concerns?" Donald replied, "It may sound rather trivial—although I guess what makes one person happy or unhappy can sometimes seem rather trivial to others—but I felt that Eric Wilson's critique of the 'mall mentality' failed to take account of the fact that, for a lot of older persons like myself, the mall is a good place to get some exercise and also to stay in touch with other people. At the mall where my wife and I walk, there are a couple of men in their early 90s who walk together almost every day, all seasons of the year. If they tried to do that in their own neighborhoods, they would probably trip on the sidewalks, and, more importantly, they would not be walking together. I appreciated the fact that Wilson also mentioned the importance of living in a 'limbo' between happiness and melancholy, and yet, here again, it occurs to me that malls may be one place where older persons help each other through various limbo situations in their own lives. Maybe we should have discussed mall walkers in our own book on living in limbo!" (Capps and Carlin 2010).

Then Donald asked Nathan if he had anything critical to add. Nathan responded: "When I was listening to Daniel Gilbert I occasionally had the feeling that his presentation was more of an overview of psychology, almost like a psychology 101 lecture, than a presentation on happiness. His talk was really more about perception than about happiness, though his linking of perception and happiness was a well-needed corrective that complicates any advice being given out on the subject of happiness. In fact, the symposium as a whole was a helpful caution against the tendency of some of us, especially those of us who are in the helping professions, to give advice to other persons about how to be happy."

Donald said he felt the same way and added, "I appreciated Bertrand Russell's refusal to claim superiority over persons in the working classes as far as the realizing of happiness is concerned. I was taken, for example, by the story he told about his gardener who experienced happiness daily because he had a running battle with the rabbits who invaded his garden. I found myself thinking that if the rabbits knew they were contributing to his happiness they might have stayed away. But I also liked his—and other presenters'—advice to avoid making comparisons between ourselves and others, especially comparisons that cause us to feel envy."

* * *

Let us imagine that by this time Nathan and Donald were both ready to go home after a long day. But they also knew that they did not want to terminate their discussion of the symposium and its effects on them. So Nathan came up with an idea, "What if we were to meet again in a couple of days—while the symposium is still fresh in our minds—and we each came up with the seven keys to happiness in our lives, based on what we heard today? These wouldn't have to be prescriptive for others, but, rather, just a list of what works for us." On questioning, Nathan admitted that he got this idea from Martin Seligman, but this was no reason not to try it. In fact, just the opposite: so two days later we find them sitting at the same coffee shop, and each has brought along his list of seven keys to happiness in his own life.

THE SEVEN KEYS TO PERSONAL HAPPINESS

They began with Nathan's list: (1) Organize your time; (2) Take time to reflect on your priorities, and act accordingly; (3) Spend time with friends and family; (4) Cultivate creativity into your life through things like writing, playing music, and building things; (5) Create a complex self-identity; (6) Don't value money or material possessions; (7) Do value experiences over things. Donald asked Nathan if they were listed in order of importance and if Nathan would say more about them. Nathan replied that they were listed in order of priority for him and that, in his experience, time is absolutely crucial, and it has risen in importance for him over the years. In high school, time wasn't a big deal for him. He'd get homework for the day and do it when he got home—there was nothing to think about. But in college the tasks become more complex. He had to set his own deadlines. The complexity of tasks increased in graduate school and this is even more the case now that he is working. He has a lot of meetings—usually three or more a week—and he needs to be flexible. So this means that if he wants to hold onto his intellectual life he needs to do so before he goes to work, so he writes from 5 A.M. to 7 A.M.—there are no meetings at this time of day—and he does this most days of the week. And this means he needs to go to bed at 9 p.m. so that he can have eight hours of sleep. This, in turn, means that he needs to be intentional and organized with his time for loved ones and friends, and for his own leisure. He noted that some people think he is too rigid with his time and that he schedules too much, but he finds the effects of time management to yield happiness for him, and it also gives him pleasure to plan out his week.

Nathan added that everything else sort of follows from this—that he needs to know what his priorities are, and then he needs to make time for them: time for love, for fun, for sleep, for work, for creative activities, and so forth. Saturday mornings are lazy for him, and he spends a lot of time with his girlfriend then, making waffles together, talking and processing, and sometimes playing video games together. He also said that once a month he likes to do something that is out of the ordinary for them, like going to a park, and that he recently took a photo at Brazos Bend State Park, some 15 miles from Houston, that gave them both a lot of pleasure, pleasure that had something to do with the fact that it seemed really lucky for them to stumble upon these animals together—a baby alligator between two turtles on a log—because this is a wild park without any fences (see below).

That they were all little, not threatened by one another, and seemingly happy and contented made Nathan and his girlfriend happy, too. And so this was something out of the ordinary for them to do. If they went there every

A baby alligator with two turtles—this photograph, taken by Nathan Carlin, depicts three animals that look happy together; the photograph also gives the authors a great deal of pleasure, adding weight to Bertrand Russell's claims about happiness being found in nature.

week they'd probably get bored with the park. He added that Daniel Gilbert made this point in his presentation, and that Bertrand Russell, too, made the point about being connected with nature. Things like this—time at the park—that cost very little are more important than having a big screen television. Experiences, he concluded, are more important than things.

Donald asked him about his fifth key to happiness—creating a complex self-identity—and what he meant by this. Nathan responded that this was important for him because he's learned, over the years, that it is best not to put all of one's eggs in a single basket. It's good, for example, to have a number of friends, so that if one disappoints you, or if you disappoint your friend, you don't slip into the trap of thinking that you are bad at friendship or something like that. The same goes for work and play. It's better to do different kinds of things at work so that when one of them goes bad, you don't think that you are bad at work, but, rather, simply bad at this one task or bad at this particular time: "I guess I'm saying, and I think Martin Seligman made this point well, that a complex self-identity is a way of cultivating resiliency."

Donald passed his list over to Nathan, and it read "Things That Keep Me Happy." He said that he got the idea for the title from William Stafford's poem "Things I Learned Last Week," and he related to Nathan what Stafford had to say about the poem in a video (Markee and Wixon 2004)—namely, how some of the things he claims to have learned last week are perhaps intriguing but not terribly noteworthy, for, after all, even if he were capable of writing a whole series of "blockbusters," this wouldn't make for a very good poem. Donald also noted that the poem consists of seven things that Stafford learned last week: "It's as if seven seems intuitively right." Here's his list: (1) A personal relationship with my wife that is based on love, trust, and acceptance; (2) A good feeling about my role as a father when our son was growing up and how we relate to one another now; (3) A few good male friendships based on trust and a mutual sense of being supportive of one another; (4) Being productive in ways that are personally engaging and neither onerous nor stressful; (5) Being appreciative and grateful for my life and not thinking about what might have been; (6) Small but daily pleasures; and (7) Focusing on the near rather than the distant future.

When Nathan asked him if he wanted to say more about any of them, Donald replied that he thought "they pretty much speak for themselves," but then added, "I'm sure I wouldn't have come up with some of them if I hadn't listened to the speakers at the symposium," that they really helped him identify things in his life that have been the source of happiness. He then noted that if he could add one more, it would be to second Eric Wilson's point about the value of irony because, somehow, he knows that having an ironic view of life is critical to his sense of being a basically happy person. And he said that if he could add another one, it would have something to do with the importance of staying in touch with the happy boy who continues to live inside of him. In fact, if there was one thing that he felt all of the experts tended to overlook—maybe because they were so engaged in the larger philosophical and scientific questions of whether happiness is genetic or a matter of temperament—it is that they didn't say anything about taking one's cues as an adult from the boy or girl you were many years ago. Maybe, he thought, this would be a variation on Gilbert's view that we should pay more attention to what others have experienced than rely solely on our own imaginations.

At this point, Donald pulled another piece of paper out of his back pocket and said to Nathan, "I found this in the scrapbook that contained the *Reader's Digest* account of the 1948 Gallup Poll that got us thinking about happiness. It's a poem I wrote in the fourth grade."

Winter

Winter is a joyful season.
It is joyful—there's a reason.
Ice and snow and outdoor fun.
Cozy nights when play is done.
Each day's more fun than all the rest.
I know—for this day is the best.
But Mother now has called us in.
I wish tomorrow would begin.

After Nathan finished reading it, Donald said, "It would be easy to say that this boy is in for a rude awakening, that there will come a day when the anticipated tomorrow is worse—maybe a whole lot worse—than today, which is already bad enough. But why should we assume that he is utterly naïve when, more likely, he is a boy with an irrepressible 'will to believe,' as William James puts it?" (1956).

Nathan nodded, and they sat there looking at the lists, the poem, and the photo of the baby alligator and the two turtles. Then Nathan, picking up on Donald's allusion to James's "will to believe" phrase, said, "It strikes me that neither of us said anything in our lists about God, as St. Augustine, no doubt, would have insisted. But I guess that is sort of implied for me. I really like the Bible verse that reads, 'I know that there is nothing better for them than to be happy and to enjoy themselves as long as they live'" (Ecclesiastes 3:12). Donald replied, "The same author said that 'there is nothing better than that all should enjoy their work' and he was critical of those who, in working for riches, deprived themselves of the pleasures that work affords, calling this 'an unhappy business' " (Ecclesiastes 3:22, 4:8). Having followed Gilbert's advice on observing the experiences of others, including the presenters at the symposium, they agreed that there was nothing more that needed to be said—at least, for now—about the human desire for happiness.

NOTES

SERIES FOREWORD

1. See L. Aden and J. H. Ellens (1990). Anton Boisen was at the University of Chicago for decades and developed models for understanding the relationship between psychology and religion as well as between mental illness, particularly psychoses, and the forms of meaningful spiritual or religious experience. Seward Hiltner was one of a large number of students of Boisen who carried his work forward by developing theological and psychotherapeutic structures and models that gave operational application to Boisen's ideas. Hiltner was on the faculty of Princeton Theological Seminary in the chair of Pastoral Theology and Pastoral Psychology for most of his illustrious career. While Boisen wrote relatively little, Hiltner published profusely and his works became notable contributions to church and society.

INTRODUCTION

1. Augustine's association of happiness with joy is one that other authors presented in this book also make. It may be useful, therefore, to note that in its comparison of happy with its synonyms (e.g., glad, cheerful, joyful, joyous) *Webster's New World College Dictionary* (Agnes 2001) states that happy "generally suggests a feeling of great pleasure, contentment, etc. (a happy marriage)," and that joyful and joyous "both imply great elation and rejoicing, the former generally because of a particular event, and the latter as a matter of usual temperament (the joyful throng, a joyous family)" (p. 647). Thus, happiness tends to be understood as an enduring state of affairs or condition, and joy tends to be understood as generated by a particular event or events.

CHAPTER 1

1. The word "fear-thought" is not hyphenated in Fletcher's book. We have chosen to hyphenate it in order to make it appear less idiosyncratic.

2. Other books by Fletcher include *That Last Waif, or Social Quarantine* (1898b), a book that deals with the topic of child abuse and neglect; *The New Glutton or Epicure* (1906), which established his reputation as an advocate of a healthy diet; and *Fletcherism: What It Is or How I Became Young at Sixty* (1913), which sets forth his dietary theories.

3. It is noteworthy that Fletcher anticipates the development of treatment methods later used with persons with anxiety disorders. Initially, the exposure method was used alone. In later decades, it has been supplemented with cognitive methods designed to create a different mind-set in a person who has an irrational fear of certain objects, locations, or social situations. What adds to the interest of this experiment is the fact that in *Menticulture* (1895) Fletcher relates the following story about himself: "When I was a boy I was standing under a tree which was struck by lightning and received a shock, from the effects of which I never knew exemption until I had dissolved partnership with worry. Since then lightning, and thunder, and storm clouds, with wind-swept torrents of pain have been encountered under conditions which formerly would have caused great depression and discomfort, without experiencing a trace of either. Surprise is also greatly modified, and one is less liable to become startled by unexpected sights or noises" (p. 34).

4. Various forms of this record-keeping method (often referred to as "homework") are used in therapeutic work with persons with anxiety disorders.

CHAPTER 2

1. In the bibliography of *Activity, Recovery, Growth: The Communal Role of Planned Activities*, Joan M. Erikson (1976) cites several books and articles published in the last decade of the 19th century and the first and second decades of the 20th century that focus on occupational therapy for mental patients. Examples include F. C. Hoyt's "Occupation in the Treatment of the Insane," published in *American Medico-Psychological Association Proceedings* in 1898; and Herbert J. Hall's "Work Cure," published in *Journal of American Medical Association* in 1910.

CHAPTER 3

1. David G. Myers makes the same point in *The Pursuit of Happiness* (1992). Citing research studies of car accident victims who suffered paralyzing injuries, he writes: "Without minimizing catastrophe, the consistent and astonishing result is that the worst emotional consequences of bad events are usually temporary. With major setbacks or injuries, the emotional after-effects may linger a year or more. Yet within a matter of weeks, one's current mood is more affected by the day's events" than by the catastrophe itself (p. 48).

2. In a footnote, Finot observes that a mother's grief for her lost child could very well threaten to last a lifetime, but he notes that he is considering here the

causes of "ordinary unhappiness" and not "exceptional" forms of unhappiness. He also adds that even the "cruelest sufferings" are eventually softened.

CHAPTER 4

1. The first verse of the hymn, the words of which were written by Samuel John Stone (1839–1900), emphasizes the sinner's longing for heaven: "Weary of earth, and laden with my sin,/I look at heaven and long to enter in;/But there no evil thing may find a home,/And yet I hear a voice that bids me 'Come.'" The second verse emphasizes that although evil is with the sinner day by day, "Yet on mine ears the gracious tidings fall,/'Repent, confess, thou shalt be loosed from all.'"

2. Russell concludes *New Hopes for a Changing World* (1968; original publication 1952) with chapters on "The Happy Man" and "The Happy World." The former, which essentially draws on themes presented in *The Conquest of Happiness*, also includes reflections on maintaining a happy disposition toward life as one enters old age. The latter emphasizes the importance of setting fear aside and embracing the world with freedom and joy.

CHAPTER 5

1. One of the authors (Capps) identifies a more benign form of envy (that of emulation) in *Deadly Sins and Saving Virtues* (2000), pp. 41–44.

2. Myers refers here to Peale's very popular book *The Power of Positive Thinking* (1952). Peale also coauthored a book with Smiley Blanton titled *The Art of Real Happiness* (Peale and Blanton 1950). It contains chapters titled "Doorways to a New Life for You," "Why Do We Love and Hate at the Same Time?," "How You Can Have Peace of Mind," "Relax and Renew Joyous Power," "How to Stay Healthy under Pressure," "How to Treat Depression and Anxiety," "How to Have a Successful Marriage," "A Solution for Problem Drinking," "Comfort and Understanding for the Bereaved," and "How to Grow Older Happily."

CHAPTER 6

1. This discussion of Catholic nuns is based on a study by Danner, Snowdon, and Friesen (2001). Similar findings from a 1999 brain-scan study of Catholic nuns who had engaged in contemplation for a minimum of 15 years are reported in a study by Newberg and Waldman (2009, p. 48). Also, a study of the risk factors for alcoholism among Catholic nuns by McKechnie and Hill (2011) found that negative emotionality (or negative affect regulation) was the only significant predictor of alcoholism.

2. This questionnaire can be accessed at www.authentichappiness.org.

3. In the appendix, he states that he uses *happiness* and *well-being* interchangeably as overarching terms to describe the goals of the whole Positive Psychology enterprise (p. 261).

4. This survey can be accessed at www.authentichappiness.org.

CHAPTER 8

1. Nettle concludes that the study of happiness—sometimes called hedonics—is a worthy form of empirical research and notes that over 3,000 empirical studies of happiness have been published since 1960. There is also a journal, *Journal of Happiness Studies*, devoted entirely to the study of happiness. The field is remarkably interdisciplinary, but Nettle's own approach, as noted, is informed by evolutionary psychology.

2. It is noteworthy that Nettle makes a case for comfort as well as joy in this chapter and in the preceding one. Since comfort was not among Ekman's six emotions—but surprise was—we may wonder why Nettle does not try to make a case for happy surprises. In any event, comfort and joy recall the well-known Christmas carol "God Rest Ye Merry Gentlemen," the first stanza of which concludes with reference to "tidings of comfort and joy."

CHAPTER 11

1. It is interesting to note that Norman Vincent Peale coauthored a book with Smiley Blanton, a psychiatrist, titled *The Art of Real Happiness* (1950). Their title suggests that they shared Dworkin's concern that people confuse "artificial" happiness with "real" happiness.

CHAPTER 12

1. Stanley W. Jackson distinguishes between melancholia and depression in *Melancholia and Depression* (1986). His chapter "Melancholia and Depression in the Twentieth Century" (pp. 188–246) is especially relevant to the case that Wilson makes here.

2. Wilson assigns Norman Rockwell to the "bright visions" tradition of Bradford, Franklin, and Norman Vincent Peale (p. 35). Richard Halpern's *Norman Rockwell: The Underside of Innocence* (2006) challenges this popular view of Rockwell, and Capps (2008) discusses Rockwell's struggles with depression and the role that they played in his art.

3. Our book *Living in Limbo: Life in the Midst of Uncertainty* (Capps and Carlin 2010) presents a substantial number of cases of Americans who have lived in, or are currently living, in limbo. For the majority of these persons, their limbo situation is primarily due to external circumstances and not to their basic personality or temperament. On the other hand, the very fact that they are living in limbo evokes the feelings of sadness that Wilson associates with the melancholic temperament.

4. Capps (2008) notes Norman Rockwell's biographer's comment that his therapist, Erik H. Erikson, encouraged him to allow his work to "flow freely out of his unhappiness" (p. 192; Claridge 2003, p. 370).

CHAPTER 13

1. Alden E. Wessman and David F. Ricks in *Mood and Personality* (1966) devote a chapter to the personality characteristics of happy and unhappy men. They found

that happy and unhappy men were clearly differentiated on Erik H. Erikson's life stages (Erikson 1950). For example, happy men displayed more initiative, industry, and intimacy. They also found significant differences in their experience and organization of time, with the happy men experiencing time in terms of ascending, upwardly soaring images. Time was also felt by them as organic composition (i.e., growth, fertility, development); was personified as a good person (e.g., a beneficent friend and wise teacher); was experienced as a bright future; as the setting for active-oriented efforts; and as filled. In contrast, the unhappy men experienced time as decomposition; as a bad person; as a dark future; and as monotonous, barren, and empty (pp. 117–120).

References

Adams, Douglas. (1995). *The Hitchhiker's Guide to the Galaxy.* New York: Ballantine Press.

Aden, LeRoy and J. Harold Ellens. (1990). *Turning Points in Pastoral Care: The Legacy of Anton Boisen and Seward Hiltner.* Grand Rapids, MI: Baker.

Agnes, Michael (Ed.). (2001). *Webster's New World College Dictionary.* 4th ed. Foster City, CA: IDG Worldwide Books.

Ahmed, Sara. (2010). *The Promise of Happiness.* Durham, NC: Duke University Press.

Allport, Gordon W. (1964). *Personality and Social Encounter.* Boston: Beacon Press.

Allport, Gordon W. (1968). *The Person in Psychology: Selected Essays.* Boston: Beacon Press.

American Psychiatric Association. (2000). *Diagnostic and Statistical Manual of Mental Disorders.* 4th ed., text revision. Washington, DC: American Psychiatric Association.

Argyle, Michael. (1986). *The Psychology of Happiness.* London: Methuen.

Augustine. (1991). *Confessions.* Henry Chadwick (Trans.). Oxford: Oxford University Press.

Ben-Shahar, Tal. (2007). *Happier: Learn the Secrets to Daily Joy and Lasting Fulfillment.* New York: McGraw-Hill.

Ben-Shahar, Tal. (2010). *Even Happier: A Gratitude Journal for Daily Joy and Lasting Fulfillment.* New York: McGraw Hill.

Bok, Sissela. (2010). *Exploring Happiness: From Aristotle to Brain Science.* New Haven, CT: Yale University Press.

Booth, Wayne C. (1974). *A Rhetoric of Irony.* Chicago: The University of Chicago Press.

Burton, Robert. (2001). *The Anatomy of Melancholy.* Holbrook Jackson (Ed.). New York: New York Review Books.

Campbell, Angus. (1981). *The Sense of Well-being in America.* New York: McGraw-Hill.

Capps, Donald. (2000). *Deadly Sins and Saving Virtues.* Eugene, OR: Wipf & Stock Publishers.

Capps, Donald. (2008). Erik H. Erikson, Norman Rockwell, and the Therapeutic Functions of a Questionable Painting. *American Imago, 65,* 191–228.

Capps, Donald and Carlin, Nathan. (2010). *Living in Limbo: Life in the Midst of Uncertainty.* Eugene, OR: Cascade Books.

de Chardin, Pierre Teilhard. (1973). *On Happiness.* Renè Hague (Trans.). New York: Harper & Row.

Claridge, Laura. (2003). *Norman Rockwell: A Life.* New York: Modern Library.

Crocker, Jennifer and Major, Brenda. (1989). Social Stigma and Self-esteem: The Self-Protective Properties of Stigma. *Psychological Review, 96,* 608–630.

Csikszentmihalyi, Mihaly and Csikszentmihalyi, Isabella. (1988). *Optimal Experience: Psychological Studies of Flow in Consciousness.* Cambridge: Cambridge University Press.

Danner, Deborah, David, Snowdon and Wallace Friesen. (2001). Positive Emotions and Early Life and Longevity: Findings from the Nun Study. *Personality and Social Psychology, 80,* 804–813.

Diener, Edward and Biswas-Diener, Robert. (2008). *Happiness: Unlocking the Mysteries of Psychological Wealth.* West Sussex, UK: Blackwell.

Diener, Edward and Seligman, Martin E. P. (2002). Very Happy People. *Psychological Science, 13,* 80–83.

du Châtelet, Madame. (1997). *Discours sur le bonheur.* Paris: Rivages Poche/Petite Bibliothèque.

Dunlap, Knight. (1928). A Revision of the Fundamental Law of Habit Formation. *Science, 67,* 360–362.

Dunlap, Knight. (1930). Repetition in the Breaking of Habits. *Scientific Monthly, 30,* 66–70.

Dunn, Stephen. (1994). *New and Selected Poems 1974–1994.* New York: W. W. Norton.

Dworkin, Ronald W. (2006). *Artificial Happiness: The Dark Side of the New Happy Class.* New York: Carroll & Graf.

Ekman, Paul. (1992). An Argument for Basic Emotions. *Cognition and Emotion, 6,* 169–200.

Erikson, Erik H. (1950). *Childhood and Society.* New York: W. W. Norton.

Erikson, Joan M. (1976). *Activity, Recovery, Growth: The Communal Role of Planned Activities.* With David and Joan Loveless. New York: W. W. Norton.

Finot, Jean. (1914). *The Science of Happiness.* Mary Jo Safford (Trans.). New York: G. P. Putnam's Sons.

Fletcher, Horace. (1895). *Menticulture or the A-B-C of True Living.* Chicago: A. C. McClurg.

Fletcher, Horace. (1898a). *Happiness as Found in Forethought minus Fearthought.* Chicago: Kindergarten Literature.

Fletcher, Horace. (1898b). *That Last Waif, or Social Quarantine: A Brief.* Chicago: Kindergarten Literature.

Fletcher, Horace. (1906). *The New Glutton or Epicure.* New York: Frederick A. Stokes.

Fletcher, Horace. (1913). *Fletcherism: What It Is or How I Became Young at Sixty.* London: Ewart, Seymour.

Frank, Robert. (1999). *Luxury Fever: Why Money Fails to Satisfy in an Era of Excess.* New York: The Free Press.

Fredrickson, Barbara. (1998). What Good are Positive Emotions? *Review of General Psychology, 2,* 300–319.

Fredrickson, Barbara. (2001). The Role of Positive Emotions in Positive Psychology: The Broaden-and-build Theory of Positive Emotion. *American Psychologist, 56*, 218–226.

Freud, Sigmund. (1961). *Civilization and Its Discontents.* In James E. Strachey (Ed.), *The Standard Edition of the Complete Psychological Works of Sigmund Freud,* vol. 21, 59–145. London: Hogarth Press. Original published in 1930.

Fuller, Robert. (2001). *Spiritual, But Not Religious: Understanding Unchurched America.* New York: Oxford University Press.

Gilbert, Daniel. (2006). *Stumbling on Happiness.* New York: Random House.

Gottman, John M. and Levenson, Robert. (1992). Marital Processes Predictive of Later Dissolution: Behavior, Physiology, and Health. *Journal of Personality and Social Psychology, 63*, 221–233.

Gottman, John M. and Silver, Nan. (2000). *The Seven Principles for Making Marriage Work.* New York: Three Rivers Press.

Graham, Billy. (1954). *The Secret of Happiness.* Garden City, NY: Doubleday Books.

Halpern, Richard. (2006). *Norman Rockwell: The Underside of Innocence.* Chicago: The University of Chicago Press.

Hart, Archibald D. (1988). *15 Principles for Achieving Happiness.* Dallas, TX: Word Press.

Haybron, Daniel. (2008). *The Pursuit of Unhappiness: The Elusive Psychology of Well-Being.* Oxford: Oxford University Press.

Herman, Barbara. (1993). *The Practice of Moral Judgment.* Cambridge, MA: Harvard University Press.

Hilty, Karl. (1903). *Happiness: Essays on the Meaning of Life.* Francis Greenwood Peabody (Trans.). New York: Macmillan.

Horace. (1959). *Satires and Epistles of Horace.* Smith Palmer Bowie (Trans.). Chicago: University of Chicago Press.

Huppert, Felicia A. (2007). Positive Mental Health in Individuals and Populations. In Felicia A. Huppert, Nick Baylis, and Barry Keverne (Eds.), *The Science of Well-Being,* 307–340. Oxford: Oxford University Press.

Huxley, Aldous. (1946). *Brave New World.* New York: Modern Library.

Inglehart, Ronald. (1990). *Culture Shift in Advanced Industrial Society.* Princeton, NJ: Princeton University Press.

Jackson, Stanley W. (1986). *Melancholia and Depression: From Hippocratic Times to Modern Times.* New Haven, CT: Yale University Press.

James, William. (1884). What Is an Emotion? *Mind, 9*, 188–205.

James, William. *The Will to Believe and Other Essays in Popular Philosophy.* New York: Dover Publications.

James, William. (1987). *The Varieties of Religious Experience.* In Bruce Kuklick (Ed.), *William James: Writings 1902–1910,* 1–469. New York: The Library of America.

Kammann, Richard. (1983). Objective Circumstances, Life Satisfactions, and Sense of Well-being: Consistencies Across Time and Place. *New Zealand Journal of Psychology, 12*, 14–22.

Kant, Immanuel. (1978). *Anthropology from a Practice Point of View.* Victor Lyle Dowdell (Trans.). Carbondale: Southern Illinois University Press.

Kasser, Tim and Ahuvia, A. (2002). Materialistic Values and Well-Being in Business Students. *European Journal of Social Psychology, 32*, 137–146.

Laing, Ronald D. (1970). *Knots*. New York: Pantheon Books.

Layard, Richard. (2005). *Happiness: Lessons from a New Science*. New York: Penguin.

Linville, Patricia. (1985). Self-complexity and Affective Extremity: Don't Put All Your Eggs in One Basket. *Social Cognition, 3*, 94–120.

Linville, Patricia. (1987). Self-complexity as a Cognitive Buffer Against Stress-related Illness and Depression. *Journal of Personality and Social Psychology, 52*, 663–676.

Locke, John. (1986). *Second Treatise of Civil Government*. Ahmerst, NY: Prometheus Books.

Lykken, David and Tellegen, Auke. (1996). Happiness is a Stochastic Phenomenon. *Psychological Science, 7*, 186–189.

Markee, Michael and Vincent Wixon. (2004). *William Stafford: Life and Poems*. Ashland, OR: TTTD Productions.

Mauzi, Robert. (1960). *L'idee du bonheur au XVIIIe siècle*. Paris: Librairie Armand Colin.

McGill, V. J. (1967). *The Idea of Happiness*. New York: Frederick A. Praeger.

McKechnie, Josie and Hill, Elizabeth M. (2011). Risk Factors for Alcoholism Among Women Religious: Affect Regulation. *Pastoral Psychology, 60*, 693–703.

Myers, David G. (1992). *The Pursuit of Happiness: Discovering the Pathway to Fulfillment, Well-Being, and Enduring Personal Joy*. New York: HarperCollins.

Nesse, Randolph. and Williams, George. (1996). *Why We Get Sick: The New Science of Darwinian Medicine*. New York: Vintage Books.

Nettle, Daniel. (2005). *Happiness: The Science Behind Your Smile*. Oxford: Oxford University Press.

Pasten, Linda. (1998). *Carnival Evening: New and Selected Poems 1968–1998*. New York: W. W. Norton.

Peale, Norman Vincent. (1952). *The Power of Positive Thinking*. New York: Prentice-Hall.

Peale, Norman Vincent and Blanton, Smiley. (1950). *The Art of Real Happiness*. New York: Prentice-Hall.

Powell, John. (1989). *Happiness Is an Inside Job*. Valencia, CA: Tabor Press.

Quennell, Peter. (1988). *The Pursuit of Happiness*. London: Constable.

Raab, Lawrence. (1993). *What We Don't Know About Each Other*. New York: Penguin Books.

Rodin, Judith. (1986). Aging and Health: Effects of the Sense of Control. *Science, 233*, 1271–1276.

Russell, Bertrand. (1968a). *New Hopes for a Changing World*. New York: Minerva Press. Original published in 1951.

Russell, Bertrand. (1968b). *The Conquest of Happiness*. New York: Bantam. Original published in 1930.

Scheier, Michael and Carver, Charles. (1987). Dispositional Optimism and Physical Well-being: The Influence of Generalized Outcome Expectancies on Health. *Journal of Personality, 55*, 169–210.

Schnarch, David. (1998). *Passionate Marriage: Keeping Love and Intimacy Alive in Committed Relationships*. New York: Owl Books.

Seligman, Martin E. P. (2002). *Authentic Happiness: Using the New Positive Psychology to Realize Your Potential for Lasting Fulfillment*. New York: Free Press.

Seligman, Martin E. P. and Schulman, Peter. (1986). Explanatory Style as a Predictor of Productivity and Quitting Among Life Insurance Sales Agents. *Journal of Personality and Social Psychology, 50*, 832–838.

Seneca. (1990). On the Happy Life. In *Seneca, Moral Essays II*. J. Basore (Trans.). Cambridge, MA: Harvard University Press.

Sheen, Bishop Fulton. (1954). *Way to Happiness*. Herts, UK: Garden City Books.

Stafford, William. (1998). *The Way It Is: New and Selected Poems*. St. Paul, MN: Graywolf Press.

Stephen, Sir Leslie. (1904). Sir Thomas Browne, in *Hours in a Library*, vol. 1, 269–270. New York: G. P. Putnam's Sons.

Veenhoven, Ruut. (2004). Happiness as an Aim in Public Policy. In Alex Linley and Stephen Joseph (Eds.), *Positive Psychology in Practice*, pp. 658–678. West Sussex, UK: John Wiley.

Vemer, Elizabeth et al. (1989). Marital Satisfaction in Remarriage: A Meta-analysis. *Journal of Marriage and the Family, 51*, 713–725.

Wessman, Alden E. and Ricks, David F. (1966). *Mood and Personality*. New York: Holt, Rinehart and Winston.

Wholey, Dennis. (1986). *Are You Happy?* Boston: Houghton Mifflin.

Wilson, Eric G. (2008). *Against Happiness: In Praise of Melancholy*. New York: Farrar, Straus and Giroux.

Worthington, Edward. (2001). *Five Steps to Forgiveness*. New York: Crown Books.

INDEX

About the Authors
and Series Editor

AUTHORS

Nathan Carlin is director of the Medical Humanities and Ethics Certificate Program at the University of Texas Medical School in Houston, Texas. His primary faculty appointment is in the McGovern Center for Humanities and Ethics. He also holds appointments in the Graduate School of Biomedical Sciences and the School of Dentistry, both of which are a part of the University of Texas Health Science Center at Houston. He also has an appointment as a faculty member in the Institute for Spirituality and Health, also located in Houston, Texas. Carlin has published numerous articles as well as one co-authored book (with Donald Capps), titled *Living in Limbo: Life in the Midst of Uncertainty.*

Donald Capps is William Harte Felmeth Professor of Pastoral Theology (Emeritus) and adjunct professor of Pastoral Theology at Princeton Theological Seminary. He is the author and editor of numerous books, including *Agents of Hope*; *The Child's Song*; *Men, Religion, and Melancholia*; *Men and Their Religion*; *Freud and Freudians on Religion*; *Social Phobia*; *Jesus the Village Psychiatrist*; and *Understanding Psychosis.* He received an honorary ThD from the University of Uppsala in 1989; served as president of the Society for the Scientific Study of Religion from 1990–1992; and received the American Psychological Association's William F. Bier Award for Contribution to Psychology of Religion in 1995.

SERIES EDITOR

J. Harold Ellens is editor of the Praeger Series in Psychology, Religion, and Spirituality. He was a research scholar at the University of Michigan, Department of Near Eastern Studies from 1990 to 2009, and is a retired Presbyterian theologian, an ordained minister, a retired U.S. Army Colonel, and a retired professor of philosophy, theology, and psychology. He served 15 years as executive director of the Christian Association for Psychological Studies and was founding editor and editor-in-chief of the *Journal of Psychology and Christianity*. He has authored, coauthored, or edited 182 volumes and 167 professional journal articles, including *Sex in the Bible: A New Consideration* (Praeger, 2006).